Rooms with No View

ROOMS
WITH NO VIEW

*A WOMAN'S GUIDE TO THE MAN'S
WORLD OF THE MEDIA*

Compiled by the Media Women's Association

edited by Ethel Strainchamps

1817

HARPER & ROW, PUBLISHERS

NEW YORK, EVANSTON, SAN FRANCISCO, LONDON

Grateful acknowledgment is made to *The New York Times* for permission to reprint "Is Television a Man's World?" by Gloria Banta. Copyright © 1973 by *The New York Times*. First published in *The New York Times,* September 30, 1973. Acknowledgments also to [*More*]: *a Journalism Review* for "Progress Report" by Terry Pristin; and to Grosset and Dunlap for "Women on the Air" by Helen Epstein, from *Survey of Broadcast Journalism 1970–1971,* © 1971 by The Trustees of Columbia University in the City of New York.

Library of Congress Catal████████ ██████████ ██
Main █████ █████ title.
Rooms with no view.

1. Women in the mass ██████ ██████. 2. Mass media—
United States. I. Strainchamps, Ethel Reed, ed.
II. Media Women's Association.
P96.W6R6   331.4′81′3803   74–1860
ISBN 0–06–014139–5

To all women in the media—the veterans, the recruits, the outcasts, the guerrillas— in the hope that those who follow us will finally win equality

Contents

Three Newspapers and Wire Services

Four Book Publishing

Five Wide-Angle Views

Six Appendix

Preface

The contributors to this book, as well as its readers, deserve an explanation for the time-lag between its compilation (early 1972) and its eventual publication. A brief recital of the difficulties that brought about the lag will, I hope, not only explain the delay, but will also shed some light on the main theme of the book—the problems of women in publishing.

In the fall of 1971, a committee of the Media Women's Association engaged me, a former Missouri journalist turned New York freelance writer, to supervise completion of the amassing of a group of essays they had already begun, written by women in the media about their jobs. I was to contact additional contributors until I had a minimum of fifty essays in hand. I was then to edit them and submit them to a committee elected by the Media Women for final approval.

The association already had a contract with Quadrangle Books, a subsidiary of the *New York Times,* which had been negotiated by a literary agent who was a member of the group on the strength of a dozen articles various members of the group had written. The contract stipulated that the copy, as finally approved by the Media Women's book committee, was not to be altered by the publisher except to make it conform to house style in punctuation, grammar, and spelling. It also stipulated that the copy was to be submitted before the end of January 1972, and that the book was to be published within six months after that.

We soon began running into serious snags. The manuscript was the first acquisition of a new editor at Quadrangle, who subsequently began to attend some of the Media Women's meetings. The association was an informal and loosely organized group, open to any woman in the business and was held together by the shared feminist activism of the members. The self-recruited Quadrangle editor seemed to fall short in that orientation. The resulting clash of viewpoints created an immediate friction, a friction that proved crucial when it came to deciding on the contents and the tone of the prospective book.

The committee met its deadline with sixty articles—admittedly not covering all possible subjects and admittedly not all written in the most polished of styles. (Some of the volunteer contributors were nonwriters—stenographers, PR people, etc.). But the committee agreed that the articles adequately fulfilled the book's purposes and approved them, along with my editing, which had been done after consulting the writers when major changes had seemed advisable.

The Quadrangle representative then informed us that there were other essays that she, personally, wanted to have included— pieces on particular book publishers and on certain aspects of book publishing that we had been unable to complete under the deadline. (The book, after all, was planned as a sampling of conditions in the media, not as a blanket coverage.) Still, the Quadrangle editor, the committee, and I managed to come up with most of the additional pieces within a couple of months; they were then edited, committee-approved, and submitted.

Next, we were confronted with still more material by the company editor—some she had selected from outside sources; others that she had composed herself. There was a group consensus that most of this was out of synch with the rest of the book—it included a *Playboy* cartoon, a Dear Abby letter, and a cutesy list of "no-no's" for bosses, written by the editor.

After the committee had formally ruled those out and had approved the additional book workers' essays, there was another long delay, supposedly to allow the *Times* lawyers time to comb all the essays for libel. (It later emerged that the lawyers concerned had been out of town for a part of that summer.)

Finally, in the winter of 1972, nearly a year after the project had been completed in accordance with the original contract specifications, Quadrangle sent the galley proofs to the agent for approval. She, of course, sent them to me, and I couldn't believe my eyes. Two of the articles we had specifically defended and insisted on including were missing; the material that we had specifically rejected was there. Many of the subtitles for the articles, which the committee and I had spent some time in trying to make apt and appealing, had been replaced with irrelevant (and irreverent) catchwords. (For example, on the Harper & Row piece, the original subtitle, "Stalled in a Wasp's Nest" had been changed to "Were You There When They Crucified Me, Lord?" The subtitle "Tempus Non Fugit," for *Time* became "The Impossible Dream: A Quest." The reader may judge for herself which subtitles are more apt. And these are by no means the worst examples.)

More serious from my own standpoint, since I was to be given conspicuous credit for the editing, were inept additions, indefensible deletions, and ungrammatical inserts in the edited copy itself. (My special field in writing and editing is English usage.)

The agent and I then met with the president of Quadrangle, and he agreed orally to observe the terms of the contract—that is, to print the manuscript as submitted. However, the fact that his editor could claim with some validity to be a member of the group (and could thus challenge the legitimacy of the committee), plus the intrusion of some other in-house politics, complicated the resolution of the conflict. Eventually the contract was canceled by mutual consent. But our story ends on a cheerful note. KNOW, a woman's cooperative based in Pittsburgh, volunteered to publish a few hundred copies of the book, without firm prospects of profiting from the venture.

Then our (moonlighting) typist, who is secretary to an editor at Harper & Row, suggested that the book might be worthy of greater distribution than KNOW could provide, and her superiors agreed. The next step, of course, was to get the original pieces updated. A great deal had happened in publishing in the intervening two years, the most drastic being the demise of *Life,* which had been the subject of one of our more enlightening essays. Most of the articles that follow have been brought up to date, either by the original contributor or by another volunteer. A few of the 1972 pieces were retained, either because the time element had no bearing on their relevance (their general tone still reflects the current situation) or because the writers were no longer with the firms they wrote about, and no substitute could be found. (Such pieces are marked with an asterisk at the title.)*

Some of the changes in the status of women in publishing that may not be covered in the articles are reflected in the following roundup by Terry Pristin, first published in [*More*]: *a Journalism Review* in August 1973.

Profits from this book have been assigned by the Media Women's Association to KNOW.

—*Ethel Strainchamps*

* Television	Magazines	Books
NBC	Harper's Bazaar	American Heritage
NET	Mademoiselle	Lippincott
	McCall's	McGraw-Hill
	Scholastic	Putnam-Coward-McCann & Geoghegan
	Vogue	

Progress Report

Media executives find themselves confronting firsthand a story they have been covering for the past several years, as women all over town organize to fight discrimination within their companies. Following is a report on one group's success and four other efforts still to be resolved.

Traditionally, newsmagazines have been bastions of male supremacy at its most blatant—where the "girls" in the office not only supplied coffee but also dug out "facts," leaving creative processes and loftier thinking entirely in the hands of the men. More than three years ago, *Newsweek* women elected to overturn the pattern by filing sex discrimination charges with the federal Equal Employment Opportunity Commission. The complaint—the first such challenge by a group of women employed by the media—was dropped when management promised "substantial, rather than token changes." But by May 1972, after insufficient progress had been made, fifty-one women filed a second complaint. This June, the EEOC complaint was withdrawn as *Newsweek* editor and chairman Osborn Elliott and six representatives of the Women's Committee signed a Memorandum of Understanding designed to right some of the inequities.

The Memorandum covers hiring, promotion, and training and provides specific goals, timetables, and procedures. By the end of 1974, under the new terms, one-third of all writers and domestic reporters must be women, and no major department will be permitted to be without a woman writer for more than six consecutive months. One out of every three foreign correspondents named in 1974 must be a woman. Most important of all, by the end of 1975, a woman must head up one of the magazine's seven major editorial divisions. In an attempt to deghettoize the research category, the agreement also stipulates that "the percentage of all researchers who are men shall be approximately equal to the percentage of all writers who are women." Eight men have become researchers since the original complaint was filed in 1970.

Three times a year, management will be required to submit reports with specific information about its efforts to hire and promote women. Differences between the Women's Committee and management will be referred to a Joint Review Committee and will go to arbitration, if necessary.

Though women at *Newsweek* are delighted with the agreement, many would also like to rid the magazine of sexist language and photos. An obvious example is the July 16, 1973, cover photo for the "games singles play" story, which showed a voluptuous, bikinied blonde against the backdrop of a California singles complex. "We were not at all pleased," says writer Maureen Orth. "We know that sex sells, but we felt that if they wanted to use a picture of a vulgar female, why not have a vulgar male, too?" Several weeks ago, when they first saw the projected cover, Orth and photo editor Joan Engels brought their objections to managing editor Edward Kosner, who set up a meeting with three people who had worked on the singles story, among them, reporter Phyllis Malamud. "To me it's a crotch picture," says Malamud. "I'm not happy about that. But I couldn't argue that it was a sexist cover. It fairly represented what the story was about—the emergence during the past ten years of the single woman and her sexual attitudes." Malamud's okay apparently ended the argument, but it scarcely resolved the issue.

In May 1972 the National Organization for Women filed a petition with the Federal Communications Commission to deny the license of WABC–TV, the flagship station of the ABC network. No doubt action on the local level had sensitized corporate management to some of the concerns of ABC women. Meetings between both sides began last summer, and a "company-sanctioned" Women's Action Committee was formally established in the fall.

In the intervening period, the women have accomplished several of their lesser goals. New job openings (except those above the middle-management level) are now publicized within the company. A computerized "skills bank" has been set up to facilitate mobility within the corporation. Grievance procedures have been created, although, interestingly, the women feel that none of the complainants thus far have had bona fide discrimination cases. A woman—Mary Jean Parsons—has been appointed employee-relations counselor, and another—Eleanor Riger—has become the first female staff producer for ABC Sports. The employment picture has indeed improved somewhat. In March personnel director Marie McWilliams told the Women's Action Committee that since September, twenty women had been added to the "officials and management" classification and another twelve to the "professional" category.

Such achievements, however, still amount to tokenism. Management has acknowledged that at present no department has a single woman earning more than one-half of that department's highest-paid man. At the beginning of 1973, a generalized "affirmative action" plan was distributed company-wide. Yet thus far, no specific goals and timetables have been made known to the Women's Action Committee. "If we had that, we could kick them along," says Hope Gaines, a secretary in the news department. "That's why they don't want us to have it. Till the time we do, our accomplishments will remain vague."

NBC, according to its Women's Committee for Equal Opportunity, employs some 800 women, of whom 600 or so hold secretarial and clerical positions. Only 200 women—or less than one-tenth of the company's work force—have technical, professional, or managerial jobs. In February of this year WC-EW became the first broadcast group here to file sex discrimination charges with the EEOC.

That was not the route originally intended by the handful of women who began meeting quietly more than a year before. As their base of support increased, the women sought remedies from the personnel department. Getting nowhere, they say, with their numerous proposals, in September 1973 they delivered a formal presentation before the company's President's Council, headed up by NBC chief Julian Goodman. They suggested, among other things, that NBC appoint a female compliance officer to implement an affirmative-action program; that job vacancies be posted; that a skills inventory be developed and utilized; that the secretarial system be restructured (secretaries are now paid according to their bosses' titles); that the company publish a newsletter including information about training programs; and that the tuition refund and loan program be liberalized to allow people without college degrees to take undergraduate courses. This last suggestion was the only one implemented to the satisfaction of the women.

Management attempted to refute the discrimination charges in the time-honored corporate manner—by preparing a slide show. "They had one of those Carousel projectors, with slides done up by the art department showing graphs in lots of colors," recalls Lois Farmer, a programmer and systems analyst. "After it was over, everybody sat there speechless. The next Monday, we filed our complaint. There was no sense in talking anymore." The city's Human Rights Commission is now investigating and hopes to issue its findings well before the end of 1974.

CBS women, the late-starters in the push for equal rights, are currently organized into three disparate but cooperative groups.

Meeting at Broadcast House are two units—one for news personnel, the other mainly for secretaries. Across town is a third group of women who work at Black Rock, the corporate headquarters.

The first rumblings came from network newswomen earlier this year, after CBS President Arthur Taylor "threw down the gauntlet," as one of them put it, by issuing a February policy statement many considered condescending as well as inaccurate. "Women and men have the same opportunities for employment and promotion at CBS," wrote Taylor. "There is a single standard of qualification for employment and for treatment after employment, for men and women."

Network newswomen rebutted this and other generalities in an April 9 response to Taylor. They pointed out the glaring inequities in their own division, where only seven of the 86 on-air reporter-correspondents are women. As of June 30, female network-news employees included six news writers (out of 25, three film editors (out of 64), one film crew member (out of 92), and 21 in the category of producer (out of 126). There are no female directors, although not surprisingly, all 92 secretaries are women. (CBS News president Richard Salant, conceding his "conscience was raised rather late," says he is trying to rectify this dismal situation. Among other improvements, two women have been added to the previously all-male graphic arts department and a female cameraman has recently been hired.)

Though they criticized Taylor sharply in the April memo, CBS women have kinder words for him now. On July 19 Taylor met with their representatives and listened to a presentation outlining a number of recommendations. At the end of the two-hour session, the CBS president promised to respond to every issue the women had raised. "We were extremely encouraged by his attitudes and the commitment he expressed," says Priscilla Toumey, manager of press services for the CBS Radio Division.

In a thoroughly clandestine atmosphere, some 80 *New York*

Times women from various departments have filed sex discrimination charges with the EEOC and the City's Human Rights Commission. There appear to be no John Deans among the tightly knit team players, who say only (in an official statement) that the complaint involves salaries, hiring, and advancement and follows attempts "for more than a year to resolve the matter through discussion with management." Their lawyer, Harriet Rabb, says that so far the women have limited their talks with her to employment patterns—not whether female reporters get good assignments and are allowed to travel. Among the activists in the *Times* movement are Betsy Wade, head of the foreign copy desk, assistant metropolitan editor Grace Glueck, and reporters Grace Lichtenstein, Rita Reif, and Lesley Oelsner.[1]

—Terry Pristin

August, 1973
Reprinted by permission.

---

[1] In January 1974, as the result of a class-action suit brought by *New York Times* women, the *Times* management submitted a plan for affirmative action in favor of women and minorities. The government had not ruled on the plan by June 1974.

Foreword

Back in the sixties, as women began to wonder about the validity of their traditional roles, one of the most natural questions to arise was: Where do women get their images of themselves? Laws? Schools? The church? The family? They found that all these traditional institutions were indeed guilty of reinforcing stereotyped notions about men vs. women, but they discovered that the most ubiquitous, the most insidious, and therefore possibly the most powerful force dedicated to the maintenance of the status quo was not one of the long-established social institutions, but a fairly new one—the mass media. All the media—books, magazines, newspapers, broadcasting, advertising—day in and day out, in boldface type and in living color, pound home the message that men are men—active, hardworking, curious, intelligent—and that women are women—frivolous, seductive, motherly, domesticated. The ancient myths had merely been put into modern dress.

In light of the power of the media to affect women's views about themselves, it is particularly ironic that women have traditionally had so little power within the media. Late in 1970, the Media Women's Association was formed in New York City with the aim of tipping that balance of power. Some of the original members had previously been affiliated with older feminist groups; others had planned and participated in the landmark "sit-in" at the *Ladies' Home Journal;* some had contributed time and effort to various new feminist journals; for others membership in the group was the first involvement with the women's movement. From the outset, all were aware that every branch of the media discriminated against women, not only in its employment and promotion policies, but in the image it projected of women as members of the human race.

In our exchange of facts and impressions, however, we discovered that things were far worse than we at first thought. As the months wore on, we found ourselves contributing *amicus* briefs in sex discrimination suits, sending angry letters to advertisers and editors about their inaccurate and exploitive treatment of women, helping women in individual companies to organize, and finally setting up an informal employment network to alert group members and other women to job openings in the field.

Recalling our own exalted expectations when we were looking for jobs, and our disappointment and bitterness when we discovered that belonging to the "wrong" sex was to thwart our dreams and ambitions, we agreed that Media Women had to do whatever was possible to help women who planned to enter our field and to encourage those already disillusioned to fight for change. And we thought it high time that the media barons themselves were told precisely how women felt about their discrimination policies.

A good place to begin, we thought, would be with a broad-ranging survey of the media. Since our own experiences varied and since cold statistics often do not reveal the essence of a situation, we decided to assemble and publish as many individual articles as we could about representative publishers and broadcasters. Each article would be written by a woman who was working, or had recently worked, for the company she discussed. In this manner we hoped to convey an accurate as well as a personalized picture of what "it really feels like" to be a woman employee at any one of these places.

Some of the contributors are members of Media Women, others are sympathetic volunteers. Some are published writers, others have had no writing experience at all. But all the contributors have a firsthand knowledge of their subject. That certain themes are echoed over and over only proves beyond any lingering doubt that sexism is not an idiosyncrasy of a particular publisher, television studio, or magazine, but the accepted policy of the industry. That the majority of the pieces are anonymously written proves that even women associated with an industry dedicated to communication may not feel free to communicate candidly without fear of reprisal. (This apprehension prevented us from obtaining even anonymous reports on certain companies.)

This book is our contribution to the spontaneous, nationwide feminist effort to bring the exploitation of women to public attention, and thus help to bring about reforms. We are proud to have played a small part, through other group activities, in the meager progress that has already been made toward our goals.

We would like to acknowledge with particular gratitude our editor, Ethel Strainchamps, our agent, Susan Protter, and all our contributors, without whose efforts this book would never have come to fruition.

Media Women's Association
New York City

The Television Networks

IF THERE WERE EVER ANY DOUBT that sexism is rampant in American society, off-camera developments in television broadcasting have dispelled it.

Starting out in the fifties with a clean slate, this newest of our public-information media had an excellent opportunity to junk all the old myths. Even if the profit motive did compel television broadcasters to respect the old pieties in what they fed to the public, they had the chance to be wildly innovative in their behind-the-scenes policies—to utilize ability where they found it, without regard to age, color, sex, or physical appearance. But they muffed it. They were either already firm believers in the propaganda they peddle on the screen, or they have been corrupted by constant exposure to it.

A clutch of the top executives of a given network would, except for the unfamiliarity of their faces, be indistinguishable from its on-camera spokesmen: white, male, middle-class, middle-aged squares.

As they are viewed each by an intelligent woman from the inside, the three commercial networks are as monotonously similar in their attitudes toward women as they are in their programming policies. The publicly supported network, National Educational Television, is slightly more advanced on both scores.

An article in our "Wide-Angle Views" section presents facts and figures that demonstrate the dismalness of the national tele-

3

vision scene. At local stations women do much of the essential drudgery, but they are effectively barred from the prestigious, high-paying jobs.

There have been no organized protests by women on the network staffs, and protests by other feminists against certain shows and commercials have not been spectacularly effective.

No Fillies Running in the Main Event

ABC NEWS

It's the first Tuesday in November and you're watching television for the election results. A woman has just finished describing the mood of campaign workers inside the hotel and signs off: "This is Marlene Sanders with candidate John Smith . . . and now back to ABC election headquarters. . . ." Sounds impressive, doesn't it? Election headquarters? Actually election headquarters, space headquarters, and news headquarters are all located in the same area and are often the very same studio with different sets.

ABC News is located on West Sixty-sixth Street between Central Park West and Broadway, not in the corporate showcase on Broadcast Row (Sixth Avenue). Almost all of the buildings on Sixty-sixth Street have some sort of history. One used to be St. Nick's Arena, as fight fans will remember. Another stabled horses. Today, 7 West Sixty-sixth Street stables news executives. On the fourth floor of this gray building, in tastefully decorated offices, are president Elmer Lower and three (male) vice-presidents.

The Evening News Show is corralled on the second floor of the same building. Most of the offices are windowless and painted operating-room white. However, the ban on putting up decorations on the wall is not too strictly enforced; there are some maps and pictures around. Gathered there, too, is a staff ranging from executive producer Av Westin and anchor man Harry Reasoner (the other anchor man, Howard K. Smith, and his staff are in Washington) on down to desk assistants—two men who do most of the legwork (gathering and distributing copy, getting coffee, sandwiches, etc.).

Notice, no females so far!

In the Special Events Unit, there are five women: four secretaries and one researcher. The secretaries usually function as assistants to the producer and get screen credits as such after election and space shows. But, except for overtime figures on the base of their secretarial salaries, they receive no additional money for the extra responsibility. One former researcher who functioned as an associate producer, and was so listed during a recent Apollo mission on all internal communications, was denied associate-producer screen credit. For that particular shot, a freelance associate producer, female, had been hired. "We can't have *two* female associate producers," said one of the news executives. Males fill all the producing, writing, directing, and editing slots on Special Events.

In between these extremes are: the writers who prepare Reasoner's on-camera stories and the lead-ins and -outs of the film pieces. All men. Next come three producers who are responsible for the daily overall content of the news show: three men. Then there are the associate, or field, producers. In 1971 they were all men. By 1973 the numbers had improved; three men, two women. There are also assistant producers, called production associates now. That started out as a female-only job, but there's been some reverse integration. One of each sex now. They're responsible for packaging the individual two- or three-minute film spots.

There are two women researchers now. There used to be a male one but he was soon promoted out of that job. The film editors at Evening News are all male—six of them. The production assistants are male too. Their job is to keep scripts and visual material in order. The secretaries are still all women. So there are eight women in all working on the Evening News show behind the scenes. In 1971 the number was six.

Also essential to the production of a news show are the Assignment Desk and the Graphics Department. In New York the Assignment Desk was recently integrated, and now boasts one female. The Washington Assignment Desk has two women. The Graphics Department, too, has recently added a woman to its New York staff, so now there's one woman in New York as well as one in Washington.

In Documentaries, Av Westin has taken over as vice-president and is making a lot of changes, many of them progressive for women. Marlene Sanders and Pam Hill are full producers of documentary programs, with the same responsibilities and salaries as their male counterparts. There are two female associate producers in the unit—one male. Three females are production associates. One male has the same title. There are also five female film editors in the documentary unit. In 1971 only one woman was there. Most of the researchers here are female, but there is one token male. All in all, while the numbers in Documentaries are not perfect, they're the best at ABC News.

For a total picture: In 1973 there are some 600 people working for ABC News in the United States (bureaus in New York, Washington, Chicago, Miami, Atlanta, and Los Angeles). One hundred and fifty are women. Most of those are secretaries. However . . . there are seven female news writers or news editors; five female associate producers (there are twenty male AP's); thirteen female researchers (two men); six full producers are female (thirty-two are men); and there are five female production associates. Of ABC's stable of forty-seven television correspondents, five are women. There used to be only one or two. And as for ABC News "management," nine women qualify. And ABC News now finally has a female cameraperson trainee.

ABC is improving, albeit slowly. There is an active women's

group, with a steering committee that meets regularly with ABC corporate management. Whatever they accomplish, it will not be overnight.

But There Sure Are Some Producers Who
Should Be Women (Laughter)

CBS NEWS*

Everybody out there in Videoland must be aware by now that some consciousness-raising has been going on at CBS News. But there are probably few who would bet on living long enough to see a headline like this: ANCHORWOMAN TO TAKE OVER CRONKITE SLOT IN CBS ELECTION COVERAGE.

Where women are and where they are not: In the fall of 1973, of the fifty highest level CBS News people, only three were women—director of special projects, director of religious broadcasts, and the associate archivist. (The first two have been in those jobs for close to twenty years now.) Of the more than 60 network correspondents and reporters, only five are women; of the 25 at the New York City local station (WCBS), three are women. Out of approximately 25 network news-show producers (including hard news and documentaries), three are women; of the 30-odd associate producers (again including hard news and documentaries), fewer than ten are women; of 22 researchers, eighteen are women; the Special Projects Library staff is entirely women. The picture at the various CBS news bureaus in other cities and at WCBS in New York is no better. It goes without saying that the secretaries are all women.

Some of the jobs: The Special Projects Library used to hire

---

* See Appendix for agreement between CBS management and women employees.

people (i.e., women) right out of college, start them at the bottom at $75 a week, and offer promises of good promotions. The hierarchy was rigid however, and the new recruits would do little more than clip newspapers for years and then be promoted to filing their successors' clips. A couple of those women did eventually move up to better jobs on news shows, but most left early because they just couldn't stand it. A reorganization of the department was in the works in the fall of 1971, and rumor had it that the library was going to function much more formally as a library and would be hiring trained librarians—in other words, that the jobs would be much better-paying and on a much higher professional level, and presumably would no longer be considered the bottom rung for recent college graduates.

The Broadcast Research Unit was created in 1970. To be hired as a researcher, one must have had some journalism experience and/or a field of expertise. A second language helps, as does a graduate degree in African studies, Far-Eastern affairs, or the like. Rarely are researchers hired fresh out of college, and some attempt is apparently being made to keep an equal ratio of men to women. Research jobs are looked upon as stepping stones upward to the writer, reporter, producer level—at least they're looked upon that way by researchers. Although it's not impossible for women to get out of the research unit (indeed, the last people promoted from there had been women), one senses that men are *groomed* to get out of it. The top producers will fight all the way up the ladder to get a promotion for a man, but often they must be pushed very hard to do the same for a woman.

The research job itself can vary from answering one-sentence questions to preparing lengthy background reports on new issues for distribution throughout the news division to spending up to a year working with a producer on a documentary film. How women are treated often depends on the personality of a particular editor or producer. Differences in researchers' salaries do not break down along male-female lines. Researchers all belong to the Writers'

Guild, so salaries are fixed by union contract. In 1971 the range was from $160–$225; who got what really depended on experience, not sex.

The associate-producer level is something else, however. Each person individually negotiates his contract with management—the range is $300 to $400 per week—and it's said that women almost always come out $1,000 to $1,500 behind men over the year. More than one woman has had the experience of having a company spokesman look over his glasses and remark, "Now, a pretty little thing like you doesn't need any more money."

Regarding full producers, the most popular theory is that the few women who have made it did so purely by coincidence—had there been a man available, it would never have happened. Not surprisingly, these women are superqualified and supercompetent.

How one gets to be a reporter or correspondent seems to be a mystery, but whatever the process, it is clearly less open to women than to men. "But what if we had to send you to a riot?" is a remark apparently no less commonly heard around broadcast-media offices than around city newspaper desks.

The atmosphere: The problem is no less how an individual woman is treated and thought of than how women as a group are treated and thought of. Some examples: At a staff meeting prior to the August 26, 1970, strike (Note: No woman is in a high enough position to be included in staff meetings), CBS News president Richard Salant is supposed to have asked whether CBS had been remiss in not promoting qualified women, and whether in fact there were any women who should be producers. One of the vice presidents quipped in response, "There aren't any women who should be producers, but there sure are some producers who should be women." At another staff meeting it was announced that a research report on the women's movement was going to be significantly expanded into a book. Another vice president remarked, "We're not going to dignify that subject by publishing a *book* on it, are we?" Although an important book written by two women and partially underwritten by CBS did finally appear, the equally important and serious CBS documentary on women is still to be produced. The attitude toward women manifests itself in another way: news events involving women are not treated with the same seriousness as those involving war, peace, the poor, or minorities. The August 26, 1970, strike—the biggest political demonstration by women in the history of the United States—was covered in a haphazard and thoughtless manner. CBS News coverage of the 1972 Democratic Presidential Convention, in which women activists made political history, was a national scandal.

In early 1971, when the Supreme Court decided the first sex-discrimination case ever to be brought under the 1964 Civil Rights Act, not one CBS-network news program covered it. When the Communist Chinese delegation to the UN arrived in November 1971, Walter Cronkite kept referring to the female members as "the ladies" of the delegation. Little if any attention is ever paid to the Equal Rights Amendment, abortion law repeal, child-care center legislation, equal-pay suits, and so on. In his 1972 interview with President Nixon, Dan Rather did include some questions about women—predictably in the last minute and a half. His lead-in to the subject, sadly, was also predictable: "I'm going to be in trouble at home if I don't ask you this. . . ."

It would be unkind and untrue to indicate that nothing has happened at CBS since the emergence of the women's movement. Some changes, conscious and unconscious, have occurred. More women are being promoted with far fewer battles; the Walter Cronkite Evening News hired its first female associate producer; perhaps the strongest program in a news series for young people was on Susan B. Anthony; the local New York station began a morning show for women completely staffed by women; and the women themselves are no longer afraid to talk to each other about jobs, money, and their own aspirations.

When all is said and done, however, CBS is not very different from any other medium of journalism. It is clubby—male-clubby.

And although department heads, producers, and writers are now far more sensitized to the situation, it would be hard to imagine the day when a woman is the CBS domestic-news editor, the executive producer of the Cronkite news, or the president of CBS News. Indeed, it would be almost easier to envision a woman as president of the United States than one in Walter Cronkite's slot.

Corporate Handmaidens

NBC NEWS*

NBC is a man's corporation where women are relegated to subordinate positions: coffee-snack-meal-getter, personal maid, details-organizer, mail opener, morale-booster. Except for a few women in the public eye (Lucy Jarvis, Barbara Walters), most women at NBC, whether they last for one year or twenty, never reach the top; and women are barred entirely from many areas. There are no women working as camera*men,* engineers, radio hosts, technical directors, sound*men,* supervising editors, stage-hands, unit managers, or in top management. There are female associate producers because NBC has benefited from women working harder and longer for less pay than a man on the job. Many women have worked as associate producers for ten to fifteen years and have never seen the other side of a producer's desk—not because they lack initiative or drive, but because they are women.

I came to NBC with a diploma cum laude from Vassar, where I had held such positions as drama director, English teacher, and college-news reporter. I told the NBC Personnel Department that I wanted to work in television news. They asked one question: "Can you type?" My employment agency had

* For update, see "Progress Report" by Terry Pristin, page xix.

warned me beforehand to expect this, and I had practiced furiously to reach the golden "50 WPM" that NBC required. I was given a typing test and sent to the NBC Spot Sales Department to be interviewed for a job as sales assistant. I was told that no one ever entered the production end of NBC from the outside—that I would have to do a stint in Sales before being given the privilege of working for News. The Spot Sales Department almost barred me from working there because I was a college graduate. If that had been the case, I would *never* have been able to break into NBC production.

The NBC Spot Sales Department has sixteen male salesmen and sixteen female sales assistants. The salesmen hustle television spots (sixty- thirty- and ten-second commercial breaks) to advertisers. They sit in individual windowed offices. The women are crowded (all sixteen of them) on to the outer-office floor. The noise of sixteen typewriters, telephones, and voices on that outer floor is almost deafening.

I had worked for three months in the Spot Sales Department before I learned that my "assistant's" job was officially designated "secretarial" by NBC. In the mystery that is NBC's grading system, secretaries are paid less than assistants and are not promoted as easily. By this time, such deception was the least of my worries. I was learning the hard facts of the working-woman's world.

My boss expected me to get his coffee and lunch and run his personal errands during my lunch hour. He constantly cracked jokes about my (and every other secretary's) legs, hips, and breasts, and so did the other men. One day a new secretary with a large bust was hired. My boss called me into his office, wide-eyed and panting and asked, "Did you see that?" stretching his arms straight out in front to indicate a mammoth bust line. This woman was still being ribbed about her figure when I left the department.

The childish chauvinism of the salesmen was rather endearing when compared to the terrorizing dictatorship of the department head. He would scream obscenities at the salesmen and completely ignore the women in the department. Once he walked past our desks at lunchtime to find only two of us sitting there. We had a "back-stop" system for answering phones ("I'll answer your boss's phone from 12 to 1 if you'll answer mine from 1 to 2") which was inconvenient and sometimes impossible in actual operation. The raging boss called a meeting of all the salesmen that afternoon and fumed, "When I walk out there at lunchtime, I want to see eight pairs of tits." Did any of our loyal bosses protest this abuse? Never a word. The department hierarchy created a male-female situation that I suspect is repeated in American offices and households everywhere. Psychologically whipped and beaten by tyrannical bosses, male employees shuffle back to their own desks (or homes), gradually regaining their dignity and sense of ego by abusing their secretaries (or wives).

Several women (now raised to the status of assistants) in Spot Sales actually sell time for NBC. They are sharp and shrewd and often work overtime for no extra pay. In the Sales Department, three women in particular do the same work their bosses do. The agency representatives know them and deal with them directly. Why are the women willing to do a salesman's work for a secretary's pay and no commission or credit? It's still a mystery to me, but I imagine it's because they are paid high salaries for secretaries (sometimes as much as $200 per week) and because they have been brainwashed by a male-dominated society.

Recently a black woman was promoted to a nebulous semimanagement job to quell the rising discontent among certain NBC women. Her new salary is one-quarter that of a man's in a similar position. Because she is black, her promotion raises the percentage figures for two minorities. (NBC must present an annual report of such statistics to the FCC.)

After six months in Spot Sales, I was permitted to approach the Personnel Department with a request for transfer into production. I was sent to be interviewed for a position as production assistant in a news documentary unit. Thrilled beyond words, I accepted, no questions asked.

In my job as production assistant, I had to work as personal secretary for my boss, the unit's producer. I made out his checks, handled his checking account, gift-wrapped and mailed his presents, made his doctor and dental appointments and personal restaurant and theater reservations. (I was also appointed "double checker"—ensuring that these dates were kept.) I mailed news clippings to his relatives and friends, picked up his personal mail at his home when he was away, got his cigarettes and lunches, stocked his office refrigerator, sharpened his pencils, wiped his desk, etc., etc. In addition, I played hostess to his visitors (business or personal)—offering them drinks, taking their coats. He once chided me for neglecting to offer a cold drink to a visitor. In the producer's words, "It was a source of great embarrassment to me to have to get him a drink myself. You should have offered him a drink, supplied a napkin, and seen to it that he was totally comfortable. That is your job."

In addition to duties as personal and unit secretary, I carried a full load as production assistant (taking notes in the editing room, ordering the transcripts, coordinating those on location with those in the office). And from time to time, I was called upon to do research. As a result, I worked an average of eleven hours a day for my first four months in the unit. I was expected to start work at 10:00 A.M. even after nights when we had worked until 1:00 or 2:00 A.M. The associate producers, unit managers, and editors, would arrive much later, of course, and would often browse through newspapers and magazines as I typed, phoned, filed, researched, and scripted fast and furious. Our producer would arrive at 3:00, 4:00 or 5:00 P.M.—or wouldn't show at all. Often, when the producer wasn't looking, other men in the unit would load their work onto my desk, and go on to read the *Times* or to work on some personal project.

When I entered the unit, a woman was associate producer. Not once did she ask me to do any of her personal work. She would type a rough draft of her letters rather than dictate, in order to allow time for my other duties. On the other hand, the man who became associate producer when she left would use my time ravenously, without concern for the immense load I carried without his contribution. The female associate producer had had to begin as a secretary and production assistant herself and probably knew only too well what being unit lackey and scapegoat felt like.

Besides the official duties, women at NBC must maintain a calm and comforting atmosphere for their male bosses. The duty of morale-booster is assigned to NBC women and the role is essential in keeping male producers, executives, and brass on their feet. The unspoken command is "Smile!" and the woman who doesn't smile each time her boss enters the office (or elevator or cafeteria) and who doesn't smile regularly (God forbid she should actually frown!) in the presence of her boss is chided with "Don't look so sullen," "Whatsamatter, Sourpuss?" and similar remarks. Two weeks after I began working as production assistant, my boss turned to me with a patronizing smile and said, "You are in charge of laundry and morale." Taken by surprise (Personnel had described the job as slightly more meaty) and terrified of him, I laughed and bit my tongue.

In a similar vein, the NBC radio station, in a particularly chauvinistic promotion week, dressed up a number of young women in abbreviated cheerleader uniforms and sent them bouncing in and out of elevators and hallways embracing executives and squealing, "Have a Happy Day!"

The number of women who have stayed at NBC for ten, fifteen and twenty years is relatively small. They are faithful, punctual, poorly paid, and rarely promoted. To me, they are a sad lot. In private, most of them speculate that their salaries are far lower than those of equally qualified men.

NBC men shrink from the idea of a female boss and are quick to gossip about any woman in a position of authority— about her bitchiness, her cuckolded husband, her man-eating nature. I have seen these same men yell and scream, call names and whine, throw tantrums and knife each other in the back. It is these men who mechanically and passionlessly report women's activities to millions of Americans.

In March 1971 WRC-TV, NBC's Washington station, charged NBC with discrimination against women. The complaint went to legal agencies and to the FCC.

Two months after this action by the women at WRC-TV, NBC sent the late Aline Saarinen to Paris as correspondent. The New York NBC radio station promoted a woman to a managerial position. Early in 1972, a special memo was sent to NBC brass warning that more women, as well as other "minorities," had to be promoted to managerial positions. And—minor point—Reuven Frank, president of NBC News, distributed a memo to all news staffers asking them *not* to refer to tropical storms as *she*.

Despite these promising signs, the vast majority of NBC's women will never be paid the kinds of salaries they deserve and will never be promoted to the positions they merit. They will enter and leave in their enticing costumes, they will smile on cue, and they will learn that NBC hires women to serve its men: to be in charge of Laundry and Morale.

Small NET Gains

NATIONAL EDUCATIONAL TELEVISION*

A Fable—Part 1

Once upon a time, a Learned Gentleman from Peking, visiting the United States for the first time, found himself in a New York office with the letters NET on the door. Not understanding English,

* See Preface, page xv.

he could only trust his perceptions to reveal the nature of the work of this peculiar acronym.

Opening the door, he saw before him a long corridor. Branching off on either side were small cells, which he found to be inhabited by men dressed in variations of a basic uniform. Seated at a desk at the doorway to each cell was a woman, wearing clothes of indeterminate ethnic origin. Quietly he observed the behavior of the two sexes. The men prowled, lonely in their isolation, while the young women called gaily back and forth to each other from behind their desks.

Very strange, he thought. He searched his mind for clues among the other experiences in this unfathomable country. Finally he recalled a tour he had taken of a hospital. He concluded that these Cellmates were American men who, rapidly aging, had contracted a contagious disease. Confined to their small rooms, they were cared for by this cadre of young Guardians, able to work the complex machinery that sat on their desks.

When he returned to NET some months later, our friend was surprised to find that while the same inmates inhabited the cells, a number of the Guardians were no longer there. He concluded that he must be observing a training ground for young Guardians, who periodically left to be promoted to stewardships of higher responsibility, perhaps at the Pentagon. He remarked that they seemed strangely immune from the disease that forced the men into the cells, for in the months ahead, he never found a Guardian who had moved into a cell!

What the Learned Gentleman didn't realize is that National Educational Television is the major supplier of national programming to the public television network. It is also the place where I have worked for the past three years as an associate producer. I was attracted to NET partly because of its reputation as a producer of quality television, with a heavy emphasis on investigative documentaries and the arts, and partly because I liked its atmosphere—relaxed in tone, liberal in its policies.

Because of its image, one would expect that NET would be a leader in eradicating discrimination against women. And in fact, when I began to write this article, I thought that, while still not exactly a paragon, NET had nonetheless begun to take steps toward major reform; certainly there were visible signs of women's mobility. But still, my boss is male, his boss is male, and so on through several rungs of the corporate ladder. When I looked more closely at the facts of life at NET, I discovered the persistent pattern of doors closed to women by the force of male attitudes and strictures. And so I began to trace the source of both my illusion and my discontent.

Several years ago, NET was rife with all the standard inequities. The glamour jobs in production were virtually closed to women. There was a glaring salary disparity between men and women. Men were frequently imported into the organization at a high position in the hierarchy while qualified women languished behind their typewriters. Women were expected to remain behind to answer the telephones while their bosses roamed freely in the outside world where knowledge and skills were to be gained.

When I recently looked at the employment figures compiled by women at NET in the spring of 1970, I saw again the blatant fact of discrimination. The statistics on corporate employees indicated one president, male; five vice presidents, male; ten department directors, male; three attorneys, male. Then began the steady gradation from "assistant" jobs through clerical workers, and the concomitant rise in the number of women employed. The largest number of employees in any single job category? Thirty-one secretaries, all female. As for production personnel—the core of NET —thirteen executive producers, male; twenty-three producers, eighteen male; three directors, male. When the list dipped into associate producers, the number of women swelled, increasing again in the ranks of researchers and production aides. There were no mechanisms for promotion; the lower down on the totem pole, the more dependent a woman was on the whims of her boss.

That spring, the women at NET, myself included, got mad. When we began to share our grievances, we discovered that behind the statistics of inequality lay deep-seated male prejudices. And they were legion: our bosses simply assumed that we were constitutionally incapable of doing what they were doing. This was translated into the nitty-gritty of office politics: no matter that NET presented an informal and idiosyncratic veneer, a secretary was still a vital ornament in her boss's accumulation of property and status. If a woman wanted to break into the field of news and public affairs, she encountered an attitude, peculiar to television journalism, in which a "hard nose for news" was an extension of a phallic machismo. If she was given more responsibility, she was frequently made to feel not proud, but grateful. While it was relatively simple to perceive discrimination as it was laid out on payroll sheets and personnel forms, it was more wrenching to perceive the thousand subtle ways in which we were constantly relegated to inferior positions and conditioned to accept our own inferiority.

A Fable—Part 2

Time passed. The concerns of the Learned Gentleman from Peking brought him back to NET. On this occasion, he discovered an empty corridor, although the inmates were still in their cells, pacing back and forth. He heard their anxiety as they muttered, "Where the hell is she?" Had they been able to leave their cells, they would have followed the trail of murmuring voices that told our friend that the Guardians were gathering. Peeking through a keyhole, he was overjoyed to see some of his favorite faces.

Was this a reunion? A new and drastic scheme of therapy for the Cellmates? He could judge meaning only by the tones of the voices, by the angry inflections. Certain words reappeared: "secretary," "discrimination," "list of demands."

The Learned Gentleman felt disquieted at this breaking of the umbilical connection between Guardian and Cellmate. He wondered: Would the magic machines rust without the touch of the Guardians' nimble fingers? Would the Cellmates die without their ministrations?

The new consciousness engendered by the women's movement threw the situation into high relief. The women at NET organized; our group represented a sizable number of women.

including secretaries, producers, publicity writers, administrative assistants. We drew up a list of demands and chose a committee to negotiate with NET's administration. We asked that salary disparities be corrected, that a central phone-answering system be implemented to free women from their desks, that job categories be professionalized and duly respected, that equal opportunities in terms of transfers and promotions exist for men and women. At the time, the justice of our demands as demonstrated by our statistics was painfully obvious. Our negotiations were successful and we concluded an agreement that promised improvements.

It's two years later. What has happened?

First, why did I think that the situation for women at NET had markedly improved? Well, because some things *are* better. To begin with, there is the simple truth that women are getting more aggressive and are creating new opportunities for themselves. Another important change for the good was the appointment of Janet Simberg to head up the Personnel office.

Originally hired as a secretary herself, Janet has been an innovator in encouraging people to hire male secretaries (a practice that hasn't yet caught on) and in trying to implement a policy of hiring from within by circulating a "house" bulletin advertising a job as soon as it becomes available. Recently, the bulletin carried, for the first time, a notice for a producer's slot, but at this writing no high executive position has been so advertised. Again, as the Personnel office is responsible for setting the tone of an applicant's first encounter with NET, Janet would never dream of asking a woman if she is getting married, but instead encourages her to talk about her ambitions and willingness to work. Janet's energy, rather than corporate policy, has been a constant force for change.

Meanwhile, here's what has happened to our official demands as a women's group—the plus side, that is. The salary situation was improved by the creation of ranges for each job category. On the whole, women are now paid somewhat less than men in comparable jobs. At least no longer are there the horror stories of a woman making half the salary of a man doing the same work, with the same experience.

A Centrex phone system has been installed; however, the executive wing is still not covered by the service. Job categories have become more professionalized, if not always duly respected; for instance, a new job, that of production secretary, has been created to distinguish between the traditional desk-bound secretary, the clerical role of following a program through from inception to broadcast which is the job of the production secretary, and the on-location duties of a production aide.

Producers still tend to take advantage of secretaries by sending them out to do picture research, and secretaries still allow themselves to be used this way in the hope of getting ahead, but there is a growing sophistication about this particular game of exploitation. Also, secretaries are more frequently attached to a functioning unit, rather than being the property of a single individual. One other factor for change has been the formation of a major new program unit, "The Great American Dream Machine" series, in which a number of women were rapidly promoted into upgraded production jobs.

But do equal opportunities in terms of transfer and promotions exist for men and women? In the year and a half following the first meeting of the women's group, the only change in the top ranks of NET was the appointment of Joan Mack as director of development. Other than that, the situation of power and control was exactly the same as it had been before we met.

How has this happened? In the nine months immediately following the women's meetings, one executive producer, one vice president, one department director, and one attorney were hired, not one of them female. Of course, women have been hired in droves to "man" typewriters and switchboards. Also in those months, twenty-nine producers were hired, some as members of the staff, others for brief tenure on contract. Of the twenty-nine, two—that's right, two—were women. Recently, a new public-affairs series, "This Week," headed, of course, by a male executive producer, built up an entire staff from scratch, and the staff hired is classic in its purity—all the producers are male, all the associate producers female!

So, you may well ask: If women were sold down the river this way, how come you all allowed it to happen? What was the women's organization doing all this time?

The sad truth is that the women's group never met again. As a whole, I think it fair to say that we allow ourselves to be co-opted by the illusion of mobility. The movers and the shakers of the group were a core of women who had felt particularly stifled in their secretarial roles; many of these initiators had since been able to move out of their restrictive jobs and taste the heady wine of production. Also, the demands we put forth in the name of women were largely labor issues. Because we had failed to examine the persistent attitudinal problems from the point of view of a sustained feminism, it was possible to further oneself, to note other examples of promotions, and to fail to recognize that women are still kept from the real decision-making jobs.

Recognizing that decision-making is a relative process in any case in a corporate structure, what is it like for those women who, by using every ounce of talent, energy, and stratagems at their command, have made it to the "permissible" upper levels of production?

As an associate producer, a woman may be doing responsible and original work only to find that she is performing as a hand-maiden to a male producer who gets every ounce of the credit. It is no accident that women frequently rest at this convenient level of accomplishment; besides, it is highly unlikely that a woman will ever find herself groomed to rise above this point. I know of one classic story in which a man and a woman, both producers and colleagues for many years, jointly developed an idea for a series; she, in fact, authored the proposal that was ultimately accepted for production. When the time came for structuring the unit, he was appointed one of two executive producers; the other was another male. She was assigned to work as a producer under the two men.

If a woman does make the leap and become a producer, she theoretically will have the money, authority, and responsibility for making her own show. But even as a producer at NET, a woman is likely to find that she is treated as less substantial, less powerful, than a man. As a female producer said to me recently: "How much control does a woman have when her program ideas have to be okayed by her male boss, when even the authorization to employ a film crew must be signed by a man? There is not a single woman in television, with the exception of Joan Ganz Cooney [president of the Children's Television Workshop], who has any real control over the direction of her own work." I have heard a job described as "producing" when a man is doing it, as "expediting" when a woman is doing it.

Although the above observations are difficult to document, it has struck me that women producers are more expendable than men at budget-cut times and that they are prey to a variety of tactics that serve to keep them in their place, such as fostering an artificial competition between themselves and other women. Certainly, the snide remarks of male coworkers will not magically cease, nor will the sniping of those women who have swallowed the myth that one woman's achievement will shut out all other women from the tiny space of success allotted to our sex.

A Fable—Part 3

Events in the Learned Gentleman's native land prevented him from returning to America for the better part of a year. Curiosity having suggested another visit to NET, he found himself again in the long corridor. He saw a new crop of Guardians, but fewer than before. Seeking to be reassured by the familiar presence of the chronic cases, he wandered down the hallway. But when he looked into the cells, he received another shock—many of the cells had become wards, each inhabited by two or three people. And among them were several of his favorite old Guardians. To his amazement, Guardians and Cellmates were to be found talking to one another as they moved between corridor and cell. More people even seemed to know how to operate the magic machines.

Our friend from Peking walked away, shaking his head, hard put to make sense out of this new development. Had the disease abated, making it possible for everybody to inhabit the same rooms together? But perhaps, alas, the reverse was true—the Guardians themselves had caught the contagion and so had finally moved into the cells. Or, was it possible that the Guardians had developed new immunities, which might allow them close proximity to the illness while remaining un-contaminated?

The Learned Gentleman was reassured to see a sign of the old, therapeutic order, when he noticed a very young Guardian bringing cups of the steaming brown medicine into the cells. Pondering the ambiguities, he wondered: Perhaps the sickness had indeed spread, but was it true that now everybody might have an equal chance to catch the disease?

Some small changes seem to indicate the glimmerings of opportunities just beginning to open up to women in media; and, as in the Fable, there is always the chance that with increased opportunity to work as colleagues, the sexes will come to regard each other with a new equality. But I'm afraid that unless we can effect these changes on our own terms, with a sense of our own values, then we're doomed to catch the sickness that infects men in their work.

But where to forge these new, immunizing values? What concerns me most at NET is not the specifics of salary and promotion, but the effect of discriminatory attitudes upon women—the implicit acceptance of inferiority, the internalizing of a degraded self-image. And so I feel that when a woman works at NET, she will continue to arrive at a critical juncture when she will look beyond the equivocal picture presented by employment facts and ask herself whether she will be able to chart an alternate course—with its own values—within a structure that provides few models and little encouragement.

2

MAGAZINE PUBLISHING

Magazine Publishing

As EMPLOYERS OF WOMEN, magazines fall, predictably, somewhere between newspapers and books. Their policies vary widely, but few magazine publishers are as Neanderthalic as book publishers, and few are as progressive as, say, the *New York Times* or United Press International.

Of course magazines are more dissimilar than other media. The output of one TV network is notoriously indistinguishable from another's, and newspapers all do the news. But to lump *The New Yorker, Newsweek,* and the *Reader's Digest* together is like adding apples, butter, and cheese.

But there is one thing that makes most magazines kin: they are run by men who have low opinions of the ability of the women who work for them. In a way, this betrays a pathetic lack of self-esteem on the men's part. Like Groucho and the country club, they seem to be saying, "I don't want to hire a woman who is stupid enough to want to work for me." A curious thread runs through the articles contained herein on both magazines and books: men are more willing to give responsible jobs to women who began their careers with other firms than to those they have hired themselves. The upshot is that the best way to get the job you want with the firm of your choice is to accept a less desirable job with another publisher.

The real female ghetto of magazines is one that female editorial staffers on most of them are kept mercifully ignorant of—

subscription handling. The *Reader's Digest,* an exception, houses its editorial and subscription departments together, and is perhaps given unfair attention here as a result. The other large-circulation magazines tactfully keep this seamy side of their operations out of the view of their editorial elite. Who knows what hells are maintained out there in Boulder, Colorado, or Dayton, Ohio, or Livingston, New Jersey?

Boring from Within

COSMOPOLITAN!

by Nancy Weber

My bathroom door and walls are plastered with memorabilia. There are funny letters from Norman Mailer, Willie Morris, Barry Goldwater, George Segal, and my brother (only my brother knew he was being funny); J. Edgar Hoover's last Christmas card and a Feiffer original; clippings, valentines, crazy postcards, lists of all sorts. Not even the kangaroo in my bathtub gets more smiles than this note from an editor at *Cosmopolitan:*

Dear Nancy,

Just got your story and am going to wait until I have enough time to read it through without interruption. I'm on my way out now to a Christmas shooting, but wanted to get these magazines off to you. Some of them are in pretty bad shape, but your article is intact in all of them.

Your idea about what famous men like in women intrigued me, but Mrs. Brwon [*sic*] says she's through with that sort of theing [*sic*] because it gives us normal girls a big dose of inferiority. And, we did one some months ago, only to get reams of mail from girls telling us that most of our eligible bachelors are *queer*. What are you going to do?

Are you interested in going back to work on a 9–5 basis? We have an editor's opening coming up—would be decorating, food, and other features. I don't know anything about the salary yet, but thought I'd sound you out. . . . Mrs. Brown likes your work so much. (I know you probably don't want to give up your glorious freelance freedom, but it never hurts to *ask*.)

Talk to you soon,

You know you can find *her* editing *Cosmopolitan*. You can tell by the *italics*. (Do Cosmo editors have an italics quota, like cops and parking tickets?) *Every single article* I wrote for Cosmo grew italics between my desk and the newsstand. And they put in all those exclamation points, too!

The terrible thing isn't that *Cosmopolitan* editors tamper with your writing and thinking. It's that after a while they don't have to. I mean, I'm a novelist. The author of poetic prose. A girl of wit and depth. And there I was, asking to do a piece on what famous men like in women.

One day it got to me, and I swore that nothing would ever make me write for them again. With breathtaking synchroneity, my editor called to tell me they were going to buy a crazy short story of mine—publish my first fiction. The next time it was a long take from my actual journals, something I'd barely dared hope Cosmo would want. So it goes, at tantalizing intervals, for all their regular writers: three for them, one for you; two for them, one for you—just enough to keep you in the stable.

To wonder why a writer would want a story she really cares about in a magazine she finds mostly unreadable is to overlook one of the great joys: infiltration. Paul Krassner once told me that he knew his pieces for *Cavalier* were in a way more important than his pieces for *The Realist* because a good many of the readers of *The Realist* already agreed with him about most things. For every Cosmopolitan Girl who wrote to tell me that I was a dreadful creature, another wrote that I had turned her head around. I can't exactly claim that I waged a revolution from the slick pages of

Cosmopolitan, but I got a few people to reconsider a few of their givens, no question.

You can be revolutionary in Cosmo; you cannot be Political. Cosmo sanitizes references to contemporary history *ad hilarium.* In that hunk of journal I sold them, there was a reference to passing an antiwar demonstration . . . and then a reference to going birthday-present shopping at A La Vieille Russie. I said in the piece that I didn't join the demonstration; but my sympathies were obvious, and my editor said the whole paragraph was "well, a little too *Russian,* you know what I mean." She let the paragraph stand only because I managed to convey that A La Vieille Russie is New York's most exquisitely capitalistic emporium, a throwback to the workmanship and acquisitiveness of the czarist era, not exactly the place where you would expect to find Ho Chi Minh hanging out.

A while back I said that *Cosmopolitan* bought my first short story. A great deal that they bought before and after was also fiction. The first time I made up an article for them (six girls sitting around my apartment talking about married men were actually six girls sitting around in my head), I told my editor what I was doing, and timidly asked for absolution. She laughed and laughed. But if Cosmo's editors don't much notice the difference, or want to notice the difference, between reporting and inventing, other editors do; and a portfolio of clippings from Cosmo is not always a girl's best resumé. Once, in Israel, which I thought was far enough away, I tried to persuade an editor to let me write for him, and my "credits" did me in. *"Cosmopolitan!"* he scoffed. "No one ever really did any reporting for them. If they chained all of their writers in the middle of the ocean, it would all come out exactly the same."

About money. *Cosmopolitan*'s fees have traditionally swung all over the place—high for the famous, low for the unknown; high for research pieces (even when they aren't), low for first-person pieces; higher for most men than for most women. I had very warm working relationships with several editors there (the woman who wrote me the funny note was incredibly responsive and helpful when she wasn't italicizing me); I didn't want to make things less warm by using an agent, and Cosmo took advantage of that. Acquired world magazine rights, when I thought they were acquiring first North American magazine rights (and sold my pieces to foreign magazines without having to pay me); once gave a piece to an anthology, even though they had no anthology rights, lost me my copyright on it forever, and let the piece be used to make a point I would never have permitted it to be used to make. Then again, they never said a word about the $200 walking-around money they gave me when I went to Israel to do a piece I didn't turn in.

You cannot write for *Cosmopolitan,* or talk about it properly, without knowing something about Helen Gurley Brown. She is a maddening woman, all the more so because it's impossible not to like her. Back in the days when I was writing for Cosmo with some frequency, Helen called me to ask me to do a piece on Why Lying Is More Elegant Than Telling the Truth—4,000 words, and could I turn it in by 10 o'clock the next morning? You're the Only Person in the World Who Can Do It, she said, and I unmade plans for dinner, and did it. The next morning she had decided that Truth Was More Elegant, and because I hadn't used an agent, or my head, I didn't even get a kill fee. I no longer write for *Cosmopolitan,* but if Helen called me right now and put on her Iron-Butterfly act and told me I was the Only Person who could do a piece about why anthologies on writing are dangerous, I would probably pull this piece out of the typewriter to accommodate her by ten o'clock tomorrow morning.

There are frustrations in store for anyone who decides to become a regular contributor to *Cosmopolitan;* and frequent doses of Mencken and Strunk and White will be needed to offset the damages to thought processes and prose style. But once you're in, the work will be steady . . . and you'll have more funny stories to tell than you otherwise might. A couple of years after I started writing for Cosmo, I was scheduled for some reasonably serious surgery. Just as a joke to distract my mother, I said that I was going through with it mostly so I could do an article on How to Be Sexy in the Hospital. I called up my editor to share the joke—and instead of getting a laugh, I got an assignment. So off I went with champagne and Shalimar and incense and my entire erotica library . . . and then this *dreamy* doctor walked in, and you'll *never* guess what *happened!!!*

De-Squaring the Circle

FAMILY CIRCLE

Family Circle doesn't fool around with your twenty-nine cents. In addition to exquisitely detailed instructions on crafts, cooking, etc., the reader occasionally gets a free bonus, such as an in-book dress pattern, discount coupons to motels or restaurants, or a packet of flower seeds.

Departmental editors are conscientious if not always imaginative. Regular features vary in quality. The astrology column, by Santha Rama Rau, appears to be more reliable than the health column, by Lawrence Galton.

While *Family Circle*'s raison d'être is still the old-fashioned "service" article, Executive Editor Beatrice Buckler, a Lucy-Stoner, has striven to introduce some feminist content: *Family Circle* paid $30,000 for first serial rights to Caroline Bird's *Everything a Woman Needs to Know to Get Paid What She Is Worth.* Among other feminist articles of some distinction was Ann Eliasberg's "Are You Harming Your Daughter?" which appeared in February, 1971. That piece has been anthologized and was one of the first mass-media efforts to explore sexism in children's literature. Buckler says, "I'd hope that *Family Circle,* and all women's magazines would encourage women to become more independent, to free themselves from the constant need to *please,* to become more aware and more critical of the stereotype society presses upon them, to have more pride and self-esteem. In short, I would like to see *Family Circle* continue to help women grow."

To some extent, Buckler has succeeded. One reporter made a content analysis of *Family Circle* at five-year intervals—from 1953 to 1973. The later issues depicted women as more autonomous, recognized that many mothers are employed outside the home, and sometimes introduced androgyny into needlepoint, cooking, and home-repair features (e.g., Burt Reynolds's favorite recipes).

Opportunities for freelancers: Family Circle rarely assigns full-length articles to persons who are not established writers. Payments average $1,500 plus expenses. Feminists are advised to query Beatrice Buckler or Patricia Curtis. *Family Circle* buys first or second serial rights to some nonfiction books, especially in service areas. Linda Dannenberg is book editor. Fiction is published only occasionally, and is most often by a big "name," such as Joyce Carol Oates, Maurice Sendak, or Jacqueline Susann.

Staff and atmosphere: While most of the departmental and contributing editors are female, five of the six top-of-the-masthead editors are male, Buckler being the only exception. Having recently been appointed vice president, Buckler is also the only influential woman on the corporate or business side of the magazine. Department editors average between $15,000 and $20,000 a year. Until recently, male personnel tended to receive higher salaries than females with equivalent responsibility. It is not clear whether or not this has been corrected. *Family Circle* rarely has openings at the senior-editorial levels. Two editors who left recently were not replaced.

At the associate-editor level, openings do occur. These jobs are part secretarial, part editorial. The opportunity to learn editing and writing (as opposed to just filing and typing) varies substantially from department to department. The pay is low, starting at about $140 a week. Applicants are expected to type, and are usually college graduates with some editorial experience. In recent years, several young associate editors, including Linda Dannenberg, have been promoted to senior levels.

Family Circle has an interesting history. It began, in 1932, as a food-store throwaway distributed by two chains in the New York and Washington, D.C., areas. In 1946 the price rose from zero to five cents. Thereafter, the price and circulation have continued to rise, and the magazine has gradually started to take itself seriously. In the early 1960s it was purchased by Cowles, which, in an effort to raise money to save *Look* Magazine, sold it to the New York Times Company in 1971.

Family Circle now has the fourth or fifth largest circulation of all periodicals published in the United States. It is sold at supermarket checkout counters only, and is not available by subscription. Presumably, this means that every copy bought is also read.

Women of (Mis)Fortune

FORTUNE MAGAZINE

Just ask any female employee of *Fortune* Magazine what it's like to work there and the answer will most likely be an ambiguous combination of praise and criticism. The education a writer or researcher gets from working on *Fortune*'s variety of stories is not easily matched anywhere else. But this is offset by the fact that *Fortune* Magazine has always been operated by the Time Inc. system, which has traditionally channeled men into writing and editing, and women into secretarial and research positions.

Fortune is headquartered on the eighteenth floor of the Time-

Life Building. Some people find the offices cold and sterile, but, that aside, there is privacy, quiet, and an abundance of support systems that range from the best possible research library to a maintenance service that will supply a calculator or tape recorder on very short notice. Every phone hooks up to a secretary's desk, so messages do get forwarded. Offices and cubicles (as some deserve to be called) shoot off narrow hallways, with the highly prized window offices going to veteran staff members. The office atmosphere is very free, with most staffers keeping their own flexible schedules. People come and go, stay late, leave early, with no monitoring and no second-guessing. Writers and researchers can write or type their notes at home. The staff is small, about 100, so most people know each other, at least by name. Because people work independently, there is little social contact between staff members. Monthly staff coffee meetings, once initiated for the purpose of making individuals feel that they were part of one big family journalistic effort, have petered out.

Fortune's editorial structure is simple. The managing editor and assistant managing editor sit on "Editor's Row" with three other editors. Together they process the monthly barrage of stories. The Board of Editors, a larger group composed of the editors, the chief of research, and a number of select writers, is an advisory group to the managing editor. The bulk of the staff is made up of associate editors (twenty-nine), most of whom are writers, and reporter/researchers (twenty-five).

There is an editorial clip desk which has always been manned by a young female college graduate with little or no previous work experience. She sorts through the daily newspapers cutting out articles that are relevant to ongoing stories. This is generally considered a training slot for research, although the work does little to prepare one for that job. Another trainee job that has always been held by a young woman is on the wire desk—where all the cables going to and coming from correspondents and stringers are coordinated. "Women are better coordinators."

Neither the clip-desk nor the wire-desk job is carefully defined, and both jobholders perform a variety of small chores on the magazine. There are several secretaries, who usually work for more than one person. The Art Department has its own small hierarchy.

Once it is decided that *Fortune* will do a specific story, the assignment is given to a writer-researcher team. Ideally, both members of the team start gathering material from the library and calling prospective contacts on the phone. One of the researcher's principal complaints has been that writers often leave these preliminary and more menial tasks to the researcher, treating her as if she were his private secretary (or maid). Researchers have felt this would never happen if they were men instead of women.

After this early research stage is completed, an interview and travel schedule is arranged. Generally the writer and researcher attend all major interviews together. Though not essential, it is often necessary to divide up the less important interviews in order to cover more ground. When the team is interviewing together, both can ask questions, although the writer is considered to be in charge of the interview. The researcher later types up the notes for all the interviews at which she was present. At last the writer gathers together all the research and notes and begins to write. Desperate requests for missing information are relayed to the researcher. Finally the manuscript arrives and is edited.

Next comes the checking phase, and that can strain even the most compatible researcher-writer relationship. The researcher carefully checks each spelling and fact. She may also argue about the way the facts are used. Disagreements about concepts presented in a story are often the most traumatic experiences. The basic psychological make-up of both writer and researcher are bared during this face-off. How liberal is the writer with the truth? How picayune is the researcher about checking-points? This varies with every writer-researcher combination, and it must be said that one of *Fortune*'s greatest assets is the variety of personalities on its staff. At last the manuscript goes off to the proof-room—the last fail-safe stop—where proofers catch virtually all the remaining errors and close the story.

This is the basic cake. The frosting is that *Fortune* allows a two-month lead-time for most stories and spares no expense to make sure that the reporting team covers all the ground necessary to get the full picture. If a writer or researcher wants to go to California for one important interview, he or she is free to do so. Air Travel cards supplied by the company facilitate impromptu travel. Both writers and researchers have generous expense accounts, can stay in excellent hotels, and may entertain story sources when they wish at a restaurant of their own choosing. And, of course, *Fortune*'s well-earned prestige automatically opens doors and wins access for its reporters to the top people in every field.

In May of 1970, twenty-nine *Fortune* women, including twenty-five out of twenty-eight researchers, joined representatives from other Time Inc. editorial divisions in filing a complaint of sex discrimination against the company with the New York State Division of Human Rights. The settlement that was eventually reached called for hiring and promotion without regard to sex, awarded credit lines to researchers, offered researchers an opportunity to try out as writers, and gave recognition to exceptional researchers by making them associate editors. The title "researcher" was changed to "reporter/researcher," a more accurate description of the job.[1]

It is more interesting to look behind the printed settlement to see what has really happened at *Fortune* since its adoption. It is fair to say that with few exceptions the female editorial staff was a most unliberated group until the women began to organize around this job action. Only a few women had pushed themselves forward into the writers' ranks. One woman with a graduate degree in journalism moved slowly but steadily from a research job to assistant chief of research and then, without great fanfare, became a

[1] See Time Inc., Agreement, page 278.

writer. Today she is the only female writer on the Board of Editors. Another woman with previous writing experience spent eleven years as a *Fortune* researcher. She had made it known that she was interested in writing, but this desire was ignored until one day her notes fell by chance into the hands of the managing editor. Soon afterward she was given a trial writing assignment which turned into an award-winning story. Eventually she was promoted to associate editor. A third woman did a stint on the clip desk and worked for over four years as a researcher. She left *Fortune* in 1967 to do freelance writing for *New York* Magazine and was very successful. A year later *Fortune* hired her back to write the Personal Investing section. These three women had obvious talent, drive, and perseverance. It was interesting that none of them was among those who joined in the legal complaint filed by their female colleagues.

During the negotiations between *Fortune* management and the complainants, the managing editor promoted the assistant head of research to a writing position. This woman had spent six years writing for newspapers but was hired by *Time* Magazine, and then by *Fortune,* as a researcher. Any man with a similar background would have been immediately hired as a writer or correspondent. During her seven years as *Fortune*'s assistant chief of research, she was given small writing assignments that demonstrated her talent. But it was made clear during the negotiations that her promotion to a writing job was simply a response to the pressures of the complaint.

The first candidate selected by management to "train" to become a writer was a researcher of nine years standing. Before coming to *Fortune,* she had been a correspondent in the Boston bureau of *Business Week* and was the author of several feature stories, including cover stories. Her writer-training period was interrupted when *Fortune* offered her the job of story-development editor. *Fortune*'s latest writer-trainee is a woman who previously spent eighteen months writing for *Life* Magazine. It seems obvious that while *Fortune* management is following the agreement to the letter, one should not be dazzled by the progress being made. These women have long been qualified for the jobs they are only now doing.

In the year following the agreement, *Fortune* hired five writers. Two were veterans from the ranks of *Time* and two others had been wooed away from other business publications. A fifth was fresh out of the Columbia School of Journalism. None were women. Management admits that they "have not been beating the bushes" to find qualified women writers, but claims that they are not actively recruiting male candidates either. If this means that they are waiting to see who walks in off the street to apply for a writing job, then the situation is shocking for two reasons.

First of all, management has repeatedly stated that *Fortune* is a "writer's" magazine. One would think that they would be tracking down the best writers in the business. Secondly, *Fortune* has never hired a female writer from the outside. To do so might help to win back some of the lost good faith of the female staff as well as to correct a situation that has proved to be a public embarrassment. Surely there is a qualified candidate either at one of the journalism schools or presently working for a daily or weekly periodical.

While the editors have made no visible effort to hire women, the chief of research quickly responded to the settlement by hiring two male researchers. They have been assigned to both male and female writers and have been asked to work on solid, exciting, middle-of-the-book stories as well as on assignments that require the long and dreary compilation of statistics. Women of *Fortune* feel that their chief of research has played an active role in boosting their case before management. This has not been the case in many of the other divisions of Time Inc.

To many women on *Fortune,* the settlement won from management in 1970 seems like a token victory. Others sense a real change in the attitude of management and in the working relationships between the men and women on staff. In most cases the male writers are now treating the women more like professional colleagues. Offhand comments like "I'll get my girl to do it" just aren't heard any more. In fact, some men will bend over backward to make sure that a woman working on a story is not excluded from story conferences or business lunches. But certainly the magazine has not become a paradise for women. And as for the hard-core male chauvinists, they will always be with us. They have pulled in their consciousness and dug in their heels.

Women who have recently joined the research staff seem to have an entirely different attitude from those who have been here four or five years. They feel the doors to all jobs are open. "Anybody who's good can make it," they say. The woman who has been at *Fortune* a long time is still her own worst enemy. Many who should be taking up the writing challenge lack the gumption—and fear the consequences of rejection. They are essentially products of the system that taught them, and taught them well, that a researcher is a researcher is a researcher.

Fortune Magazine's coverage of women in business is less than extensive. In the July–August 1971 issue of the *Harvard Business Review,* Charles D. Orth and Frederic Jacobs discussed the question of women in management and presented the following statistics:

A 1970 national study of the employment of women showed that in 82 percent of the companies surveyed, more than 10 percent of all employees were women; and in 31 percent, more than 50 percent of the employees were women (this includes secretaries, file clerks, etc.). But 83 percent of the same companies reported that fewer than 10 percent of their first-line supervisors were women; and 91 percent reported that fewer than 10 percent of their managers were women.

Each month *Fortune*'s aptly named "Business*men* in the News" section highlights the careers of newly appointed company presidents and board chairmen. When it decides to write a story about one company, it is the chairman, president, division managers, etc., who are interviewed and quoted. Since so few of these jobs are held by women, female faces rarely appear in the magazine.

There have been exceptions. A few years ago when Mary Wells formed her own advertising company and miraculously boosted the revenues of Braniff Airways with clever ads and gimmicks—such as painting the airplanes different pastel colors—*Fortune* wrote about her success story in glowing terms. There has apparently been some discussion in story conferences about a major *Fortune* issue on women's liberation as that has affected business, but thus far nothing concrete has been scheduled.

Time Inc. management, still unnerved by the actions of its own female employees, is eager to project a modern editorial attitude toward women. In 1970 the editor-in-chief of all Time publications expressed concern over, and nearly canceled, a story entitled "There Are Sex Differences in the Mind Too" which was bound to enrage most women. The concern, of course, was aroused by fears of damaging the company's public image rather than by doubts about the basic premises set forth in the article.

In summary, females working for *Fortune* are unfortunate.

Bad Staff Keeping

GOOD HOUSEKEEPING

Good Housekeeping's Good Housekeeper has a high-school diploma, at least two children, a devoted husband, a germ-free house, and a freshly mowed lawn. (She may also have a dog and a station wagon, but these are optional.) One of thirteen million readers, she does not travel outside the United States; instead, she focuses her energies on things that immediately affect her home and the well-being of her children. The Good Housekeeper is an idealized American institution—the middle-class mama whose chief joy is a happy hearth, a hubby, and lots of little ones. Her service magazine is *Good Housekeeping,* and editorial management continues to give her hard-hitting reports on items like the basic facts about carpet padding or "The Right Way to Fix a Leaky Faucet."

At *Good Housekeeping* it is editorial policy not to rock the money-making boat. The monthly is the most profitable women's magazine on the market because, as the top editors often remind the staff, those in administrative positions *understand* the reader. The Good Housekeeper would not "enjoy" articles about divorced women who are satisfied with life or people in ghetto areas who are suffering. The few controversial pieces that the magazine has carried, about issues such as Kent State or abortion reform, have received low readership, subscription cancellations, and hordes of irate letters. Who is to blame for that?

The editors rely on their monthly reader-survey reports to tell them how women react to past features and what they want in the future. And the women they polled shun provocative pieces and want more fiction and practical service articles. So far, by going along with the polls, the editors have continuously boosted profit margins.

As things look now, *Good Housekeeping* will change only if, for some reason, monetary losses require editorial revision. But any woman who is willing to work for the Good Housekeeper might well be able to move ahead at the magazine.

The staff is organized into ten departments: Fiction, Articles, Features, The Better Way, Home Building and Decorating, Fashions, Editorial Production, Art, Art Production, and Copy—and each one is headed by an editor with an associate editor and an assistant or two. There are six female and four male editors representing the ten departments, but the top executive positions are retained by men.

One female exception is a woman named Willie Mae Rogers, the director of Good Housekeeping Institute. The Institute operates on a floor with test kitchens, model rooms, a laundry, a beauty salon, a sewing center, and God knows how many other facilities for evaluating advertisers' products. However, no matter what type of household item is discussed in the magazine, the Institute is a story that would take another chapter to describe. But it is worth mentioning that Willie Mae Rogers does rank as a *Good Housekeeping* executive, although her bailiwick is the Institute and not the editorial workings of the magazine.

The important decisions are ultimately made by the men. And since the Hearst Corporation, which owns *Good Housekeeping,* is still a private business, it has chosen not to abide by the Newspaper Guild regulations governing wages and promotions. There is a Hearst Employees' Union for secretarial and office workers, but editors and writers have variable salaries, with no definite standards. Raises are given when titles are changed, and occasionally for something called merit. Mostly, increases are left to the discretion of the individual editors, subject to approval from management. Generally, women are hired for less money than men.

One woman with several years' experience in medical writing was hired as an associate editor and, six months later, a younger male was employed as a staff writer. Although her job was of a higher rating, he was started at $1,000 more in salary. When the woman complained, she was told that her many years of experience did not compare with the three months that the man had worked on a newspaper. Shortly after that, the younger staff writer was promoted to associate editor and given an office of his own, while the female associate editor shared desk space in a room with three other people.

For another example of inequity, a woman who had been a

staff writer for almost three years requested promotion to a recently vacated associate-editor position. She was told that she could not have the job while she was pregnant. The woman told her superiors that she would not quit, that after the birth of her baby she would need a job and would welcome the increased responsibility and income. "You can tell me that my work is below par," she argued, "but don't say you're not going to promote me because I'm pregnant." Upon investigation, she found that there was a strong bias among the editors toward hiring a man for the position. Still, she persisted, and after two months the promotion finally went through.

Considering that the magazine is dedicated to serving women who are wives and mothers, it is surprising that pregnancy should be used against a woman. However, there are no worthwhile maternity benefits available from the magazine; having a baby only means time off without pay or using up vacation days. And vacations are not that plentiful. The first year that an employee works, say from May to May, she gets two weeks off; after five years, three weeks; and after ten years, four weeks; that is the limit—vacations do not exceed four weeks for anyone.

Because the magazine is broken into departments, there is no general research staff or typing pool for a woman to work her way through. A new employee would probably be hired as an editorial assistant or assistant editor, or possibly as a secretary (the two women who are currently employed as secretaries to the editor have Master's degrees), and would be assigned to a specific section of the magazine. From there, she could work her way up within the department as vacancies occur. Usually promotions will come from within (the woman who has the nebulous title of assistant managing editor was once a staff writer), but there will be occasional hirings from the outside. As in the case of the woman who was pregnant, a woman has to make herself heard and understood.

Citizen Kane Redux

HARPER'S BAZAAR*

Harper's Bazaar is a matriarchy comprising about sixty women. However, don't look for familial comforts or a sisterly ambience; the $97 a week you will receive as a secretary/assistant is the only straightforward and stable exchange made on the premises. All other forms of communication are analogous to Frost's version of the apocalypse: fire or ice.

Don't expect to learn the overall workings of a magazine here, since each department jealously guards the secrets about whatever mysterious function it has. However, if you have a fairly resilient ego, job experience at *Bazaar* carries almost enough prestige to compensate for the trauma. The magazine usually promotes from within: chances are that you may go on to better things after several years as a secretary/assistant, but the upper-echelon staff will probably never let you forget your humble beginnings.

Raises are almost unheard of—the Hearst Corporation doesn't belong to the Newspaper Guild. As slave laborer, you can only retaliate by booing all the way through *Citizen Kane*. Old movie reruns are all you'll be able to afford on your salary anyway.

Carrying the White Man's Burden

LADIES' HOME JOURNAL

The editorial message driven home by the *Ladies' Home Journal* to date is that women are meant to be totally passive, ever-suffering, second-class citizens whose greatest fulfillment in life is

* See Preface.

having their collective psyche divined by the out-of-touch-men, the editors and advertisers, who determine the content of this magazine.

The *Journal* has a paid circulation of 6.9 million, with probably double that number in actual readership. According to a recent survey, 1.2 million readers of the *Journal* are black, but the magazine ignores its black readers: in the past year it has printed one article by Mrs. Medgar Evers and an occasional photograph of a black athlete's wife in a fashion spread. This is the total sweep of the *Journal*'s social concern, aside from the statement from Mrs. Nixon endorsing the idea of volunteerism, "The heart has reasons the mind knows nothing of."

"The Magazine Women Believe In" deals superficially, unrealistically, or not at all with the actual problems of today's women: job opportunity, child care, abortion. Though one out of every three adult women in America is single, divorced, or widowed, the *Journal* depicts no alternative life-style for the American woman aside from marriage and family. (One editor explained it: "Those women don't buy the refrigerators.")

Consumerism and inflation are twisted into *mea culpa* pieces, like Sylvia Porter's "Why You Can't Live on Your Husband's Salary." Family relations are reduced to tips on deception, as in a story explaining football, "Impress Your Husband with How Much You Know—Without Knowing Much at All." The politics of the nation are covered by stories like the one protesting the virtue of the girl who drowned in Senator Ted Kennedy's car.

This peculiar idea of women's needs is the vision of John Mack Carter, who holds the dual title of editor and publisher of the *Journal*. He is exemplary of the man who has built an entire career telling women how they could better come to know themselves. John Mack Carter has edited at *Better Homes and Gardens; Household* (published at Topeka, Kansas); *American Home; McCall's;* and since 1965, the *Ladies' Home Journal*. He is a member of Sigma Delta Chi, a journalism society which until very recently barred women. According to a profile in *Business Week,* John Mack Carter runs the *Journal* with "freedom and an iron hand."

There is no doubt about John Mack Carter's long hours and dedication to his job. The question is whether he is qualified for the job at all; he admittedly sees women through male eyes. In keeping with this view, three of the four top editors of the magazine are men. The token woman above middle management, Lenore Hershey, was hired from *McCall's* because of her contacts in the Nixon and Johnson administrations to add to the "prestige" of *Ladies' Home Journal.* John Stevens, the second managing editor at the *Journal,* was promoted from a production position at the magazine. The third managing editor in this proliferation, Dick Kaplan, was employed by *Saga, Playboy, Coronet,* and *Pageant* before he assumed the white man's burden of editing for women.

Not only has John Mack Carter surrounded himself with male editors at the magazine, which "Never Underestimate[s] the Power of a Woman," he also doles out more than half of the magazine's article assignments to men.

Within a period of fifteen months, the *Journal* by-lined seventy-six men, compared with sixty-seven women. (These numbers do not include men writing under female pseudonyms, a practice that is quite rampant.) Since February 1969, only twenty-five percent of all service articles—advice on food, fashion, sewing, medicine, and decorating—have been credited to men.

The *Journal's* psychological and personality pieces typically place all the burden of compromise in man/woman relationships on the woman. The magazine's constant message is that if the husband throws his dinner at the wall, it is always because the wife's food is lousy, her hair is rotten, her kids are unmanaged brats.

Food and beauty stories resound this theme by promulgating standards that are by definition unrealistically lofty and geared to evoke female self-contempt. The pictures of "real" women are retouches of the most flattering work of highly paid photographers who use movie make-up men setting up "candids."

If the foregoing indictment of *Ladies' Home Journal* sounds familiar, it's with good reason. It was taken from a press release prepared by the Media Women who engaged in the sit-in at the magazine's offices in March 1970. The demonstration was not entirely in vain. It focused the attention of the public and of other publishers on the Neanderthalism of women's magazines and contributed to the reformation of some of them.

But not the *LHJ*. Except for a few specific figures, the indictment is as pertinent today as it was when it was first formulated in the spring of 1970.

In fact, John Mack Carter boasts, in a 1974 radio commercial, that nothing about *Ladies' Home Journal* has changed except its size.

Old Wine in a New Bottle

McCALL'S MAGAZINE*

McCall's Magazine is housed in one of the loveliest buildings in New York. The lobby reminds you of the fifties—the beige marble walls, the old-fashioned chandeliers that drop from the ceiling two stories above. This building, backed by the modern Pan Am building and the bustle of Grand Central Station, symbolizes the *McCall's* state of mind. For this magazine, which proclaims itself "First Magazine for Women," retains the trappings of an old era—the lavishly decorated offices for the top few editors, the general concern for status, and the jealously guarded power rights

* See Preface.

—while the magazine struggles to find a new reading market to assure its very survival.

The new market, hopefully, will be composed of moderately liberated women: they will want to read serious articles (for example, Gloria Emerson's report from Vietnam) and will appreciate service departments—rather than depend on them—for glamour and innovation. They will want stories about divorcees, women bringing up their "illegitimate" child(ren), instead of just life in a nuclear family. After Shana Alexander's one-year tenure (1969–70), also known as the "reign of chaos" because it seems that more than half the staff left during a six-month period, Pat Carbine, formerly an editor at *Look* and now at *Ms,* established order and commitment to the new themes. Pat is a charming, eloquent, tough woman—one who is receptive to new ideas.

Since the fall of 1970, when Pat first took over, women have filled almost every editorial position, although two top spots—managing editor and art director—are filled by men. Since concern for the budget has pared down the staff, many women feel that the nucleus remaining is the most professional and most competent staff *McCall's* has had in recent years. The people here work very hard, so *McCall's* is not a gay or even a very loose place, but none of the tension can be attributed to sexism.

What about jobs and opportunities for freelance writers? To start with the happiest side, the magazine is looking for people to submit queries and to write freelance news stories for the "Right Now" section. An eight-page newsletter that runs as an insert, "Right Now" began in February 1970, and the staff generally considers it the liveliest and most open section of the magazine. "Right Now" pays from $150 to $300 for a 700-word piece.

On the other hand, expect very tough competition on the "national" (or full-length) articles level. Payment for a full-length article may run up to $1,500 or even $2,000. With so many magazines failing or cutting down on their staffs, the market has been blitzed with top professionals looking for freelance assignments.

You need a contact or an in with an editor for your article to have a chance of being printed.

Now on getting a job—*McCall's* hires recent college grads for editorial-assistant jobs, but it takes much determination and effort ever to move up from those spots. Better to have three or four years' experience on your résumé—then you may be considered for a junior-editor position. It is worth your while to make an appointment with an editor (not with Personnel) for a job interview. It is not a waste of time to talk to editors here—they don't just file and forget you—and, generally, they're honest and helpful to applicants. Again, keep in mind that approximately twenty to twenty-five people in editorial put out the magazine, and turnover is fairly light. Should you land a job at *McCall's,* don't expect a great salary. *McCall's* pays no more than you need to exist—unless, of course, your name is Lynda Bird Johnson Robb.

McCall's is a quiet place: the offices themselves, usually large and roomy, tend to separate people and to muffle outside commotion. Generally, it is not a place where there is intense pressure. If you come to *McCall's,* you will work hard, and if you're ambitious and offer ideas, a job here could be a very exciting prospect. It is definitely a place oriented toward women—and most women find the atmosphere positive.

Eustace Tilley Is a Closet Chauvinist

THE NEW YORKER

There are two *New Yorker*s: *The New Yorker* of the writing staff and *The New Yorker* of the editorial staff. For women, the two have little in common, except for the genial and paternalistic atmosphere of both realms. Battered veterans of other magazines and newspapers agree that *The New Yorker* is a comparative paradise. For a large percentage of the women on the staff, however, the fruits of this paradise are unavailable. The magazine is so enlightened about most other things that it is clearly a lack of understanding of the problem, or more accurately an unwillingness to even see that it *is* a problem, that allows it to continue its discriminatory policies unchanged. So far, they have also been for the most part unchallenged.

The New Yorker is extremely fair to its women writers: the pay is equal for men and women. The magazine considers its writers its greatest asset, and it is talent, not sex, that matters, when a writer is being hired or published.

For the women on the editorial staff, however, discrimination is fairly classic and complete. There are just two women editors, and only one of them is officially called an editor. All the rest of the editors (sixteen) are men. (Fact editors tend to be large men, fiction editors medium to small.) On the editorial staff too, as the magazine quite correctly claims, the pay is equal for equal work. But the statement is, of course, made absurd by the fact that all the higher-echelon jobs are held by men, and all the lower ones by women. No women—except for one fiction editor—have any decision-making power of any kind.

When secretaries are hired, they are discouraged in very plain words by their bosses from contemplating anything but the tiniest hop up the ladder. The researchers, called "checkers," are all women except, typically, the department head. Perhaps the best-known and most professional research team in publishing, they are nevertheless preposterously underpaid and are never rewarded with better jobs. In the past, when there were men in the department, a checker occasionally became an editor. A few went on to become staff writers. The personnel manager insists that there were simply more jobs available in the good old days. True, but a year or so ago, when it looked as if there might be room for one more editor, the lone man in the department (capable and hardworking, but no more capable or hardworking than several of his senior female colleagues) was given the opportunity to train for it. The editorial proofreaders are also all women. They are somewhat better paid than the checkers, but they are still underpaid—and very much handmaidens to the editors. They, too, either remain as proofreaders or leave.

Not only are women denied any upward mobility, they have also traditionally been reprimanded in a particularly vicious way for complaining about it. Only editors are really crucially important to the editorial staff, petitioners have been told repeatedly. Therefore, it has been suggested, *"Don't* ask for more money, *don't* ask for a better job, above all *don't forget that you are replaceable."* This weapon has been used often and with remarkable efficacy in recent years to silence people whose requests for raises have been turned down even in pre-wage-freeze days. Incidentally, editors at *The New Yorker* continued to receive handsome annual raises in their bonuses during the recession, while lower-paid employees— most of them women who felt the pinch more acutely—did not.

The man who was personnel manager until his recent retirement seemed to be a true believer of the "women-are-ruled-chiefly-by-their-passions" faith, and was stubbornly unresponsive to any evidence to the contrary. Another of his articles of faith seems to have been the curious conviction that women were *creative* and men were *responsible,* and while men were occasionally endowed with both qualities, women never were. Thus a staggering file has grown over the years of women of ability and talent who weren't given more responsible jobs or who weren't hired at all, simply because they were known to be writers of novels or publishers of poetry. ("I have in my hand a list, a list of thirteen published short stories.")

The new personnel manager is a much younger man, also a working editor, who is well aware of the bitter feelings of a lot of the women on the staff. It is still far too early to tell what changes, if any, he will instigate, but thus far his attitude toward the problems of women seems to be one of bemused detachment, behind which lurks an ill-concealed irritation. Like the rest of the extremely fuzzily defined group that the term "management" doesn't quite seem to fit at *The New Yorker,* he thinks things are quite splendid the way they are, and he doesn't really see what all the fuss is about. The health-insurance plan is excellent, the hours (10–6) are comfortable, and really, *every* link in the chain counts, doesn't it?

The fuss is about the fact that all the best jobs—the most responsible ones, the best-paid ones—are held by men and re-peatedly and unreasonably denied to women. The way things are now, you don't have to begin at the bottom at *The New Yorker,* but if you do and if you're a woman, you're expected to stay there forever or find a better job elsewhere.

The $150 Kvetchin'

NEW YORK MAGAZINE

I am the photozaza at *New York Magazine.* It's a title I gave myself in September 1969 when I took the job of secretary to the art director, was listed on the masthead as editorial assistant, and found that none of my duties were editorial. I do photo research. The art director receives a sheaf of articles scheduled to appear in future magazines, decides whether he should assign an artist (who may need reference photos) or photographer or use extant mate-rial from picture archives, libraries, news services, or another publication. He then tells me what we are going to do. It is never mine to decide which artist to use or which picture to run, and if I feel a pang of impotence in surrendering the pictures to someone else, I can say I did not go to art school—so how should I presume?

The part that is my province, and mine alone, is returning artwork and photographs before they get lost; cutting, pasting, and mailing tear sheets to design contests; ordering art supplies; sending work out to be photocopied; maintaining an ongoing intimacy with the messenger service; and other equally absorbing things that I hope not to be doing when I am an old lady. But for the first year it was with pride that I called myself the photozaza: what the job lacked in responsibility, it gained in the contact with photographers, artists, and intellectuals; what it lacked in decision-making, I ignored—speaking from what must be the most appealing, eccentric, informal atmosphere in town. Whether or not I welcome the realization that people and fun are not enough, I'm afraid it's here to stay.

With the exception of two writer/researchers, who make $175 per week, the other editorial assistants are secretaries to editors, at $150 per week, and lunches together more often than not turn to kvetching about this fee (there are no raises on a regular basis—in fact most of the decision-makers are sorely remiss in asking themselves if someone is ready for one). The talk does not always begin and end in a coffee shop. Some of these bright young women have approached their bosses with the problem: "More money, and/or hire another assistant to do what I've been doing for a year or two so I can take on more fulfilling responsibilities, such as editing, attending idea meetings, etc." Here arises a twofold problem. For one thing, though I have never been present at the encounters, I have a feeling that some of the passion, bravado, and clarity expressed yapping "with the girls" is dissipated by the time they are telling it to the men they work for. Secondly, we are typed. We were hired to become proficient "helpers," and the men would rather hire new, experienced "thinkers" than rethink the image of their assistants.

The first problem is the more pervasive and defeating one, for

I am sure that if any one of these women, myself included, began to change radically, throwing out million-dollar ideas casually on their way to the ladies' room, the editors would soon take notice. Clare Boothe Luce tells of how she was having trouble making her enthusiasm and capability believable at *Vanity Fair* thirty years ago, until the editor dared her to come in on Monday with fifty new ideas, and she did. (The rest of the story is that he thought a man must have helped her, but *we* know what became of her, no matter what he thought.) Misspending energy, wishing this women's lib movement had burgeoned when we were kiddies, is easier than changing our self-image to "able" and our behavior to dynamic, positive, and aggressive.

New York Magazine is not undemocratic, it is simply not going to go out of its way to discover unblatant talent. The only aspect of the editor's alleged sexism that I am around to witness is that he is quick to give audience to a woman, initially just because she is an attractive woman. If he is then taken with her mind, she will be put to work for the good of the magazine. The early operation, five years ago, was staffed (understaffed) primarily by women. Anybody who had any ideas and the capacity to work hard was right away given every opportunity to use her talents. It is now only slightly more difficult for a woman to make herself invaluable by demanding more responsibility because there are fewer slots to fill. Some editorial assistants have become writers; one of us became editor of Best Bets; and one former photozaza became senior editor.

If I, a woman, am to view my office as a microcosm of the professional world, I feel O.K. There is nothing to stop me from saying anything to any editor—and without even making an appointment to do so. Meekness and butterflies are more formidable enemies than are men and the system.

In a Time-Honored Tradition (Lucely Speaking)

NEWSWEEK MAGAZINE*

The fact that most researchers at *Newsweek* are women and that virtually all writers are men stems from a newsmagazine tradition going back almost 50 years. (*Washington Post,* March 17, 1970)

This was Editor-in-Chief Osborn Elliott's analysis when confronted by the announcement that a large group of *Newsweek*'s female editorial employees had filed suit with the Federal Equal Employment Opportunity Commission alleging that *Newsweek* was discriminating against women by "maintaining restrictive job categories and limiting promotional and training opportunities on the basis of sex." It was the first such suit in the industry· and as such got a substantial amount of media coverage. Pressed by the publicity and the threat of formal action on the legal suit, the editors of the magazine met with a negotiating panel of the women and their lawyer, Eleanor Holmes Norton of the American Civil Liberties Union (since appointed Human Rights Commissioner for New York City).

Briefly, the understanding reached between the two sides was that *Newsweek* would "undertake an affirmative accelerated policy of recruitment" of outside women with demonstrated ability for positions of writer and reporter and also that it would "substantially increase" the number of tryouts for these jobs for qualified women currently employed at the magazine. Concomitantly, "affirmative efforts" to employ men as researchers would be made. The college summer-trainee program would be expanded to include positions for three *Newsweek* women as reporters in the domestic bureau for three months. Finally, continuing bimonthly

* For update, see "Progress Report" by Terry Pristin, page xix.

consultations were arranged to review the implementation of the agreement between management and the women.

At the time of the suit, there was one woman writer. Since then, eleven women have had writing tryouts (four current *Newsweek* employees, seven outsiders); three of them have been hired. At the time of the suit, there were eleven women reporters. Since then, seven women have taken part in the summer-trainee program; six have "passed." Three of these researchers, plus a fourth who didn't have to go through this internship, have been placed in bureaus. A couple of women reporters from outside the magazine have also been hired, and the total number of women in this category has increased to fourteen. At the time of the suit, there was one male researcher. To date, seven men have been hired. The proportions are as follows: women make up approximately 10 percent of writers, 19 percent of reporters, and 90 percent of researchers. There are no women editors (figures as of November 10, 1971).

As for the professional advancement of women at *Newsweek,* the women's action has had some very modest success; but it was a solid beginning. In terms of women's liberation, the same can be said. There is heightened awareness of the sexist attitudes and atmosphere in the work situation and in the magazine itself. And slowly, a broader consciousness of how, when and why women are oppressed is developing.

But there are strong—in fact, dominant—elitist attitudes among the women themselves. The most heated and the only really bitter arguments within the activist group arose over the efforts of a small number of the women to broaden the issue to include better opportunities for all women, including secretaries, receptionists, filers, etc., who were not yet even in the preferred position of the researchers. The lawyer indicated that this would not be legally feasible, but many of the women further opposed the proposal with an argument that categorized women in these other, less "advanced" positions in just the way we were protesting against for ourselves. They claimed that these women were in a *different* situation, that they might *like* their jobs—that for some, in fact, these were pretty good jobs—and, anyway, if they wanted to change their situation, they should show some initiative and form their own movement.

The bimonthly meetings have not been as productive as hoped. While management has learned the language of women's rights, it is not yet ready to embrace the practice. The women, as a result, have become increasingly militant. At an anniversary meeting of the whole group, "sense-of-the-meeting" votes revealed that no one felt there had been any real changes in the job situation, the attitudes, or the atmosphere—and everyone was angry and impatient. The panel and the group's new lawyer, Harriet Van Tassel, have increased pressure on the editors with renewed threats of legal action, and recently management has seemed to take the issue more seriously.

Prospects for the woman college graduate with no experience to get the job she longs for in reporting, writing, or editing are still gloomy. Editing she should forget. The senior editors (who perform the real function of editing) have almost all worked up through a good many years as writers at *Newsweek;* the exceptions have had extensive experience in other media. Writers most often have had some solid writing experience (journalistic, freelance magazine, etc.) before coming to *Newsweek.* But since the main recruiting technique is word-of-mouth and friends of friends, a modicum of experience and a generous helping of personal pull just might land a writing tryout. Beware, though, of trading too heavily on this mixture. Professional experience and competence really will count in getting the job, your clout notwithstanding.

Reporters have also usually had some prior experience, but it may have been as a particularly active college journalist, a *Newsweek* campus stringer, or a summer trainee under the *Newsweek* student-trainee program. To work up to either reporter or writer from within is about as good (or bad) a strategy. Advancement time from researcher to reporter has varied from nine months to five years. If female, allow at least four years. Only three women so far have been promoted from within to the job of writer. For them the climb took four to five years.

One new barrier to working up is the integration of "traditionally female" jobs, such as researchers, from which women could start their climb. The women's group is pressuring *Newsweek* to integrate all job categories, including research, and in this, ironically, *Newsweek* has been somewhat overdiligent. They have been considering only men (or women already at the magazine in other jobs) for the new openings in research.

Setting aside these forbidding statistics for a moment, *Newsweek* appears to be a rather informal and friendly place to work. Everyone is on a first-name basis with everyone else. There is a good deal of time for general office discussions, personal errands, doctor's appointments. The lunch hours are loose, and almost no one is expected to be at her desk constantly from ten to six. The work philosophy seems to be that one should be available to do whatever needs to be done when it needs to be done. The weekly deadlines are pretty regular and create a work schedule with periods of intense pressure alternating with slack time. The reasonable assumption is that after a while you know when you'll be needed and will be there.

Judging by office space, women have low-status set ups. In sections like National Affairs, International, and Business, where there are many writers and researchers, space is arranged with an open (windowless) area in which all the researchers sit, with the writers' private offices opening onto it. In the other sections, where there is generally only one writer and one researcher in each department, the two share one small office (writer by the window, researcher on guard near the door).

Other reflections of hierarchical, sexist attitudes emerge clearly over time. When a phone rings, a woman is expected to answer it whether it's hers or not. Most ordering-out for morning "coffee and Danish" is expected to be done by women. In the meeting that senior editors have with the writer of each story to discuss the emphasis and organization of the piece, the researcher is generally not included.

There are, naturally, individual variations of discrimination against women. Hopefully, the atmosphere will change as it begins to reflect changing hiring patterns. But only a couple of months ago, one of the most open and friendly writers could walk into the National Affairs area where several researchers were working at their desks, survey the empty writers' offices, and say, "So everybody's gone out to lunch."

Queen of the Damned

PHOTOPLAY

I think I was about 13 the last time I read a movie magazine, but here I am, poring over the latest issue of *Photoplay*. I am reading *Photoplay* because, after weeks of post-graduate job hunting, this is the first real possibility. I won't have to type and file; they won't pay me $90 a week. They'll pay me $135, and all I'll have to do is write and edit. *Photoplay*. It looks like the work of a madman.

Finding *Photoplay*'s East-Coast office is a task in itself. The magazine isn't listed on the building directory, although the company is: "Macfadden-Bartell Corporation—7th floor." But the seventh is Macfadden's machismo territory—*Sport* Magazine, *Discount Merchandising,* and General Advertising, Public Relations, President and Publisher. You have to go up a flight to find the female ghetto, or "Women's Group," as our magazines are called:

Photoplay, Motion Picture, TV-Radio Mirror, Silver Screen, True Story, True Love, True Romances, True Confessions, True Experience, and *Pageant.*

Here are created dreams for blue-collar wives, the beauty-parlor fantasies that need no parody. To women's liberation it's an enemy camp—ironically, but predictably, staffed almost exclusively by women. And here an intelligent woman's problem is not getting *into* the bastions of editorial power, but getting out.

I arrived at *Photoplay* at the age of twenty-two, through the recommendation of an older and wiser friend who knew that I would learn far more, far faster, at a smaller magazine. Once this "connection" was made, the hiring procedure was exceptionally fair. I was given a test to prove my writing ability and potential editorial skill.

I must admit feeling a certain unadulterated pleasure in my work during those first weeks as a story editor. After all, I'd just struggled through a thesis on Samuel Richardson, and the adventures of Elizabeth Taylor brought easy release from the torments of Clarissa Harlowe. Then, too, the magazine's bizarre editorial framework offered a constant challenge.

Usually, *Photoplay* simply romanticizes or sensationalizes factual material. But when the facts are unobtainable . . . There was the day a coworker received a layout entitled, "Why Julie Nixon Eisenhower Hasn't Had a Baby Yet." She asked for the manuscript and was informed that it was to be housewritten—by her. Another: "Liz Gets Advice from an 80-Year-Old Grandmother." A coemployee was the grandmother.

Whatever moral or aesthetic qualms I felt were somewhat allayed by my financial need and the knowledge that I *was* learning—a hundred times more each day than my contemporaries stuck in secretarial slots on more prestigious publications. I wrote stories, captions, blurbs, titles; I proofread, ordered art, and—endlessly—rewrote the contributions of West-Coast illiterates blessed with the right "contacts." The subject matter may have been absurd, the chances for printed perfection slight, but the rudiments of publishing remained; the proverbial "experience" was there to be gained.

Six months later, through a strange combination of luck and ability, I was promoted to a responsible job. I had assumed that there would be some objection to my age and lack of tenure, but the promotion went through on the recommendation of *Photoplay*'s editor, always willing to advance her staff. As for me, it meant $19 more per week and a chance to expand my "experience."

The reaction of one of my literature professors at this point is telling: "My God! She's the only one of my students to become a *success* in publishing!"

For the few women of talent and ambition who stumble into the fan-magazine field, opportunities for titular advancement are frequent. And, depending on the company involved, financial compensation can be decent, occasionally good, or—if one rises to the position of editorial director—spectacular. (At Macfadden, salaries begin to reach the realm of reason only at the editor-in-chief level. Good editors remain simply because Macfadden publishes most of the few respected fan magazines.)

Getting out of the field, however, can be a different matter. As far as I can gather, those who accomplish great escapes go to the "slick" women's magazines. The transition is natural: Just take "Did Jackie Get Onassis Back Into Her Bedroom?" and call it "The Strange Onassis Marriage," or change "I Have to Beg Ryan for Love" to "Can This Marriage Be Saved?"

Maybe this is the true curse of the "experience" I've gained working among the "damned" these past two years. We who take the world's abuse are quick to discern the abuses others endure: while I once would have jumped at the chance to write for one of the more reputable women's magazines, I'm now acutely aware of their limitations. And as for transferring to a publication demanding more honest journalism, it seems I've simply acquired a third handicap. To be young and to be a woman is difficult enough, but to be a fan-magazine staffer—in the eyes of personnel directors, I might just as well have been lobotomized.

The Most Forgettable Characters They Ever Met

READER'S DIGEST

The home of the *Reader's Digest* nestles in the gently rolling hills of Westchester County. Its editors work in elegantly appointed offices decorated with real Van Goghs, Renoirs, and Chagalls. Twenty-five lounges, each with its own special decor— the South Sea Lounge, the Garden Lounge, the Pink Shell Lounge —exist for their use. In the springtime, dogwoods bloom all around; tulips, daffodils, and jonquils nose up out of the ground; and everybody gets Friday off all through the merry month of May.

A carillon rings out at noon, and subsidized lunch is served in the company cafeteria. Vacations are more than generous, and a plump turkey is given to each employee for his Christmas dinner. After ten years of service, a woman receives a gold-circle pin ensnaring Pegasus, the company symbol, to wear proudly on her neatly tailored suit. Clearly, Mr. and Mrs. DeWitt Wallace, the owners and founders of the *Digest,* want their employees to be happy, and the employees pay them back with a devotion and loyalty that are rare in this century.

Surely, in this opulent setting you would expect women to be well paid and held in high regard. But nothing could be further from the truth, if your criteria are equal employment opportunity and equal pay for equal work.

Until February 1972 when the fiftieth anniversary issue of the

Reader's Digest appeared, the masthead of the nation's most widely read magazine was a testament to discrimination on the basis of sex. Of those who headed the list—the chairman, the president, and assorted senior editors—only one in twenty-five was a woman, a grand total of 4 percent. Yet even that one woman could not be regarded as a symbol of egalitarianism—for she was Mrs. Wallace.

Since American colleges have been turning out literary women for over a hundred years, and since 70 to 80 percent of the employees at the *Digest* are women, the lack of even a token 10 percent at the top of the masthead hinted loudly that prejudice and not performance was determining who was and who was not qualified. In fact, the entire structure of the *Digest* is geared to keeping women down.

It is no secret that the majority of *Digest* articles are commissioned, and half of them are planted in other magazines so the *Digest* can pretend to find them. The remaining third are zealously searched for by the editorial staff. Picking the right article, or better yet, dreaming up a good idea for one, then removing paragraphs and sentences from it, is what *Digest* editing is all about. Men trained in this art become senior editors. Sitting in their posh suburban offices, reading magazines, they form ideas about the world in which we live, and they have the prerogative of hiring writers to execute their dreams. This is the beginning of true power. Somewhat more powerful are the three to six men who take turns being issue editors—controlling the general contents and each specific word in one month's entire issue. Ultimate control is exerted by the managing editor and the editor-in-chief who veto the ideas of issue editors and substitute their own.

Women, on the other hand, read and clip magazines endlessly with no advancement at all. Some are allowed to edit departments like "Picturesque Speech," "Life in These United States," or "Press Section" where only a few paragraphs or sentences are involved. With one exception, the associate-editor level is as far as any woman has gone in half a century. The names of these women have appeared in the same lowly spot on the masthead for fifteen, twenty, even twenty-five years. Two women have been associate editors for over thirty years.

In fifty years of *Digest* operation, only one woman, Audrey Dade, was ever made a senior editor. After many years of taking her turn along with men at supervising the cutting and polishing of articles, a job that customarily brought senior-editor status to men, she too was given the title—recognition she had to fight bitterly to achieve. Furthermore, men who have done the final editing have usually taken their turn at running issues afterward. It is common knowledge at the *Digest,* however, that women who do final checking are not thought capable of running issues. It is illogical, but men are known for their clear thinking along these lines.

Women get a clear shot at copyrights and permissions, editorial correspondence, indexing, fact-checking, copy-editing, and other ancillary housekeeping chores. After toiling away in these all-female departments for the requisite number of decades, some women have come to head them.

So much for the female success stories at *Reader's Digest.* For fifty years, no matter how obvious a choice a woman has been in terms of seniority, experience, and skill, she has been ignored. It's as though the succession of some medieval monarchy were at stake.

Did no women wish to advance? Were none qualified to make the grade? With beguiling mock honesty, management males would sadly insist there were none. And then an amazing thing happened. Ever since women began having meetings to discuss sex discrimination, the masthead has been in a constant state of flux as some heretofore unsuspected female talent suddenly was "discovered." In February 1972 the heads of research, the copy desk, and the excerpts (jokes and fillers) were listed on the masthead as senior editors—among the men—rather than in their usual places at the head of their all-female departments. In July a fourth female senior editor appeared as if by magic, and another popped up in August.

Genuine recognition, long since overdue, has at last been given these women, and the editorial territory, so long defended as a male preserve, has been violated. Glorious new titles are also being appended to the same dreary old jobs, in an effort to make window-dressing reforms. The contents of one all-female department were even dumped into the associate-editor slot, making the *Digest* look like a wonderland of opportunity.

Not satisfied by this hogwash of the masthead, a small group of women filed a complaint with the EEOC (Equal Employment Opportunity Commission). More thoroughgoing and profound changes are needed, for the whole tissue and fabric of the corporation's organization sorely needs reform.

Women, who have no idea of the limitations on advancement at the *Digest,* are routinely hired into all-female departments where they are generally expected to stay put. None of these departments is a training ground for editors, or even a talent pool to tap—as far as management is concerned. When editors are wanted, men are hired. Years go by before women work themselves out of their assigned slots, and most never do. For them, these departments are ghettos where they are segregated because of their sex and where they are inevitably economically deprived.

One of the most charming of these ghettos, if one is to believe the description published near the front of the March 1968 issue, is the Research Department. Members of "our nosey harem," it croons, "are almost all college graduates of exceptionally high scholastic achievement, and all are pretty. In fact several of our younger editors, after a little checking on their own, have taken them as wives."

After all, what is a harem for?

Although researchers spend days conferring with the company lawyers to protect the corporation from million-dollar lawsuits or solitary hours rewriting hopelessly mangled articles, they are paid less than gardeners who trim and spray the trees at Pleasantville ($7,500 to start). A promotion for a researcher is moving from an inside cubicle to a window office. The view is spectacular, pollution permitting, and it's hers, if she wants it, till she turns sixty-five.

There are other problems, as well, that women contemplating a career at the *Digest* should consider. The headquarters of the magazine that reaches 105,000,000 people in thirteen languages tends to be a tight-knit, closed-off community where one's working associates and one's social circle are likely to be identical. With no fresh faces and no fresh ideas, gossip can mushroom in the fetid atmosphere. Uniformed men patrol the grounds—guarding the paintings from thieves and possibly the personnel against Communist attack. If an employee's car does not bear an American-flag decal, the license number is taken down. Latecomers, even if they are senior editors, are reported. At the company cafeteria, men tend not to eat at the same table with women. One woman was startled on her first day of work when her male cohorts introduced her to some women and, with a "see-you-after-lunch," were off. For these reasons, several women, having thoroughly satisfied themselves that they were beating their careers against a sexist wall, transferred from Pleasantville to the offices in New York City.

The Book Department, divided between New York and Pleasantville, produces the condensed book that appears in the back of each issue of the magazine. It is kinder to women. Little distinction is made there between men's work and women's work. But before declaring this to be one of the few enlightened corners of the corporation—the Byzantium of an otherwise *Dark Age Digest*—one might look a little closer.

The major wheeling and dealing there is (of course) done by male senior editors. Although women assume equal—perhaps more than equal—responsibility, they get nowhere near equal pay. One woman, a model of diligence and fidelity, worked hard (and long—twenty-five years) in the Book Department without advancement and with less pay, in the end, than young men being hired every year. She is now retired and her pension is based on that pay. Women who imagine that long and faithful service will earn them recognition and rewards should remember Ms. Fidelity. Recently, a few of the more flagrant pay inequities have been somewhat ameliorated—word having reached the Westchester estates of the owners of some newfangled laws being passed in Washington and Albany.

Nevertheless, with no union to enforce ethical standards of remuneration, employees are paid as little as possible, and no more. Raises are refused, retarded, and never retroactive. Secretaries and assistants have been hired with the promise that they would be given a raise in six months. When it finally comes, after a year or even more, it may be to the tune of $5 to $10 a week. Older women have been given a $2.50 hike after a two-year wait—an annual increment of $1.25 a week.

The *Digest* is one of the richest privately owned companies in America, a heavy contributor to many charities, and the owner of a $1.8 million jet. Such exploitation of women by such a company is inexcusable. Granted, it's a game the *Digest* did not invent, but it's one it well knows how to play.

Thus far, we have mostly been discussing the professional women on top of the masthead, the part of the iceberg that shows. Imagine the lot of the others, those who form the great majority of the proponderantly female population here.

Separated by a tunnel from the pretty building with the paintings inside is a factory where the women handle the voluminous flow of mail that 18,000,000 subscribers generate. At a public hearing before the New York State Legislature's Committee on Labor Problems, a *Digest* employee testified what it was like to work with fifty women in a "drab, dreary, poorly ventilated room." "We were to raise our hands," she said, "to ask permission to go to the rest room. We were not to talk or make any noise. We had to queue up to get our coats at the end of the day, then return to our seats and line up again to be dismissed. . . ." She listed eleven such points. The pay for this work is $88.50 a week.

As is the case with all *Digest* employees, fifteen percent of even this pitiable salary is withheld until the end of the year. It is doled out in January and is called a bonus. (All salaries mentioned in this article are the full pay, including the "bonus.") Until recently, if you left the *Digest* before December, you were out of luck and, of course, the *Digest* was in.

Meanwhile, top-management males are getting real bonuses and lavish ones, sometimes several in a year. Twenty years ago, *Time* reported the following *RD* salaries: "Senior editors reportedly get anywhere from $20,000 to $50,000 a year and sometimes half as much again in bonuses. One year the executive senior editor drew a salary of $34,000 and a bonus of $87,000." Another year "Wally" sent out flagpoles—fifty feet tall—as Christmas presents to the boys who put out the magazine—their lawns are spacious enough to accommodate this sort of bagatelle. Christmastime also brings an *engraved* invitation to a "special lunch." The jokes last year at this all-male affair were about "women's lib."

Even as the laughter rang out, the silent ones in the factory toiled on. Far from being liberated, they can't even plan their own lives. With no advance warning, they may be ordered to work late, or on Saturdays—previous commitments to their families notwithstanding. Those inclined to refuse remember the "SR" threat: when business is slow, they may be told, "Stay at home tomorrow and go without pay." *"Supervisor's Request."*

Music is piped in periodically each hour, but tensions build up that it cannot allay. There may be no raise if you're sick and none if you're slow. Always, there is the unrelenting pressure to produce, as management twists the screws.

If you want to work for the *Digest,* and if you have an outside source of income, a servant mentality, and an indifference to social injustice, the place is tailor-made for you. If you wish to be an editor before, not after, you receive your gold-circle pin, try to start out in Reading and Cutting (and pray a lot). If you are ambitious, avoid the female ghettos.

A better bet by far would be to aim for the condensed-book club or General Books, where books about nature, history, and other subjects are assembled. Both are in New York City, both have a female senior editor, and both are heterosexual departments, where the men and women even manage to dine together. Though far from perfect, in neither place is the morally contemptible sexist prejudice that permeates the magazine staff quite so strong.

One hundred years after a war was fought over the fundamental rights of human beings, there is still a "peculiar institution" in this country, and *Reader's Digest* is capitalizing brilliantly upon it. Women here are used as a cheap source of labor on dull, monotonous, demeaning jobs.

Perhaps a hundred years hence, people will look back at the handsome plantation-style building and the lush appointments at the *Digest* and console themselves that at least, at this place, decent quarters were provided for the help. Yes, the bathrooms are exquisite, the turkey at Christmas is really plump and, instead of banjos strumming, we have a carillon. But those hardly make up for the pay withheld and the opportunities denied. Happily, with the filing of a complaint with the EEOC, the struggle is on to bring about the greening of this corporation—that is, to make the *Reader's Digest* a company that is just.[1]

Subtle Exclusion

REDBOOK

Of some fifty staff members listed on *Redbook*'s masthead, thirty-six are women. Men hold the following positions: editor, art director, managing editor, articles editor, home-furnishings editor,

[1] The *Reader's Digest* case had not been decided as of June 1974.

senior editor (two men), and contributing editor (three men). The Fiction, Women's-Service, Copy and Production, Beauty, Food, Fashion and Home-Sewing Departments are headed by women.

The oppression of women working at *Redbook* is subtle. The attitude of the men in power is paternalistic and permissive rather than hostile, although a certain amount of grousing surrounds any attempt by a woman to be "too aggressive"—about more money, or more power, or more of any other male preserve.

"They listen, which is good, and last fall they acted on a number of suggestions we made to improve policies," said one former editor. "But you always know that you can't ask for too much—like for more money for women employees across the board, or for drastic changes in the image of women portrayed in the magazine. Some change is possible, though, and that's why I stayed on for several years."

A number of secretaries have become assistant editors and associate editors over the past few years, so *Redbook* is a place where you *can* begin as a secretary, learn editing, and eventually become an editor, although the salary increases with the title are not significant. Women on the senior-editorial level and beyond are fairly well paid; associate editors make around $10,000 to $14,000.

Many of the younger staff members are feminists or, at least, supporters of the movement. Some of the older ones are too. But, although editors are allowed some autonomy and some leeway for creative thought, all ideas must be finally approved by the editors in charge—mostly men. So, more often than not, the really decent ideas are simply dismissed—with the noncommittal explanation that they just don't "fit *Redbook*'s editorial framework."

It's permissible to fight for your point of view, but you rarely win. All you will get in rebuttal is some elaboration of the "editorial-framework" gambit. Whatever that happens to be on your day of confrontation, be prepared for frustration at *Redbook*.

Teachers on the Rocks

SCHOLASTIC MAGAZINES, INC.*

Scholastic's hiring procedures are, to say the least, erratic. The Personnel Department, which is entirely female, is more than glad to interview any individual who might walk in off the street. *Scholastic* advertises many of its openings in the employment section of the Sunday *New York Times,* which brings in a great proportion of the applicants. Applicants should know what job they are applying for, since the Personnel Department is not accustomed to fitting an individual into the notch he is best qualified for. *Scholastic* puts an almost ludicrous emphasis on teaching experience. They would, apparently, rather hire a math teacher with no aptitude for writing or editing than a polished writer who is also capable of communicating with students.

Scholastic does not discriminate against ethnic minorities and is, in fact, on the lookout for applicants from such groups. Unfortunately, this attitude does not extend to women. A Yale graduate, fresh out of college, might be given the job of editorial assistant, while a Smith graduate is given a typing test and made a "gal Friday" with vague promises of quick promotion (few of them kept). Of the men interviewed, none have been given a typing test. All women without extensive teaching and/or editorial experience, have been.

The company will consider graduates from any obscure college for important positions, and has placed several noncollege graduates in them. But many men in authority are wary of placing women in responsible positions who have graduated from any Seven Sisters college. ("Nobody wants one of those 'bright girls' working under him.")

* See Preface.

The founders and executives of *Scholastic* seem to have had an inordinate number of children and grandchildren, and all of them are considered for summer or even full-time positions if they show up and ask. This is understandable—but infuriating to equally qualified applicants who are not given the same consideration.

The ideal applicant for a job at *Scholastic* is a black male who happens to be the son of one of the vice presidents and has had three years' teaching experience. The job seeker who should avoid the company is a female college graduate who is unfortunate enough to know how to type.

The salary scale at *Scholastic* is the kind that inspired the French Revolution. Employees starting out are not paid a livable salary according to New York City standards. It's hard to gauge the extent of the discrimination at clerical and secretarial levels, since men are not hired for such positions. The pay for both men and women at the editorial level is considerably better, but there is a tendency to pay men more on the higher levels since "they have families to support."

Scholastic tries to hire its employees at the lowest salary possible (an addiction here), but if the company has its heart set on procuring a specific kind of individual, as in the case of black studies, sudden disparities are evident. One such editor was hired at $165 a week, although his duties were comparable to those of a female employee who had been with the company for one year and was still making $115 a week.

There is no such thing as a training program at *Scholastic*. People are either hired for advanced positions outright or they work their way up through the company. More of *Scholastic*'s thirty magazines are edited by women than by men.

Beyond the position of editor, women don't do very well at *Scholastic*. There are no women executives and no female department heads. The men who run the company feel that women are not attuned to the "dollars-and-cents aspects" of the company, and they restrict them to editorial duties.

Ostensibly, the company considers employees for promotions before looking outside the company for new material. However, as one wide-eyed young lady in the Personnel Department put it, "In this market, we can get anything we want. And we will." Many qualified women are passed over when men can be hired instead because the company would like to "equalize its staff." Personnel chooses to ignore the fact that fifty/fifty is not equal when 40 percent of the women have clerical jobs.

Women in authoritative positions are not under any special kind of pressure; they never get high enough to become a real threat. Women can rise only so far. After that point, they will notice their salary checks rising slightly, but not their titles. At this juncture a woman may choose to move on to another company, but she is under no pressure to do so. One of the considerations that may encourage her to move on is the fact that it is considerably harder for a female editor to get an assistant, or even a secretary.

Scholastic Magazines, Inc., regards itself as one big, happy family, and it does make an effort to keep its employees content. The hours are very lenient, and most people can make their own schedules, so long as they get their assigned work done. Every employee is allotted ten sick-leave days. The company pays for part of the health program which, unfortunately, does not include pregnancy benefits for women who have conceived before being hired. However, the company will grant a six-month maternity leave of absence (without pay).

Any mode of attire is permitted. The employees have never been noted for being particularly well-dressed. Working conditions are extremely relaxed (to the point of encouraging laziness), and most of the employees are on a first-name basis, even with the officers. Unfortunately, the lines of communication often break down and a certain amount of antagonism exists between employer and employee, since the latter is never quite sure of where he stands.

Scholastic Magazines, Inc., adopts an extremely paternal attitude toward its employees. Unfortunately, many of those employees, especially the women, suffer the attendant consequences of being thought of as children.

That Great Locker Room in the Sky

SPORTS ILLUSTRATED*

Journalism at *Sports Illustrated* is of the frontier school—circa 1920, before the era of Heywood Broun and the American Newspaper Guild. (The union is recognized at Time Inc., but the contract, unlike stronger pacts at the New York newspapers, does not provide for a Guild shop, meaning that editorial employees can choose to receive the benefits without paying dues. Most writers and all but one editor at *SI* are free riders.) Rugged individualism is still very much alive in these offices, competition being as integral to the game plan of the magazine as to the action reported each week in its pages.

This jock code of every-man-for-himself-by-any-means-necessary is hardly calculated to encourage the talents of women or their participation in the editorial processes—most of them have since childhood been trained in nonaggressive techniques and conditioned to wait patiently for favors to be bestowed. Add to this the deeply entrenched notion that the world of sports is a man's world and you've got a hell of a lot going against a woman who seeks to advance a career at *SI*.

When you come right down to it, forgetting women's sports (which the editors tend to do anyway), the sports world is only slightly more male-dominated than other fields where women as

* See Preface.

journalists have been excluded for superfluous reasons. ("Women can't get into executive board luncheons" is the financial world's equivalent to "Women can't get into locker rooms.") *Sports Illustrated* has in fact—more than any other of the sports media—opened the door of sports reporting to women. Relatively high numbers of female researchers and a few female writers and editors have long been part of the magazine's staff. Coaches, public relations directors, and athletes long ago accepted it as routine to talk to women interviewers from *SI*. Thanks as much to *SI* as to any other medium, acceptance has been won for women in most press boxes and at news briefings (a few pockets of resistance remain).

This paradox has created a dilemma for the magazine. Male editors cherish an image of *SI* as a heavy in the fast-moving professional-sports picture. Women, given the present stereotyped concept of sex roles, don't fit the scene. It's okay for young female researchers to use their charms to go out and get a quote from Joe Namath or an agreement to pose from Mario Andretti, but when these same women reach a level of experience and ability that should qualify them for equal masthead billing, equal pay, and equal bylines, that's too much for both the *SI* image and the male editorial ego, which is basically not much different from the man who discovered that his friend's daughter was an *SI* reporter. "She was a fine, talented young girl," he said, "and so feminine-looking. I never expected her to find employment on *Sports Illustrated.*"

The reason women were employed in relatively equal ratio to men was partly that the staff structure was modeled closely after the Time Inc. pattern, especially *Time* Magazine (where all researchers were women), and partly because of the Newspaper Guild contract which contained an antidiscrimination clause. "Integration," however, was mainly on the lower rungs. The high-paid categories were top-heavy with males. Most of the women hired went into conventionally female jobs. Nevertheless, the first masthead in 1954 did list one female associate editor and one female writer in addition to the nine female researchers (reporters). As the size, reputation, and circulation of the magazine increased over the years, even this ratio of women to men in the higher-paid categories deteriorated. Also, the rate of advancement, slow as it was, declined after the early years.

In the first decade of *SI*'s publication (from 1954 to 1964), a total of seventeen women were hired or promoted into the two highest Newspaper Guild pay categories (Groups 10A and B— writer/reporters, writers, editors), but in the next seven years, or until legal action charging discrimination was brought against the entire company (see page 278), only six additional women reached writer/reporter status or above. That women did get ahead in the early years was not due to any system of natural progression based on editors' encouragement and expectations, but on an exceptional combination of drive and talent on the women's part, and the fact that resistance to women's aspirations had not yet hardened.

As for the rest of the women on the staff, their second-class status was as obvious as the functions they performed. As throughout Time Inc., women mainly typed, clipped, and filed newspapers; researched and checked stories; read copy; answered phones and made coffee. Men mainly handled traffic; took pictures; directed production; reported; wrote and edited. That was, and still is, the basic table of organization.

It was the women in the *SI* researcher category (as at so many other magazines) who were angriest over their relegation to inferior status in the way they were interviewed for the job, the assignments they were given, their level of pay, and their opportunities for advancement—as compared to men.

At the outset *SI* hired three men and nine women as researchers (euphemistically called reporters on the masthead). *Time* Magazine had never employed a male in its all-female pool of researchers, so this integrated setup looked like a step forward . . . until it became apparent that the job was to be a training ground for aspiring men and a "career" (closed-circuit!) for women. Within a few years, in fact, the men in the slot were doing so much writing (in violation of Guild provisions) that a new job title had to be invented as a way station on the road to writer category. When the writer/reporter classification went into effect in 1957, five men and no women were promoted into it. Within three years three women had been promoted and eventually a few others followed, but the men, with few exceptions, moved in and out in relatively quick order while women remained in the slot for years before further advancement.

Meantime the researcher (reporter) category became an almost all-female group. (In 1956 there had been seven men and seven women.) Two or three men hung out there, true, but seldom for longer than two years before promotion. The men once lodged a complaint because one of them had had to spend three and a half years as a reporter before being advanced, whereas the average time there for the few women who made it out was six years. It used to be ironically observed by the women that if one of them made a checking gaffe she got fired, while male researchers who made errors were bounced up to writing. Though exaggerated, the bitter sentiment was reinforced by the fact that male reporters were interviewed by editors before being hired and were evaluated on the merits of writing samples submitted, while women were interviewed only by the head of research, with no consideration given to their writing potential. One of them was once told by her boss, "Thank God, you're not one of those researchers that wants to write!"

It's not that every woman on *SI* wants to be a writer. Just as all complainants were glibly dubbed "women's libbers" (thanks to male chauvinism, Time-Life style, most of them are by now), so all researchers were assumed to be frustrated writers. In fact many researchers have no inclination and some lack the talent for the expert writing demanded by *SI*. What they did want, and asked for, was "fair recognition in status and salary" for the performance of special assignments of a nonwriting character.

There are women reporters who have scouted story locales (on travel allowances), interviewed, collected, and evaluated research and prepared the backgrounding and working script for major text pieces and color essays—responsibilities clearly equivalent to those of many editors. These women are still "researchers" by designation and pay. Others, in addition to their regular research and reporting tasks, have been handed managerial and administrative duties during long-run, on-location assignments like the America's Cup, the Kentucky Derby week, the Olympics, and so on.

In May 1970 when 150 women at Time Inc., in a joint action with the state attorney general, brought legal action against the company for sex discrimination (see page 278), twenty of the fifty-plus women on *SI*'s editorial staff signed the complaint affidavit. Nine of these were researchers. The rest came from among the ranks of secretaries, newsmarkers, proofreaders, and copyreaders. That more than half the female staff did not want to participate in the action surprised no one. Many excuses were advanced, but the gut reason was: she who had made it preferred to believe she had done it on her own. (And if there was some help along the way, well, who wants to bite the hand. . . ?) Those who hadn't made it still hoped to be discovered. And indeed chivalry among men is not dead at *SI,* or at least chauvinism is not, for of the six women who have been promoted into high-pay categories since the legal action was initiated, five were noncomplainants.

The list of charges compiled by *SI* women cited ten discriminatory practices in hiring and advancement procedures for researchers and writers. One instance was of a female researcher with a degree in journalism and five years' previous experience on three newspapers as a reporter and writer who was hired as a typist at $85 a week, later "promoted" to the clip desk, and six years later advanced to *SI* researcher—her terminal station.

One of the factors perpetuating the kind of preferential treatment described in the complaint action is the male-dominated managerial hierarchy. Of the ten departments, only three (two when the complaint was filed) are headed by women. The art director and picture editor have always been men, as have the assistant managing editors and the managing editor. Two men and one woman were hired as layout artists between 1954 and 1956. The men are now associate art directors. The woman is still a layout artist. (The second female layout artist in seventeen years was just recently hired.) In the picture department the two women who began in 1954 as picture assistants are still picture assistants. Four successive picture editors have been male, as have the deputy picture editors.

Six weeks after the complaint had been filed, and despite an eighteen-page plea by Time Inc. management for its dismissal, the director of the State Human Rights Division announced a determination of "probable cause" and ordered management to negotiate an agreement or submit to a public hearing of the case.

When the *SI* women's representatives sat down to talk to their editorial maanagement, they found their managing editor absent. He was the only top editor of the five divisions of Time-Life who, until threat of a walkout was finally brought because a stalemate had been reached, refused to appear personally at the negotiations.

The women presented a list of nine demands: (1) training and tryout programs; (2) no more hiring of overqualified women into dead-end jobs; (3) integration of traditionally female groups like secretarial and typing; (4) job mobility; (5) public protest by the editors when equal access to sports events or facilities (except locker rooms!) was denied them; (6) nondiscrimination in job interviews and job referrals; (7) orientation for writers on what are—and are not—the functions of a researcher; (8) reclassifications in the reporter category to provide advancement opportunities; and (9) a permanent committee of the women's representatives and editorial management to act on complaints of sex discrimination. These demands were, of course, in addition to the general demands of all Time Inc. women covering equality in interviewing, hiring, promotion, and pay.

Ten grueling months later, an agreement was signed. The terms were hardly earthshaking: (1) No training program provision was made for "writing tryouts to be arranged where possible"

("This is not a school of journalism"—managing editor). A tryout recently resulted in the promotion to writer/reporter category for a woman who had been a reporter for ten years. (2) Employment of overqualified individuals in jobs with slight opportunities for advancement will be discouraged. (3) No progress toward getting management to seek out male secretaries and typists ("Men just don't apply"). (4) The effort to create mobility between departments and job functions, from researcher to secretary for instance, met with considerable resistance. ("Secretaries need ambassadorial talents that are less critical for a researcher. . . . I don't think a person good at one job would be good at the other"— executive editor), but *SI* does promise "to encourage mobility for staff members who have the desire and aptitude to be promoted. To help such individuals in becoming trained for other jobs, they will be enabled to familiarize themselves with work in areas other than their own when this can be done within their regular responsibilities and the requirements of *SI*'s editorial schedules." (5) *SI* will "protest and combat (but not publicly) the denial of any reasonable press facility to any member of its staff." (6) Newly employed writers will be briefed on the functions of reporters, who "are not expected to do secretarial chores such as making appointments, travel arrangements, writing letters for writers, etc." (7) The background of all prospective reporters will be evaluated by an assistant managing editor as well as by the head of research. 8) Reclassification of reporters along the lines proposed by the women was refused. ("There is only one way to be an editor on this magazine and that is to write. And the only way to write is to write"—managing editor.) (9) A permanent joint committee to act on complaints of sex discrimination was authorized.

What has actually happened since? Basically, not very much. There have been encouraging steps. Whether it is mere tokenism remains to be seen.

In the two years after May 1970, when the complaint was filed, six women were hired or promoted into the top pay groups (10A and B) and a seventh was given a tryout in the writer/reporter category—more than had been advanced in seven years! Female college graduates are no longer being hired to clip newspapers. The ratio of women to men has leveled off in the researcher category to an equitable five men and five women, and assignments and travel opportunities have been more fairly apportioned. Bets are open on whether this will continue after the semifreeze on travel expenses has been lifted. Meanwhile, men have learned to check stories.

Instead of the editor-equivalent category asked for by the reporters, a mock status group called senior reporters was created —for the masthead only. The six women selected (no men) received no pay increases.

Preferential treatment for men continues in the writer/reporter category. A man with no special knowledge of winter sports was assigned to go to the Winter Olympics in Sapporo, Japan. The female writer/reporter who had expected to go had consistently covered these sports and written on them. She was later signed on by NBC to report the games for them—on vacation time!

Overall, the view from the masthead is better than the view from inside. (Views, too, are chiefly a male prerogative since men occupy most of the window offices.) Today, months after the discrimination charges were brought, the pattern of sex inequality at *SI* is as marked as ever: the lowest wage groups (Nos. 1 and 2 in the Newspaper Guild contract scale, ranging from $111 to start to $138.50 after two years, and including clerks and typists) have an equal number of men and women. In the middle groups (ranging from $132 to start to $205 after three years, and including production clerks, newsmarkers, copy typists, secretaries, and layout artists), women outnumber men two to one. But in the highest paid groups (Nos. 9 through 10B, from $159.50 to start to $314.65 after two years, including researchers, writer/reporters, writers, and editors), men outnumber women two to one.

For men at *Sports Illustrated,* the twentieth floor of the towering Time-Life building is still the great locker room in the sky.

Tempus Non Fugit

TIME MAGAZINE

If you're young, female, and a recent college graduate with an interest in journalism, what's one of the first places you think of to apply for a job? It's almost got to be *Time* Magazine—if you're interested in New York City and in print. And it's almost got to be *Time* for another reason: the magazine has for two generations been an employer of women on a large scale. *Time*'s female employees have been very well educated, very well informed, very highly qualified. And they have been restricted to only a few of the job categories that the Newspaper Guild covers on this huge weekly.

For years in the past, the traditional entry to *Time*'s Editorial Department for a female college graduate was to go to the Personnel Department for a typing test. She would then be sent to be interviewed for a newspaper-clipping ($118.50 a week) or editorial-secretary's job ($132). Or she might be sent to see about a job as clerk on *Time*'s copy desk or as traffic-desk secretary in the Photo Department. A new college graduate, if female, would never be hired directly into a higher Guild category, such as staff correspondent or writer (at a weekly starting minimum salary of $247.50) or as researcher, staff correspondent, or writer-trainee (at $159.50). A male would.

Men were never hired as researchers, newsmarkers, or secretaries. Women have been told that in the lower-ranking, lower-paying positions, they would find excellent opportunities for training for higher-level jobs, and, sure enough, a substantial number of the reporter/researchers on *Time* Magazine today came "up" by just exactly that route.

Now, here's the catch, if there hasn't seemed to be at least one before. That first job, that "foot-in-the-door" job, which might lead to the coveted researcher spot, was (and still is) just about the only step that can be confidently taken by a woman on the magazine. Oh, sure, there are other possible steps: from editorial clerk to secretary, from researcher to head researcher. But scarcely anyone is affected by such barely perceptible movement. Most generally, once she acquires the job, a reporter/researcher can do considerable reporting if she wants to—in addition to the office-bound library research and story checking that is admittedly still the essential part of her job. The back-of-the-book researcher can undertake some aggressive lobbying with her senior editor or her writer—who are, by the way, almost without exception male—to try to get local reporting assignments. The reporter/researcher who has been successful at lobbying and covering stories can rack up invaluable experience in reporting and writing in that way. But she must technically remain a researcher. It is even today considered unseemly by the editors and executives at *Time* and Time Inc. for a woman to do such "unwomanly" work as story writing or covering news events—under any name, that is, other than the acceptable one, researcher. The woman at *Time* has stepped through the door and onto a treadmill whose mechanism is the vicious circle.

Almost invariably, she holds the job now called "reporter/ researcher." It is true that there have been, and are, female writers at *Time*. Some of them managed to work up from secretary and researcher in as little as five or six years after college graduation. And there have been, and are, women correspondents with *Time*'s News Service. Some of them, too, have been out of college for less than ten years. But most of the women who either write or cover stories for *Time* have gone through a long, slow, and frequently painful struggle to get the jobs they now hold.

Because of a legal complaint charging sex discrimination in job placement brought by women at Time Inc. in 1970 (see page 278), there have been a few changes from past practices. But for the most part, the old way of doing things (from hiring to moving of copy) is still firmly embraced by male management, and the picture of career possibilities and opportunities for advancement for women at *Time* is not encouraging.

At the end of 1971, in an execrable job market, the job situation everywhere was in rather special circumstances. At *Time* Magazine a certain trend had begun, perhaps as a result of the complaint: male college graduates were being hired as newsmarkers and researchers. (Women college graduates were still the ones being hired as secretaries.) Women with professional writing and reporting experience were being hired from outside the company as reporter/researchers. Women from outside the company were *not* being hired as writers or editors under any circumstances, whether they were experienced or not. One woman researcher had been promoted to writer in the year and a half following the filing of the legal complaint. No women were formerly, and none have since received promotions to senior editor. Of the total seven female correspondents in the News Service, not one was hired after 1969. None of the seven has been promoted to bureau chief. In contrast, one man was hired directly after college graduation as a writer. Nine men, some newly graduated, some with and others without professional experience, have since been hired as correspondents by the News Service.

There are few trainee positions to be had these days. When there were more such jobs, they all went to men. Now that there are fewer than ever, they still all go to men. Salaries at *Time*—for all the Newspaper Guild guidelines and minimums—vary widely, with inequities between one man's salary and another's; women rarely do quite the same job as men and they can usually be assured that in pay, too, they will be a little less equal.

The daily atmosphere at *Time,* for all the gloomy career prospects here, is good. Strict hours are not kept, but editorial employees are expected to know when they have work to do and how to meet deadlines. In general, editorial staff are at their desks by about 10:00 A.M. and they stay around until they have done their work. Sometimes that allows a generous two-hour lunch, plus the option of leaving early in the afternoon. Sometimes it means that the editorial worker gets in at 8:30 A.M., takes no lunch, and works right through until the next morning at two. Hours, therefore, are flexible, but a member of the *Time* staff is expected to be responsible about their work. The Guild contract covers late-work expenses for meals and transportation.

Generally "group journalism" as practiced at *Time* works like this: the senior editor, writers, picture researchers, reporter/researcher, and news-service deskman meet for a story conference. The writer and news-service deskman come there from outside-window offices. The picture researcher comes from an office with window—perhaps. The reporter/researcher's office is an interior cubicle—windowless. All participants are welcome to suggest story ideas at a conference. Once a list is drawn up, the writer (or the reporter/researcher) may draft a query which the researcher then types and sends to the News Service for coverage by bureau correspondents.

Sometimes a reporter/researcher takes the query herself, to provide some reportage in addition to gathering clippings, books, articles—background material—for the writer. If she reports, the reporter/researcher must type up her files, of course. Research librarians, who are almost equally male and female, provide library and source material at the researcher's request. The writer sifts the gathered material and, out of it all, constructs a tight, concise story, which is then edited twice—first by the senior editor, then by managing editor Henry Grunwald or his assistant. After the editing process, the reporter/researcher goes over the story with the writer for accuracy and tone. Often writers look upon the researcher's role as that of adversary—her confrontation coming, as it does, face-to-face over the copy, rather than indirectly, *on* copy, as the editors' changes do.

Female copyreaders and copy editors read stories for style;

female picture researchers have assigned or tracked down the photos that illustrate the stories. Layout artists (for the most part male) have pasted the stories up, and the entire process has been okayed and overseen by male editors.

The two highest ranking women on *Time*'s masthead are associate editors, and both have been at the magazine for well over twenty years. They are not in policy or decision-making positions, although one of them heads a staff of twenty-five at the copy desk in addition to handling her responsibilities as copy stylist.

One thing is sure at *Time* Magazine. There is only one way for things to go for women there now and for the women who will, one way or another, join the magazine later. Things have to get better. They can't get much worse.

Upward Mobility, Ltd.

VOGUE AND MADEMOISELLE*

One day a few years ago a wide-eyed, newly hired *Vogue* secretary went bouncing into an editor's office with a package and said, "Hi," at which the editor is supposed to have cringed and finally snapped, "We don't say that around here!"

> From *"Vogueland" in Fame and Obscurity*
> by Gay Talese

A *Mademoiselle* secretary moves up literally and figuratively if she becomes a *Vogue* secretary. She moves from the eighteenth floor at 420 Lexington Avenue to the nineteenth. At the same time, she moves from a young professional woman's magazine to one regarded as sacred writ by the world's diamond-decked "beautiful" people.

* See Preface.

Both magazines are owned by Condé Nast Publications, whose stable also includes *Glamour, House and Garden,* and *Bride's* Magazine, as well as *Air Progress* and the science-fiction monthly, *Analog.* Since Condé Nast bought *Vogue* in 1909, it has remained a pantheon of the beauty and fashion industry, while *Mademoiselle* has aimed, by definition, to woo eighteen- to twenty-five-year-olds as much with its features and fiction content as *Vogue* does with its clothes and make-up. The differences between working on the two are distinct, but the way to get a job on either is essentially the same.

Applicants should write to the Personnel Department of Condé Nast rather than to a specific editor. The department's amazingly efficient staff grants an interview to almost everyone who requests one. Many applicants meet the department's kind motherly head, Mary Campbell, who is almost as much of an institution as *Vogue* itself. Occasionally someone does slip in with no test, but most women must take a typing test, regardless of the positions they want. Passing is fifty words per minute, but no one really cares if she does fifty words with a half-dozen mistakes. The idea is to see whether you can bat out a letter or manuscript, and Personnel is delighted when a prospective employee can also take shorthand. A college degree is required of everyone except summer interns and those with exceptional qualifications, such as the finalists in *Mademoiselle*'s annual guest editor competitions.

More than a dozen members of the present staffs of the five main Condé Nast magazines were once guest editors, which means they were among the twenty undergraduate winners in an annual contest involving writing, photography, and art. The guest editors, whose legions have included Ali MacGraw and Sylvia Plath, invade the *Mademoiselle* offices in June; afterward, three or four of the twenty are hired as summer interns. Two or three of those then become permanent employees. A guest editorship is an open sesame to Condé Nast jobs, and hundreds of former winners have worked there over the years.

During the job interview, Personnel staffers look for spirit and pep as much as for talent, sometimes musing aloud that a woman seems, or seems not, to be "the Condé Nast type."

Salaries are incredibly low, but the "glamour" of working at *Mademoiselle* or *Vogue* is considered part of the payoff. In 1970 secretaries started at $100 to $115 per week. Raises come promptly after three or six months, but those are never more than a mere $10 or $15 a week.

The title of a new employee traditionally has been "secretary," although the job involves much more than secretarial work, and "editorial assistant" has lately been heard more often. Whatever her title, a woman starts at the bottom. Horizontal and vertical mobility are sure but slow—CNP wants a woman to prove her loyalty and dedication before making any switch. And once inducted into the CNP "family," she's always a member unless fired. Condé Nast staff and alumnae get the first crack at new job openings. Some staff members leave, put in time on other magazines, then return. A saying goes "The reason all the women on *Seventeen* know all the women on *Ingenue* is that they all worked together on *Mademoiselle*." A standard farewell goes, "We're delighted you've received a good offer elsewhere, but please come back." Many who would have liked to come back have not done so after their salaries have been nearly doubled elsewhere. Those who stay eventually move up in rank, though not everyone sees this as benefiting the magazines. Mastheads are dotted with titles referred to as "deadwood" by some of the editors: they belong to people who have stayed for twenty years and have kept getting promoted —for longevity rather than talent.

Which magazine a woman is assigned to depends on her interests and where Personnel thinks she will "fit." "I can tell in minutes whether or not a girl is the *Vogue* type," one interviewer contends. A *Mademoiselle* staffer put it differently. "You don't have to have a title or a name like Consuelo to work on *Vogue*," she says, "but it will help you get there." The *Vogue* masthead is, in fact, crowded with such unpedestrian names as Arabella von Westenholz, Constance von Collande, and Catherine di Montzemolo.

More important than a girl's name, however, is her personal sense of style. Gay Talese has pointed out that the editors are singularly uncharitable to neophytes. Women are expected to adapt to the *Vogue* way of doing things. That may mean refraining from a bubbly "Hi," presumably because the conventional office put-down describes *Glamour* staff members as "those peppy, hi people." Or a new recruit may have to alter her attire; freaky dress is restricted to models and the *Mademoiselle* crew downstairs. She will certainly have to learn to spell in the *Vogue* (i.e., British) manner: to write, for example, that a hat is a "marvellous colour."

Most important, a girl is expected to perform whatever task she is given. Though secretaries on all magazines are subject to running a vast number of personal errands for their editors, *Vogue* provides the most garish version of this women's-lib nightmare. There Mlle. Secretary is expected to follow her editor to the hairdresser to take dictation issuing from under the dryer, if her editor wishes. The secretary often spends her lunch hour in such pursuits as searching for a christening present for the editor's godchild. She trots to the Pan Am Building's Zum Zum for an editor's frankfurter. She will type all of the editor's business and personal letters and will dial her phone calls, including the three-digit extensions. A woman who doesn't like it—and remember, she has a college degree—can leave, because others are queueing up to take her place.

On *Mademoiselle,* certain editors are as patronizing as those on *Vogue,* but in both places a lucky novice will get a crack at a few quasi-creative chores—such as reading (i.e., evaluating) manuscripts, proofreading, dealing with authors and manufacturers, and editing copy. And each job offers its particular kind of brush with "glamour": a fashion assistant commutes on an editor's coattails to Seventh-Avenue showrooms. Manufacturers send beauty-staff members free lipsticks by the crate, unless lipstick is "out" this season. A features or fiction assistant speaks to Truman Capote or Jane Fonda. And eventually the secretary/assistant gets a stab at writing, or hard editing, or covering the Rome collections.

In *The Bell Jar,* which contains a thinly fictionalized account of her stint as a *Mademoiselle* guest editor, Sylvia Plath wrote: "I was college correspondent for the town *Gazette* and editor of the literary magazine and secretary of Honor Board, which deals with academic and social offenses and punishments—a popular office—and I had a well-known woman poet and professor on the faculty championing me for graduate school at one of the biggest universities in the east, and promises of full scholarships all the way, and now I was apprenticed to the best editor on an intellectual fashion magazine, and what did I do but balk and balk like a dull cart horse?"[1]

What surprises most rookies is an almost total lack of the expected dazzle. The most exciting thing about working at Condé Nast is hearing you've landed the job; after that, it's usually all downhill. "People always used to say to me, 'You work for *Vogue* . . . how exciting!' " a former editor sighs. "I used to think, 'If you only knew!' "

Many women find the low salaries and the lady-in-waiting aspect of their jobs humiliating. Others are happy merely to be surrounded by beauty and fashion—to share an elevator with Shrimpton, to see a new style six months before anyone else, to make friends with such legendary personages as Diana Vreeland, former editor, now consulting editor of *Vogue.* John Keats wrote of Dorothy Parker in his biography of her, *You Might As Well Live:* "As a staff member of *Vogue,* she was the very center of this fashionable world; she was one of those who, if only in a very minor way, were helping to establish new styles for the fashionable. New York City believed in being 'smart,' and so did *Vogue,* and so did she."

On *Mademoiselle,* the atmosphere may be a bit looser, but

[1] Used by permission of Harper & Row.

otherwise it's more of the same. Low salaries, uninspiring day-to-day chores, personal errands, with only occasional touches of glitter, are the rule. Beauty, Fashion, College and Careers, Travel, Public Relations, College Competitions, and other departments offer the possibility of traveling a couple of times a year eventually. However, Ali MacGraw once remarked that it's hard to survive on a fashion magazine's salary unless you're subsidized by a rich aunt, and the occasional glitter may not compensate for the meagerness.

Working on either *Mademoiselle* or *Vogue* has had the same effect on hundreds of women since then, as the high turnover of employees attests. Still, a recent graduate can cut her professional teeth on either magazine and enjoy it, too. The offices swarm with people—roughly 20 to 30 percent are men, mainly in advertising—who make intelligent, spirited friends. It's best to try to find one sympathetic editor who will take you under their wing and treat you humanely as you're learning. If you can't find a sympathetic editor, you can usually aim to be one—and make it, if you stay long enough.

3

NEWSPAPERS AND WIRE SERVICES

Newspapers and Wire Services

OF THE FOUR KINDS OF MEDIA this book explores, the wire services and the newspapers emerge as the most enlightened in their hiring and promotion policies.

There are two reasons for this. The first is that the newspapers covered are not really typical of those throughout the country. What is happening in New York in network television and in magazine and book publishing is what is happening *period*. But there are newspapers everywhere. The large New York City dailies are organized; the Newspaper Guild negotiates the editorial contracts, with no variations for sex differences. To keep competent employees, the suburban papers have to match the Guild terms or at least come close.

The other reason for the newspapers' comparative enlightenment is that they are not so tradition-encrusted. Their very dispersion has allowed them to innovate at will. Not that many of them have ever taken full advantage of their independence but, here and there, somebody hired a female reporter or typesetter without the roof falling in—and set a precedent.

Still, the situation for women on New York newspapers is better than the national average and is gradually improving—not without some firm prodding by the women themselves.

In their handling of the news, the metropolitan newspapers are also exhibiting signs of recent consciousness raising, mostly in response to specific criticisms. They are not yet so thoroughly rehabilitated that they can be trusted to go it alone.

The Sob-Sister Mystique

THE DAILY NEWS

Seven years ago, a girl with superb grades from one of the Seven-Sisters schools responded to a *Daily News* want ad for summer trainees. She was told, after one glance, that she wasn't qualified: she wasn't a man.

One college generation ago, a young married woman was asked in her job interview at the *News:* "What kind of contraception do you use?"

Fortunately, the days of those blatantly outrageous practices are over—although if you're female and want to work for New York's picture newspaper (or just about any other news outlet) these days, it helps if you're black or Puerto Rican as well.

Today's New York *News* is both good news and bad news. First the good news:

In the last five years, the number of female reporters on city, suburban, and bureau editorial staffs has doubled—a dramatic increase indeed—bringing the grand total up to around two dozen out of 150 *News* reporters. The Women's Department (not included in the aforementioned tally), notwithstanding some personnel changes, has remained the same size during this time, with its writing staff of twelve women. What *has* changed in the women's pages is the layout. As the first department to be overhauled under the new regime of Managing Editor Michael J. O'Neill, the women's pages are without question the most attractive in the entire paper. The content has improved somewhat as well.

Two women copy editors have recently been hired, one for the city and one on the suburban copy desk. While the addition of these two women may not seem earthshaking, their employment marks the end of nearly twenty womanless years on both desks.

The television editor is a woman who, incidentally, began her *News* career as a copy girl during World War II. In the Film

Department, all three staff critics are women, a quasi-precedent created by the first quasi-critic—who happened to be the sister-in-law of Captain Joseph Medill Patterson, the tabloid's founder.

Since we have gotten into the bad news without formal announcement, let us continue. Of the seventy-some photographers at the paper, one is female—she too was hired during World War II, when men were scarce and women were qualified—no women photographers have been hired since. The same goes for the copyboy staff. All boys.

There are no women city or suburban editors. There are no women on the telegraph desk, which handles all copy outside a fifty-mile radius of the city. There are no women executives in any areas of *News* management, but they abound in clerical positions.

Despite the increase in the number of women reporters on city and suburban staffs, Stone-Age ideas about what women can and cannot cover still permeate the place. With two exceptions (Norma Abrams and Theo Wilson), women are regularly assigned stories that do not make page-one headlines. When the biggie breaks, a woman will almost inevitably do the sidebar—that is, the tearjerk, emotional, human side of the event, rather than the event itself. While editors insist they seek the best possible reporter—male, female, black, or white—for any given job, they betray the assumption of the power people at the *News* that women are better at writing about the emotional sidelights than about the hard facts.

Perhaps needless to say, the paper's attitude toward the feminist movement is one of snide, chuckling condescension, blatantly exemplified in the page-one banner headline following the August 26, 1970, march: "Gals Unbutton Their Lib." *News*-women who protested and continued to sound off over subsequent sexist headlines, captions, and *News* style, (e.g., the Alice Crimmins-shapely-blonde-divorcee-former-cocktail-waitress-and-secretary syndrome) have earned "bitch" reputations for their efforts.

When freelance writer Claudia Dreifus, in preparation for a magazine article on the employment situation for media women in the city, asked Ed Quinn, assistant to the executive editor, why there weren't more women around the *News,* she was told, "Women have ways of their own" and "Women don't want to work nights in crime-ridden New York." He did not point out that the working shift is a matter of assignment, not choice, and that the reason there are no women working nights or lobster (1 A.M. to 9 A.M.) is simply that the *News* is shrouded in paternalism (not to mention Irish-Catholic fraternalism).

Alas, Ms. Dreifus was unable to pursue her probe into the *News* further because Mr. Quinn, after calling her "naïve," "biased," and "not normal," threw her out of his office, shouting after her, "Are half of all *firemen* women?" She later described the aborted interview as one where "he tried to pull a macho-rank trip on me."

And that's about the way it is today at the *News,* the paper with the largest circulation in the Western Hemisphere. When Managing Editor O'Neill took over the helm, an article appeared in *New York* Magazine entitled, "Can Mike O'Neill Save the *Daily News?*" For many women within the *Daily News,* the follow-up question was: save the *News* from what?

Woman/Man-Child/Adult

THE LONG ISLAND PRESS

The *Long Island Press* is an old-time rag—the seventh-largest evening paper in the United States—where it is still possible to rise from a copy boy (gopher) through the ranks of clerk, news clerk, night reporter, day reporter, rewriter, and deskman to editor and even to management. If you are a man.

The *Press* has other plans for women. Their job titles hint at it: copyBOY, rewriteMAN, deskMAN.

Unless a woman has been with another Newhouse publication for several years, she starts as an editorial assistant in the Women's News Department. Her job is to write engagement and wedding announcements, women's-club news, and feature stories on such subjects as an elderly Queens lady who collects saltshakers and the latest window display at the Gertz department store. (Guess who is the *Press*'s biggest advertiser.)

Although it's possible for a woman to stagnate in that job level for years while young men in clerk jobs are promoted to reporters, management requires a college degree for the women's news job. Not that anyone specifies "women's news" (or "social," as editor Dave Starr refers to it) on her application. General applications for jobs in editorial from men are assumed to mean sports and news. Similarly unspecific applications from women are assumed to mean women's news—even when, as in one case, the female applicant was a former war correspondent or, as in another case, had covered general assignments for two other newspapers in Asia.

It takes a while for a new female employee to become aware of the many differences between women's news and the rest of the paper. For there are some similarities. Like the other departments, women's news maintains the proper professional atmosphere of slovenliness. One female editorial assistant made the novice's faux pas of cleaning out her desk. Crammed behind the stuck drawers were letters requesting wedding announcements dated as early as 1949; yellow, rotting newspapers from the early fifties; pointy-toed spike heels; an Annette Funicello sweater; and a set of eggy eating utensils. (Remember the scene in *The Front Page* where the reporter finds dirty underwear and moldy pie in his desk?)

Now about the differences: Reporters in women's news are paid the lower salary of editorial assistants, a title made up to pacify female clerks who had been performing reporter functions. One woman who has been doing desk*man* work since the late fifties was promoted to reporter in 1969! While I was there, the woman who handled the Sunday women's pages from start to finish was paid only reporter pay, while men who perform identical functions in other departments are either deskmen or editors. Anyone who so much as questions the rationale for such inequities is branded a troublemaker and forced out. In 1969 the *Press* got rid of two women's-news reporters and the women's editor herself after they had spoken up at a union meeting requesting that the contract be held back until provision was made for upgrading women's-news employees, ostensibly on other grounds, of course.

Similarly, in July 1971, Nancy Borman, who had brought charges of sex discrimination against the *Press* under the state Human Rights Law, was offered severance pay to resign, and was ultimately fired.

In women's news, the work load is heavier than in other departments. In the Borman case, a comparative analysis was made of sports and women's news; it was found that the average daily output per person during the women's light season in July was 34.26 column inches for sports and 57.35 column inches for women's news. (It was an average season for sports.) In the same study it was found that twelve of the nineteen men in sports are paid as deskmen, while there are, mysteriously, no deskmen in women's news. By the *Press* editor's own admission at an investigatory conference on January 10, 1972, most of the sports deskmen actually function as reporters, a level lower than their pay scale. Women, meanwhile, function at levels higher than those at which they are paid. Is this discrimination? You bet your green eyeshade it is.

Because of the upward titling in sports and the downward titling in women's news, the women, who do an average of 50 percent more work, receive an average of 87 percent of what the men earn. Four men in sports, including two editors, a reporter, and a deskman, have higher salaries than the women's editor. And there are no clerks or editorial assistants at all in the sports department, indicating that those functions are distributed among higher-paid men.

On top of all this, sports has an auxiliary force of at least eight local columnists who cover events at space rates, while women's news has only one columnist. Her (society) column appears only in the Suffolk edition, and only on Sundays.

Management's explanation for the difference is that the reporting done by women's-news employees is a different, simpler kind of reporting, and that the deskman work performed by the women is a simpler kind of deskwork. "It's like the difference between children and adults," Starr explained at a Division of Human Rights conference.

His comment revealed his attitude better than any amount of statistics: women are children; men are adults. Men are serious workers; women play around.

Women's-news employees don't even work the same number of hours as those in other departments, though the length of the work week is specified in the Newspaper Guild contract. Under the 1968–70 contract, editorial employees at the *Press* were guaranteed a 40-hour work week, with time off for lunch. News reporters were permitted to take an hour off during their eight-hour day, but the women's-news employees worked from 8:30 to 4:00 nonstop, always eating at their desks. The next contract called for a 37½-hour week, and under it cityside knocked off a half-hour earlier each day, while the women's desk kept the same hours as under the old contract.

With all this going on, it's no wonder so many women have requested transfers over the years. The mystery is why the *Press* repeatedly turns them down. Most eventually just quit altogether and go to another newspaper, or start a new career. But one woman kept up for years, until the women's editor herself was pleading with the managing editor to transfer her. The *Press* finally did and got a bargain in the deal. The woman served as film critic, at reporter pay. Another woman took her case directly to the managing editor, who gave her excuse after excuse ("Women shouldn't work at night," etc.). Finally she handed him her resignation . . . and was promptly transferred. A third woman won a transfer after a long uphill fight, only to be transferred back, against her will. She quit.

The latest victim of this kind of treatment was Ms. Borman, a reporter for the Women's News Department being paid as an editorial assistant. Without knowing the past history of the transfer issue, she innocently brought up the subject with the women's editor. The editor told her not to talk about it and tried to persuade her to stay in the department, but finally agreed to "handle" the transfer. After a year, Borman was still not tranferred, nor was she being paid for the writing she was doing under her byline.

Aware that three editorial clerks, who just happened to be males, had been promoted over her in that time, she brought her request to Dave Starr. Starr said he couldn't transfer her because he didn't want to set a precedent for that kind of thing. "I have the same problem every time I hire a bright young lady," he said, adding that he would have to start hiring "dullards" for the job. (He has since denied ever making this crack.)

When she asked why she couldn't be a reporter, he said because she wasn't "getting the preparation." She then asked to be transferred to a job where she would be getting preparation. In effect, she was asking for a demotion to clerk. Starr said he would have to talk this over with the women's editor.

That afternoon the women's editor threatened to fire Borman at the end of the next week if she didn't learn to "fit into [her] niche." When it became clear that the *Press* might be able to carry out the threat (the Guild unit at the *Press* is a joke), Borman filed charges of sex discrimination with the state Division of Human Rights.

When the *Press* learned of the charges early in July 1971, it was rumored in the office that management was using every ounce of political pressure it could summon to "get rid of" the case. At the first investigatory conference on July 8, Starr contended that he and the women's editor had planned to fire Borman as early as March for "refusing assignments." But under cross-questioning, he admitted that the "assignment" was an order from the assistant women's editor in February to look up a telephone number for a reader calling in. Borman explained that she was writing on deadline at the time.

Despite affidavits from Susan Glass, the former women's editor, and several female ex-employees that they had also been discriminated against in pay and promotions, the first finding of the Division was that there was no "probable cause" to show that Borman had been discriminated against. She had been fired for "insubordination," the Division found. Ironically, she had not been fired at the time of the finding. On that basis, she had the case reopened and reheard in December and January. In the course of the new conferences, the *Press* subpoenaed its own female employees, implying that they were hostile witnesses, and paraded them in to tell how good the *Press* had been to them. Cross-examination revealed that one female editor received no expense vouchers, although this is the way the *Press* makes up for the men's low salaries in her category. Women who had risen to deskman and editor on other papers were titled "editorial assistant" when they came to the *Press*. The only testimony that any of them gave against Borman was that she had once broken into tears while being taught to do the food layout.

Borman won the first case, the newspaper appealed and won the appeal, and the case has now gone to a federal court. If the ruling is favorable, it will point the way for other underpaid women in women's-news departments to fight for equal pay for equal work.

Some pointers for women applying to the *Press:*

(1) If applying for an edit clerk's job as a stepping stone to reporter, specify news, sports, or Mr. Fixit (action-reporter) department. Or ask to be a copyboy, if you don't mind being summoned with the call, "Boy!"

(2) Specify city news, night-side, or sports when applying for a reporter's job. Women's news is a dead end here; once in, you'll never get out.

(3) Don't plan a big future at the *Long Island Press*. Its longevity seems to be uncertain, due to inroads in advertising made by *Newsday* and competition in home delivery by the *Daily News*.

(4) Don't ask questions about ABC News Service, which appears to be an independent wire service. The Newhouse chain set it up twenty years ago in an attempt to prevent the entire staff of the *Press*, and then the *Star-Journal*, from belonging to the Newspaper Guild.

(5) Don't raise any serious questions at Guild meetings (instant professional death as far as the *Press* is concerned).

(6) Take what Dave Starr tells you with a grain of salt. His nickname around the city room is "the smiling assassin."

(7) The *Press* likes reporters who are already familiar with Queens, Nassau, and Suffolk. Not very many other prerequisites.

(8) Bear in mind that many great careers were begun by people *after* they left the *Press*. Make contacts on other papers and work on getting another job as soon as you get on the staff.

I'm Newsday—Sue Me

NEWSDAY

Once upon a time before the new feminism, a female *Newsday* reporter, whose husband also wrote for the paper, asked for a raise. Management denied it. Reason: she couldn't have a raise because her husband had just gotten one.

They don't do things like that these days. It's illegal since Title VII; it's immoral since Caroline Bird; and it's so obvious.

Subtler forms of sex discrimination flourish here instead. But *Newsday* is still a promising publication for women journalists. Not because management has some inherent understanding that women reporters and editors are just reporters and editors who have different sexual appendages than men, but because the women think this way. In December 1973, *we* stopped thinking and started suing. That month we announced our intention to file a sex discrimination suit under Title VII of the Civil Rights Act.

A woman's future with *Newsday* now depends on the EEOC or the courts. But some pressure has already been applied by the *Newsday* Women's Caucus, established in 1972 and representing almost every woman reporter and editor on staff.

The caucus developed a 117-page brief outlining sex discrimination charges and backing them with dozens of pages of statistics. The caucus found: women are hired in substantially fewer numbers than men; women are generally hired for or are assigned to jobs traditionally held by women and are concentrated in the feature sections of the paper and Sunday roto magazine; women hold no upper-level editorial positions that can influence the paper's policy; women are rarely assigned to political bureaus; women are rarely given assignments with promotion and/or prize-winning potential; the few women editors on staff are in the lowest echelon.

Recently, several more women have been assigned as editors, but again, at the lowest levels. Women also have flooded the copy desk, but rarely move up to slots, and never to news editing. The paper has also begun to hire more women as news writers rather than assigning them to features. This, no doubt, is the result of pressure from the Caucus, but we also feel it is too little, granted too slowly.

About one-third of the reporters on staff are women. *Newsday* can't assign them to the women's page because the page was abolished when all the soft-news sections were combined into one feature pull-out called Part II. But *Newsday* still has women doing what has been traditionally called women's news: fashion, food, furnishings, and family-type stories. This is one of the sections headed by a woman editor. It's called the Living Section, thus its editor is the Living Editor, a title she has to choke out whenever she has to say it.

The rest of Part II covers such specialties as science, media, religion, entertainment, and business. All but two reporters and all editors are men. One woman reporter in the specialist section writes consumer news. She got the job when this area was considered "women's interest" and had it handed to her without a fight. Now that consumerism has become a hot issue, she says the paper would be less likely to hand the job over to any woman. She just got it before it was respectable enough for a man to cover. There is one woman on the entertainment section staff and one writes for the business section.

Due to the Caucus pressure, *Newsday* has become conscious of an obligation to hire more women. But a recently hired reporter said she was asked at her job interview if she intended to get married. *Newsday* has hired "working mothers," who often turn out to be a better investment than some working fathers we know. It's youth-oriented, for both sexes. Thus jeans are acceptable office dress.

Most reporters start working nights, or in the Suffolk County bureau, or both. The copy desk is another entry-level job. Usually *Newsday* wants a couple of years' experience before they'll talk to you. Potential employees are given a three-part test—writing a news story, a feature story from information provided; explaining how one would go about reporting a given rumor; and a copyediting test.

Women are generally not paid as well as men, a fact management will dispute. But there has been some action in the salary area since the birth of the Caucus.

Other benefits and nonbenefits—no maternity leave, no day care, discriminatory health coverage for single women; car a necessity; no women columnists or editorial writers. Women reporters can expect some abuse from the male executives and staff, especially in the Suffolk bureau. They can also expect to get strong support from some of the men and all of their sisters on the staff.

While the future of *Newsday* women rests with the EEOC or the courts, it would be nice to see the class of our class-action grow in the meantime.

Post-Liberation

THE NEW YORK POST

The *New York Post* has one of the best records of any major newspaper in the country for hiring women, and undoubtedly *the* best among New York media. Women make up about a third of its reportorial staff. Paradise? Not quite.

Like all New York City papers, the *Post* is forced by union contracts to give women equal pay for equal work. Compared to many other papers, the *Post* seems to be fair about giving women equal assignments, and a number of women reporters have covered "dangerous" stories. However, although there is no unanimity of opinion among the women, some feel that male reporters are usually given the bigger or more complicated stories and most of the out-of-town assignments.

One woman complained that although female reporters are paid the same as men, the woman often acts as the man's assistant when a mixed pair works together on a series. Men are generally assigned the "most interesting" subjects for the "man (or woman) in the news." And only a couple of women have received merit raises.

The *Post* has been quite open to giving young people (of both sexes) three-month tryouts, but both have had a high failure rate. The *Post* has also arranged tryouts for copyboys and girls, with about five males becoming reporters for every female promoted. However, the paper seems to be phasing out that practice and has been attempting to hire more staff members with experience. One feminist on the staff feels that this new policy will work against women, since the pool of women with experience is smaller than that of men because other papers are less liberal in hiring women.

The newspaper allows some female reporters who have worked for it for several years to work only three days a week. (One staff member calls the women with shorter work schedules "the office pets.")

The *Post* is quite flexible in its schedule demands on pregnant reporters, and has an excellent maternity-leave policy, with six months' leave (plus a possible three more months) and four weeks' pay for employees who have been at the paper at least two years. One woman, however, who was never let out of the office on assignment during her pregnancy, objected to being treated like a "Dresden doll."

Many of the women at the *Post* are feminists. They were backed by the then metropolitan editor, who encouraged them to take part in the historic march down Fifth Avenue. He has also tried to keep sexist headlines and descriptions out of the paper. The male editors seem to have resigned themselves to living with a "liberated" female staff after failing in an attempt to fire the two most outspoken feminists. In the fall of 1969, two young women refused to allow their bylines on stories about the wives of famous men. They were promptly fired, but the union backed them because of a contract clause providing that reporters can choose to have their bylines removed from stories. So they were rehired.

A number of the young, single women find many of the men, especially the older ones, alarming. "They act like Diamond Jim Brady let loose in a whorehouse," one of them says. "They ask questions like 'When did you get laid last?' 'Are you wearing a bra today?' 'How often do you have an orgasm?' "

Some of the men at the paper have even been known to send dirty notes to women, and one feminist reporter said, "Most of the

male staff members are male chauvinist pigs, but their consciousness is being raised, so they aren't as bad as they used to be." She
added that some of the younger male reporters are "heavy
feminists."

Although the *Post* has been good about hiring women, some
female staff members feel that it has not been good about moving
them around or promoting them. They feel the paper might attract
a different staff if it were known to give women a better chance to
move upward.

The *Post* has no women editors, except for *the* editor, who is
the owner. According to a profile in the *New Yorker,* Dorothy
Schiff, the owner-editor-publisher, is known for her fondness for
the writing of Harriet Van Horne and the Hollywood gossip
columnists.

"It seems to be very important for the men in the office to
denigrate her," said one woman. "The mythology of the *Post*
seems to be that everybody's failures are excused by having to
work for a woman."

The *Post* is "the apotheosis of *The-Front-Page,* anti-intellec-
tual-type journalism," one former employee recalled. Other women
say that while the *Post* is, relatively, a great place for a *woman* to
work, it's a lousy place for anyone to work.

"It is known as a cheap paper, preferring to gather news by
phone rather than sending a reporter out," said one reporter. Like
many other (male) publishers, the *Post* publisher "prefers pap and
personalities to Pulitzer-Prize-winning stories. There is very little
in-depth reporting, and the *Post* is not big on trend stories. The
archetypal series would be 'The Love Stories of Famous Reform
Democratic Homosexual Jewish Opera Stars in History.' "

The women's section, unlike the "family" pages of other
papers, such as the *Times,* is where many papers were twenty years
ago featuring "Dear Abby," Paris fashions, and astrology. But
coverage of abortion, day care, women's lib, and gay lib has
improved.

Working conditions have irritated many staff members. "The

Post is located at the ass-end of the world, in a seedy neighborhood," said one. The nearest subway is eight blocks away. A bus once ran sporadically from the paper closer to the IRT, but it has been discontinued. There have been purse-snatchings and muggings in the neighborhood. The building itself, she said, looks like a "modernized barracks, with Kafkaesque hallways."

There is plenty of room at the *Post* for a day-care center, but how many women would want to bring their kids into that sort of environment? So if you have a Black Belt in karate, own a cab, and are immune to the howling winds off the East River, maybe you can hack it at the *Post,* but you may end up being just that—a hack.

Autres Temps, Autres Attitudes

THE NEW YORK TIMES

Despite the male-chauvinist hangups of its almost exclusively male management (such as the editors who open doors and unjam desk drawers for women reporters, and those who abhor *Ms* and wonder why women need to be liberated), there are more opportunities for women on the editorial side of the *New York Times* than in its business and production departments.

The *Times,* like the other two remaining New York dailies, is obliged by contract with the Newspaper Guild to disregard sex in the payment of salaries. The contract that went into effect on March 31, 1970, provides that reporters start at a minimum of $264.54 a week and reach a top minimum of $293.54 after two years. Increases of nearly $60 were written into the next two years of the contract although the Pay Board in the terminal months of Phase Two cut them back somewhat.

The contract is based on a five-day, 34½-hour week, with overtime at time and a half in cash for work beyond the work week or beyond the six-hour-and-fifty-four-minute work day.

In the good old days, before cost-cutting, the *Times* was amenable to regular merit raises (besides the periodic union-negotiated increases) and, in its hiring, did not feel tied down to union minimums. So it is that although women's salaries as a group average less than the men's, a small number of *Times* women earn more than some of their male counterparts either because their performance has been rewarded or because they were hired away from another publication at a tempting figure. One rule of thumb for women as well as for men interested in handsome salaries is to make a reputation on another newspaper or magazine and then be wooed away by the *Times*.

However, some women *have* pulled themselves up from the rungs of clerks, news assistants, and secretaries to the level of reporter, and one woman moved from secretary to the managing editor to administrative assistant to one of the vice presidents. The *Times* does promote from within along reasonably well-defined avenues of access. Anyone wanting to be a journalist has only to show relentless perseverance and boundless energy and resourcefulness. Because of its policy of letting employees write for departments other than those to which they are assigned (and thus receive a moderate freelance fee), it is possible for an ambitious beginner to work her way up the ladder without being treated like a serf.

In any case, there are fewer opportunities in the newspaper business than in most other businesses for the free play of the male impulse to dominate. Everybody does what he is being paid to do, and menial chores for someone else are not included. Female reporters are not only exempted from requests to change their bosses' typewriter ribbons, they don't even have to change their own. That's done by someone who can do it faster and, presumably, at less than a reporter's wage.

As a morning newspaper, with deadlines in the early evening, the *Times* has always required its reporters to write their own stories. (On evening papers, with deadlines breaking frequently throughout the day, the reporter often acts as legman, telephoning in facts to a rewriteman.) In recent years, an emphasis on lively writing and interpretive reportage has heightened the necessity (and the opportunities) for reporters to score with their typewriters rather than by strength of shoeleather and shrewdness. The plums and plaudits go to the best writers, or at least to those who can gain the most space as a showcase for their writing.

So it is that a woman who aspires to make it at the *Times* should discard the traditional journalistic prejudices which hold that the newsroom is the only respectable assignment and that the women's page is a dumping ground for featherweights and sex objects.

The women's-news department, now rechristened Family/Style, has been a writer's dream showcase. The metropolitan news reporters in the city room may see their efforts whittled down to three-quarters of a column (perhaps disappearing entirely in the second edition), under the fierce competitive pressure for news space in a newspaper that is a national and international, as well as a local one. But the Family/Style reporter often enjoys two to four columns of space, with compelling illustrations, at the top of the page. Displays like this not only gain recognition for a writer within the *Times* but from the outside world in the form of free-lance writing assignments as well.

During the last decade, as its name change does not quite satisfactorily indicate, women's news at the *Times* has broadened its base to include subjects of general sociological and cultural interest, and has moved increasingly away from the four categories it used to encompass—food, fashion, furnishings, and family.

The department has also been a springboard for several female writers: Nan Robertson went from there to the Washington bureau and then to the Paris bureau, Gloria Emerson to the foreign staff (and then back to Family/Style as an outside contract writer), Marylin Bender to financial news.

Other showcases for women reporters—as specialists rather than as news generalists—are in cultural news (the umbrella for art, film, dance, music, and television news) and in science news. Lesley Oelsner brought such distinction to the legal-news beat (she had a law degree) that she was transferred to the Washington Bureau.

In the newsroom proper, the number of women reporters has also noticeably increased in recent years, although it is nowhere near 50 percent of the resident population. The thing to watch here, though, is the changing attitude toward the women who *are* in the newsroom.

Once upon a time, the *Times* had a rule (informal but still restrictive) that kept women reporters from danger or indignity. This policy served to exclude them from challenging assignments —and hours of work.

On a morning newspaper publishing seven days a week, the newsroom must be staffed weekends and holidays as well as regular weekdays; nights as well as days. The woman who wants to succeed as a metropolitan news reporter (with hopes of getting from there into national and foreign assignments) cannot complain at having to work New Year's Eve or of being given the night rewrite stint because it interferes with her social life, or because the Times Square area after dark is not the safest part of the city.

The representation of women on the metropolitan news reportorial staff, the Washington Bureau, the various copy desks and on the foreign news staff has been increasing since *Times* women organized themselves into an action group in 1972. Their efforts, together with a rash of sex discrimination lawsuits and fines against major corporations, have kindled a new attitude of receptivity on the part of management.

A woman stringer was hired for the photographic staff which had never had a female member. Charlotte Curtis had the highest editorial position held by a woman—editor of the Family/Style Department (a position that carries with it an assistant, also classified as a manager). Curtis was named to succeed Harrison Salisbury as editor of the Op/Ed Page and Ada Louise Huxtable, the Pulitzer Prize-winning architecture critic was taken into the all-male confines of the Editorial Board. A pioneering woman, Betsy Wade, sits in the command post of the prestigious foreign copy desk.

There had never been any women in the managerial pipeline, that is, in such slots as assistant metropolitan news editor, until Grace Glueck became assistant metropolitan news editor for cultural news. Nora Sayre was hired as a movie critic, adding another female sensibility to the cultural area.

Until recently, *Times* women were not noted for feminist militancy. Possibly because they enjoyed their fame and modest financial rewards as pet writers, they did not aggressively seek executive or policy-making roles. Given the climate of the *Times* (upper case and lower), the next round is theirs.

Anachronistic Bohemianism

THE VILLAGE VOICE

Working for *The Village Voice* is a little like reading it; there's a lot of crap mixed in with the good things. From a worker's point of view, sorting out the crap means separating the bread-and-butter issues from the less tangible ones.

Pay at the *Voice* is incredibly poor. Regular freelancers— those who do most of the reporting—are paid $100 to $200 an article, depending (usually) on the length and amount of work involved, although there is no set policy. Columnists, including Jill

Johnston and Nat Hentoff, who appear each week, are paid any-where from $75 to $100 per article. Theater reviewers are paid $65 for covering one play, plus $25 for others reviewed in the same piece.[1] The only writers who are paid a salary are those on staff, which altogether numbers thirteen, including the publisher, the executive editor, the news editor, the associate editors, and the staff photographer—leaving five slots for reporters. Salaries for staff start at $200 a week, which is not all that much more than freelancers get.

The real advantage to the staff writer is security. If you're ill one week, or just too tired to write, you are still paid. And if you are really sick, you have health coverage, something freelancers don't have—just as they don't have paid vacations, Social Security, or any other fringe benefits that most employees now take for granted. Ironically, once you get on staff, not only do you get more money but you also have more time to spend writing for more open-handed publications, having been freed from the need to produce a weekly article in order to get paid.

Given these conditions, which are poorer than those on any other major New York publication, why then do so many people continue to write for the *Voice?* For one thing, its ambience. The *Voice* is a bit like an overgrown family; everyone is on a first-name basis, and there's never a feeling of a big boss watching over you. Bikes clutter the entrance, dogs are chained outside—or inside, for that matter—and a continuing debate takes place to which anyone is free to contribute, à la the Chinese Cultural Revolution.

There are still remnants of the bohemianism of the fifties. When the *Voice* first started out, its writers were mainly people who wanted to paint or write or discuss politics, and only occa-sionally tell the public about their own work or the work of their friends. Nobody had much money and everyone was good at talk. But while the atmosphere may still have the tone of those days, the finances do not. The *Voice* is now making money. How much, no

[1] These figures are as of November, 1973.

one seems to know—except the accountant, who won't say. As part of the fifties hangover, *Voice* old-timers retain the feeling that making money is an anal activity that had best be kept secret; almost anyone at the *Voice* will glibly describe all the details of his or her sexual life, but no one talks about money. The net effect is that *Voice* writers are racy, but poor in pocket.

As one of the first nonestablishment papers, the *Voice* has always been ahead of other journals in having a fair share of women writers. Of the four editors, two are women. But none of the nine remaining staff positions are held by women. When the paper was poorer, a much higher percentage of staff was female. Although many women continue to write for the *Voice,* and are paid the same as men, the real powers are male. That is, the owner, the publisher, the chief editor, the accountant, and the lawyer are all men, and it's this group that determines policies regarding salaries.

Expressions like promotion, sick leave, vacation pay, expense accounts—the ordinary vocabulary of commerce—are irrelevant at the *Voice*. They imply a structure that doesn't exist there; the only general policy is arbitrariness. The first piece I submitted to the *Voice* (1968) ran several full columns. I was paid $35. Then I was given $50, then $100, then $60, and now that I write regularly, I receive $150 an article. Each article usually takes three to four days to research and write. Since that $150 includes no fringe benefits (which means that when I'm old, I'll have no Social Security and will probably be just the sort of case the *Voice* will do an exposé of), why do *I* continue to write for it?

In a word—freedom. There is no real tampering with my work. My editor is literate, and his refinements are almost always improvements. There is also prestige, at least in New York, where most of the most interesting people get the *Voice,* if for no other reason than habit. The *Voice* has a certain amount of political power locally. The politicians read it, and if you want to get something done, you usually can if you embarrass a politician who is courting the liberal vote (as most in New York do). Which is why many established political writers and social critics like their writing to appear in the *Voice*.

In contrast, novice writers choose the *Voice* for its showcase opportunities. If you are unknown but good, you will get noticed. People in publishing scan the *Voice* like talent scouts looking over the graduating class of Hollywood High. The *Voice* is a starting point for a career in journalism. Often one controversial article (whose pertinency is often gauged by the number of letters about it) will elicit offers from publishers and open doors to the magazines that pay big money. First the *Voice*, then *Esquire*, and ultimately *Playboy* or *The New Yorker* is the careerist ladder many aspiring writers calculate on climbing.

This makes it hard for people who like writing for the *Voice* as a way of life instead of a starting point. Fewer and fewer of the younger writers seem to want to sit around in a local bar with friends, boozing and talking about plays and politics, and occasionally taking time out to have a nervous breakdown, as in the old days. Times have gotten tougher in New York. Aside from getting seduced into ambition and the hustling that involves, it is much harder to be a poor bohemian and survive in the New York of the seventies. Which is why many *Voice* writers are the offspring of fathers who are famous, or wealthy, or both. One can't afford to write for the *Voice* without an additional source of income. Now that the *Voice*, with its showcase opportunities, makes it possible for other sources of income to materialize, time spent writing for it is regarded as only a short period of marking time until graduation. But during that period, there is real insecurity, which no paper, particularly one with such liberal pretenses, should impose on its writers.

The *Voice* is no longer a cozy little family, operating on a shoestring and protecting its own when they're in trouble. Some of the older people may still feel paternal; everyone remembers a writer's block and there is great sympathy if you can't get a piece out on time. But if you can, the policy of flexibility can work against you; there's no guarantee your piece will be in the current issue or even in the next. If Andy Warhol gets stabbed or some major countercultural activity takes place right before the paper goes to press, your piece—which may have taken weeks to write—sits on the editor's desk waiting for duller days. These conditions have made for a hostility that contrasts with a general spirit of friendliness. For almost everyone at the *Voice* falls within the liberal-radical range and is sympathetic to way-out life styles, even if they don't actually cultivate them except in the pages of the paper.

Other than the underlying power structure of the *Voice,* which varies little from that found at any establishment institution in being male-dominated and in keeping workers ignorant of money matters, there is no sexism. You can't sleep your way up (or down), although you *can* have a pleasant affair with someone you work with (or for) and no one will particularly notice, nor will your work get published any faster or slower. But, more important, nobody eyes you, comments on your clothing, or does any of the things that make women feel they are mainly decorative objects or supportive creatures serving the needs of men. (Mary Nichols, the news editor, has a young male assistant.)

In talking about working for the *Voice,* I should point out that only a few people work *at* the *Voice.* The editors all have offices, and there is a set of communal cubicles for the regular freelance writers to share. But most people just drop by, hang around, wait to see "Ross."

In summary, you won't be ogled by *Voice* staff, you won't get any expense accounts to wine and dine people—or even to pay for your own expenses—but you will get a feeling that you're influencing people. Best of all, you'll be read (circulation is 150,000), and if you're good, some day someone will call and offer you a job that *does* have expense accounts, that pays well, and that might even put you on staff. And then you just might get nostalgic for the days when you were able to bike over at midnight, slip your piece under the door right before the morning deadline, and go back to sleep.

Even-Handed Exploitation

WOMEN'S WEAR DAILY

Women's Wear Daily is a nice place to work—but you wouldn't want to make a career there. It's a freewheeling office, filled with diverse, intelligent people who are exploited without regard to sex, religion, age, color, or what-have-you. For, without the constraints imposed by a union, *WWD* is run under the benevolent-patriarch concept of management: the company gives you lavish benefits, such as three-week vacations, all available holidays, even limitless shopping time—and laughable salaries.

Women comprise over half of the editorial staff of the paper. It would be tempting to say that it is simply because fashion is deemed a "woman's field" that the paper hires women at all. But the reasons are more subtle—women demand less pay, and single women, in particular, are more readily available for covering nighttime assignments.

The fashion staff, all women, is the most exploited on the paper because they often attend evening screenings without pay for overtime. The premise is that the assignment involves a free movie and that the reporter will be paid for the time involved in any interviews that result. Other evening assignments for Fashion-Department reporters, which might include anything from debutante balls to political dinners, are paid for in compensatory time, but never in money. The company has an aversion to the crassness of cash.

At one time fashion reporters couldn't refuse an evening assignment, but these days, with several near uprisings behind them, management must tread more lightly.

The news staff is a heterogeneous group of men and women who cover various markets from a financial and business standpoint and write the hard-news copy in the paper. Salaries are equal for men and women of equal experience. They are all well under union scale.

While *WWD*'s methods of foisting fashion on the public exploit women, the paper's consciousness has been raised somewhat by feminist staff members. On the day of the Women's Strike for Equality in the summer of 1970, a dozen women struck the paper and made demands—some of which have been met. Management is more careful not to step on female toes in references to women in the news or in the editorial content in general.

WWD was the first paper to adopt the "Ms." style for all women, out of a desire to be *au courant* as well as from a genuine belief that marital status is irrelevant.

However, as the fount of Beautiful-People gossip, the paper practices its very own brand of sexism by spotlighting women who are "beautiful" and rich, and who lead lives with little redeeming social value.

WWD does offer editorial people mobility, and if you can prove you can write and are ambitious, you will get good assignments regardless of your sex. The paper puts a premium on a gutsy, unique approach to stories. And if they like your work, you move.

Most copy kids at *WWD* are picked with an eye to filling eventual vacant reportorial positions and, in almost every case, a copy kid is writing within a matter of weeks. Editorial spots on the general-news staff, although not occupied by women at the present, are open to them.

Working at *WWD* often requires closing one's eyes to the thrust of the paper in general, but it's the kind of place where an individual can have impact. Several women, without interference, have broadened the scope of the paper by introducing interviews with outspoken feminists and with other women in all walks of life. The Arts & Pleasures pages are a constant outlet for criticism of the media, frequently on the theme of their exploitation of women.

WWD is a good place to learn the newspaper business at a

mediocre salary, and then move on. For a woman, it provides the opportunity of pioneering new territory—because the one thing the paper is not closed to is new ideas.

Lois Lane Poised for Takeoff

ASSOCIATED PRESS[1]

Is there hope for AP when its treatment of a story about five scientists who lived underwater for weeks begins: "Five shapely aquanauts . . ."?

And what do you think your chances of making it are when there are no women bureau chiefs in an entire 171-bureau, world-wide network?

Can you live with the idea that the Associated Press is a cooperative of more than 1,500 papers and many thousands of radio and television stations, and that most of those publishers are conservative businessmen? (Fewer than one in thirty is a woman.)

It might appear that applying to the Associated Press for any job—not to mention one with prospects for a future—is futile. Happily, that's no longer true.

AP has never been avant-garde, but it could never have existed, much less grown, if its management had totally ignored change. In 1969 they recognized that nobody cared about women's news, at least not the way they—and hundreds of others—were doing it. *Kuchen, Kirchen, und Kinder* was as dead as rural America.

So they created the Living Today Department, five women and one token male who would do "now" news. The goal was "newthink"; unhappily, its launching was "oldthink."

[1] See report in Appendix of legal action taken by the Wire Service Guild against the Associated Press.

This staff was presented to well-primed editors and publishers in what could only be termed "a follies." One by one they . . . Well, let *Editor and Publisher,* the news industry's house organ, tell it:

With a giant screen flashing, in quick sequence, color photos of the subject [the emcee] introduced each of the stars on the "mod squad" with descriptions that sounded like backgrounds on *Playboy*'s playmates.

After outlining one woman's experience freelancing in Vietnam, *Editor and Publisher* polished her off with: "————, a strawberry blonde with a nice figure, will do stories on sex habits of youths."

Another mod squadder, one of the first women ever to cover the workings of government in Albany, was identified only as the winner of the "girl-every-boy-would-like-to-bring-home-to-mother" award in college.

Now one of those women admits, "They exploited those of us who were females." "But," she added, "I don't think it was so much sexist as just hokey promotion."

And, as it turned out, the mod squad and its stories on women's liberation probably did as much as anything else to raise the consciousness of AP management.

During the past few years, there has been an influx of women into AP's New York headquarters, and there have been a lot of firsts, albeit token firsts:

—The so-called "poets" of news features have had a token woman for years, but never more than one. But because stories there are assigned on the basis of what one does best, this woman is not stuck with "women's news."

—The sports department finally admitted a woman writer to its all-male club and the process was so painless that it hired another when the first one left. However, attempts to make them increase that number have been fruitless.

—The general desk, which is the control center for all outgoing news, in 1969 took on its first woman since World War II. Since then, four of the twenty-four deskmen have been women. But with luck and sensitivity to cries for equal rights, another very important factor must be credited for the change—they were having a tough time getting qualified men to New York for the general desk.

What once had been a prized showcase job is, in the seventies, viewed differently. New York is expensive and dangerous and a lot of family men are living very nicely in Denver or Phoenix on their $10,000 a year. Change that for New York? Hell, no. Not at that price.

But almost none of the eager women knocking on AP's doors had anybody to support but themselves, and they were determined to work harder and more diligently than any man "to prove themselves." When faced with an efficient and cheap labor market, what employer can resist—especially in an era of inflation? Male and female reporters are paid the same—starting salary $164.48; top scale after six years is $300—it is assumed that women staffers don't need raises to pay for extra babies and unexpected family illnesses.

So AP, confronted with females who wanted theirs and publishers who were trying to keep theirs, has been hiring lots of women. Now about one-third of the reporters in the New York bureau are female.

Of course, each editor has his own idea of what is proper woman's-work. AP's woman sports writer is not allowed in locker rooms, but its female theater critic can see *Oh! Calcutta!*

It also helps if you are good-looking. A number of women agree that AP has always been nice to its attractive women. AP likes having a pretty package speak to editors and publishers and they reaped publicity for months from one cool blonde's whirlwind trip to Vietnam.

Tokenism exists in more serious forms: there are only a

handful of black women in the entire AP network, ten out of about 900 newsmen and newswomen in the domestic service—110 bureaus. "AP is the largest news-gathering organization in the world," said one of the few. "I can't see why it hasn't developed a staff of black reporters when there are lots of talented blacks looking for jobs."

"I don't feel sexism in the media," she said, "but I do feel racism, not only at AP but out on the street too." (The "street" is where you go to cover a story.)

"To AP's credit," said a young newswoman (that term was fought for by a group of California AP women and eventually adopted), "I've covered more important people and stories and had more experience than I think I could have done anywhere else, and I've gotten to do it faster."

But to a lot of old-guard newsmen and executives, AP women are children whose careers are only temporary aberrations. One newswoman wrote the general manager a letter questioning whether the AP's political cartoons, all revealing a conservative bent, were conforming to the news service's first-through-tenth commandments—"Be objective!" The manager replied that the cartoonist's ideas were his own, adding that the newswoman should speak to the cartoonist because he had "a daughter about your age."

"If you don't get married," said one girl who did, "they wonder what's wrong with you."

"If you do," said another, "they tell you a husband is more important than a job and to go off and have babies."

"If you do, and leave," said the first, "they wonder what's wrong with you. If you try to come back, they hold it against you. It's difficult for a woman to please them."

"Yet," she said, "they give women plenty of opportunities if they're any good. But you've got to push. You can't just work eight hours and get anywhere."

And, of course, unless she becomes a feature writer or covers a 9-to-5 subject, a woman, just like anyone else, can be scheduled for any day, any time, eight working hours, with a half-hour for lunch.

There are seven national holidays recognized by the Associated Press, but if you're assigned to work on one of those days, you must, even if it's Christmas. In return, you get either pay at time and a half, or a day and a half extra vacation time. Staffers also get their birthdays off.

After you have worked at AP five years, you get three weeks off, and four weeks after ten years of service. Leaves of absence are rarely granted.

After the initial six-month trial period, it is practically impossible to be fired, for management hates hassling with the Wire Service Guild, an open shop which represents all AP employees during the biennial negotiations.

Eight months' maternity leave with four weeks' pay is written into the contract, and AP's stated policy is to grant "reasonable" paid paternity leave.

Another AP policy, as stated in article 6, section 3 of its contract with the Guild is: "The employer will continue its policy of nondiscrimination as to age, sex, race, creed, or national origin."

Make them live up to it.

Women's Writes Arriba!

UNITED PRESS INTERNATIONAL

United Press International, a wire service, is the world's largest independent news-gathering organization. It delivers news, newspictures, newsfilm, and audio services to more than 6,400 subscribers in 114 countries and territories. It operates 238 bureaus in 62 countries and employs more than 10,000 full- and part-time reporters, photographers, editors, telegraphers, and technicians worldwide—15 percent of them women. On the woman score, the domestic scene is better than 15 percent: 100 newswomen versus 564 newsmen. The situation is expected to improve. According to the UPI Affirmative Action Program, the wire service intends to "fill . . . employment needs from all available sources without regard to race, sex, age, religion, or national origin. . . ."

Back in 1971 UPI ran an ad in *Editor and Publisher,* the trade journal. It proclaimed: "UPI Supports Women's Writes." The ad showed the diversity of twelve staffers pictured. The reporting stations ranged from Vietnam to Paris; from the statehouses of the land to the White House and the Supreme Court; from London to New York. In short, the nation and the world. The diversity of woman's work at UPI probably has broadened since then.

Where assignments are concerned, UPI's women were liberated a long time ago. They draw the same assignments as men. In jobs covered by a contract with the Newspaper Guild (the Wire Service Guild, Local 222), their salary is paid according to the same pay scale—$300 a week for experienced newspersons as of January 1974. And, says UPI in its "women's writes" ad, "they deliver with the same high level of journalistic professionalism." The wire service may be a unisex service where assignments and opportunities are concerned. The UPI slogan some time ago was changed to read "UPI is at the scene." That takes the place of the old slogan—"A UPI man is at the scene."

Women are moving into supervisory positions. More than a half-dozen small—"two-man"—bureaus are headed by women. In New York, world headquarters of UPI, Dottie Brooks runs the business desk. She is assistant business editor and has twelve men and one woman working under her supervision. Gay Pauley is

Women's News Editor, Patricia McCormack is Family News Editor, and Joan Hanauer is Assistant Newsfeatures Editor. Barbara May Glickman is a national radio news editor. Patricia O'Gorman is editor of UPITN—UPI Television News.

The columnist field is dominated by male bylines, but two veteran women columnists take the top places in UPI usage surveys. Namely, Gay Pauley, who writes "Woman's View" for the afternoon papers, and Patricia McCormack, who writes "Woman to Woman" for morning papers and "Woman's World" for Saturday and Sunday papers. These are not tea-party columns. In recent months they covered such things as vasectomies, sperm banks, the birth dearth, and other developments of interest to the women and men who read the family-news pages of subscriber papers.

Helen Thomas, a White House correspondent since 1960 and a journalist since 1942, contributes to the column "Backstairs at the White House." Ms. Thomas probably is the top-ranked UPI woman. She accompanied the President to China and was the reporter most often called by Martha Mitchell when cracks appeared in the Watergate dam. Ms. Thomas is the first woman ever elected to the executive committee of the White House Correspondents Association.

Another UPI veteran on the Washington scene, Charlotte Moulton, covers the Supreme Court. And there is Margaret Kilgore, whose previous service included assignment in Vietnam. In the past, UPI has had four women on its Vietnam staff, including Kate Webb—who was captured, reported and believed dead, and then found to be alive. After convalescing from the experience as a V.C. prisoner, she asked to be reassigned to Vietnam. She was.

On the world front, few women can match notes with Aline Mosby, now in Paris. Her tours have taken her to Vienna and Moscow. She has also covered Hollywood and New York. Peggy Polk, in Rome, is another UPI stalwart.

As with the men, female Unipressers who leave the service

almost always do so for greener pastures and greater opportunities. For purposes of this report, the UPI Personnel Department was asked how many female newspersons earn over $20,000 a year. The answer: none. The supervisory and executive positions in that and higher salary ranges are held by men. These positions are not covered by the Guild contract. Such positions also include benefits of the Scripps-Howard Pension Program, better than the Guild-contract one.

Women not covered by the Guild—confidential secretaries and a few others—are covered by the Scripps-Howard plan. These include a woman news executive in the South, a personnel manager in New York, an executive assistant in California who is moving into sales, and Ms. O'Gorman, of UPITN.

The route to top management jobs at UPI is no different from that in other corporations. It is circuitous, and frequently includes experience in sales as a requirement. Not many women have expressed interest in sales work at UPI. (That is a trail that interested women might blaze. The same for the Photo Department—which is wide open for female lenspersons.)

What does UPI management think of women? H. L. Stevenson, editor, answers the question:

Women reporters have increasingly played important roles at UPI in recent years, covering virtually every type of assignment in the world. Quite a few are in management jobs or in positions where judgments must be made on breaking news copy. We've had no hesitancy in promoting them to those positions. In considering women for reporting assignments or managerial jobs, we try to use good judgment—ours and theirs—as the primary guideline.

(Write to Editor Stevenson or the Personnel Department [Dale Johns] at UPI, 220 East 42nd Street, New York, New York, 10017, if you want to know more.)

Desire and capability are the keys that unlock the doors. One final word of caution: Wire service journalism goes on twenty-four hours a day, seven days a week. It isn't stilled for holidays—not even Christmas. Before you make a move to land at UPI, be sure you are prepared to give up weekends, to work holidays, to take the lobster or graveyard shift—when it is required. Everyone at UPI has served their time in that arena at one time or another.

4

BOOK PUBLISHING

Book Publishing

IF THE YOUNG WOMEN IN BOOK PUBLISHING seem to find their jobs even less rewarding than those in other media, it is for a good reason. They come to them with greater expectations.

Mainly English-lit majors with degrees from top colleges, they have been preparing themselves since junior high to be movers and shapers in the transcendent world of books. They were encouraged in their delusion not only by their teachers, who praised their poetry, their essays, and their fiction and installed them as editors of school publications, but also by the examples of the famous women they most admired.

They came to New York with the feeling, deep down, that they would rather be a janitor at Scribner's or Harper & Row than the editor of *Cosmopolitan* or the publisher of *Time*. Once they were inside one of those distinguished places, with all their discerning, talent-seeking editors, quality would tell. In no time, they would be helping to mold the style of some less-privileged genius of their own personal discovery, while turning out criticism and books of their own for publication.

What they got was roughly equivalent to the janitor's job—if they had the right looks, the right credentials, and an ability to type. And knew somebody. Whatever their titles, women in book editorial departments begin as more-or-less menial helpers to editors, usually male, and often wind up in similar capacities, though with more impressive titles and better salaries. In the meanwhile, their male juniors pass them by. More than one contributor to this section points bitterly to skilled women who have trained their male assistants to be their bosses.

The revival of the feminist movement has had no discernible effect on book publishers in general, other than the financial bonanza some of them have enjoyed as a result of it. There are males in those places who have de-Anglicized Germaine Greer and fixed Kate Millett's spelling while remaining totally unmoved by the words on the pages. Which is a bad recommendation for the business they are in.

Expanding Horizons

AMERICAN HERITAGE*

American Heritage Publishing Company publishes two magazines (*American Heritage* and *Horizon*), a series of illustrated historical and art-history books (no more of these are planned at present), and a line of trade books. Bought several years ago by McGraw-Hill, the company has since had to cut down on its staff and eliminate many of its projects.

American Heritage is a pleasant place to work—lively and friendly and full of young people—but prospects for jobs there look dim at the moment. There are no longer any training programs for copy-editors and picture researchers, although there will probably be openings now and then for people already qualified to do these jobs.

Salaries, especially for beginners, are rather low. Secretaries with shorthand start at $140 and so-called gal Fridays at $110.

Heritage hires mostly history and art-history majors, and

* See Preface.

starts them at the bottom as secretaries and receptionists. But the company is usually willing to promote a woman who is energetic—and screams loudly. They do not display the usual reluctance to lose a good secretary to a department that will teach her to do something more interesting.

There are women in all departments of the company—as art directors, picture editors, editors and managing editors, as well as fact-checkers and secretaries. But it is also true that most of the boring, low-paying jobs are held by women and most of the interesting, better-paying ones by men. It used to be the kind of place where a young woman could work her way up—with great effort—to a top editorial job and then discover that her male assistant was making more money than she was. Now, at higher levels, women's salaries are supposedly equal to those of the men on the staff, although there are some women editors who doubt it.

On the lower levels there is not much basis for comparison because untrained men are seldom hired. The few who are seem to get the same pay as the women. These male trainees, by the way, have recently volunteered to share the lunchtime receptionist duty which female trainees and secretaries have always been responsible for.

Recently American Heritage has made a move in the right direction for its female employees: coverage under the company medical insurance policy now extends to self-employed or unemployed husbands of women who work here.

So things are changing here, and if the fortunes of American Heritage improve enough so that the company is able to expand again, there are some indications that women employees will have better prospects than in the past.

Avon Calling (Faintly)

AVON

Avon offers the woman interested in mass-market paperback publishing the opportunity to work with and develop a diverse list of adult and juvenile fiction and nonfiction, in mass and quality formats. This, in addition to the company's liberal public image, may make Avon an attractive choice for a woman seeking employment in publishing. But she will have to decide for herself, from the information to follow, what obstacles, if any, either sex-based or otherwise, she may face as a potential employee and as a staff member.

Avon's good name as a mass-market house and its impressively growing list can be attributed to the know-how of Peter Mayer, its dynamic thirty-eight-year-old publisher and editor-in-chief, who is also a vice president of the parent Hearst Corporation. In fact, youth and the quality of youthful enthusiasm have always been highly prized by the publisher and have counted heavily in favor of prospective employees. These, plus native ability, intelligence, and the appearance of being "with it" set the tone at Avon.

The company has at times served as a breeding ground for gifted people who moved on elsewhere and who were hired, in some key cases, either without experience or without full college credentials. Coincidentally or not, more men than women have been hired in this fashion. Two very able young men were plucked from their jobs at bookstores (one was a manager of the paperback section of the Doubleday Fifty-seventh Street Bookshop) to become editors at Avon. Women staffers, on the other hand, have the appropriate degrees and experience. So far, no able, intelligent women have been hired out of bookstores, or off the street, for that matter.

While the importance of previous publishing experience has varied for different individuals, it is nonetheless considered desirable. Background helps, but not too much ego, since the house demands gratitude in return for the opportunity to work for it. Avon also offers low salaries, which only less-experienced and less-ego-minded people are likely to appreciate.

Avon depends on Papa Hearst for its daily bread, which perhaps explains why salaries are usually ungenerous, often starting as low as $8,000 (salaries for secretaries had been as low as $6,000), while the top editorial salary had been only $17,000 before the wage-price freeze. The company cries poverty a lot, with how much justification nobody quite knows. The house *is* making money, and Peter Mayer's salary is very substantial indeed. Still, women's salaries do *not* suffer in comparison with those of their male counterparts. Some have even been known to make more money. The managing editor at Avon for several years was a woman (since returned to hardcover publishing) who outranked her male colleagues in both title and salary.

The world of publishing is, after all, a tightly knit community, where it helps to know someone, especially someone who can vouch for your work. A young single woman with reasonable credentials, adequate education, and, above all, contacts, approaching Avon for a job will find little or no *obvious* discrimination based on sex. There are distinctions, but it is hard to tell whether they reflect discriminatory company policy.

One such distinction manifests itself against the clock watcher, who is most often the married woman with children. Avon regards itself as a "family." (It is very self-congratulatory in this respect.) Traditionally its editorial employees have been single and have been able to fulfill the company's expectations for almost round-the-clock dedication and/or preoccupation. It is not uncommon to find Avon staffers in the office well past five, the official closing hour. A single woman can have a social life and work at Avon. (It even provides a social life, of sorts, for some.) But a married woman—whose time is probably more closely budgeted—would feel this pressure more acutely, especially if she has children. This has been true more often of the editorial department than of either the art or production departments.

The editorial staff is compact; at present an executive editor, two senior editors, a managing editor, and the editor-in-chief share total editorial responsibility for the lists. The hierarchy at Avon is not unalterably rigid. While the editors are possessive and protective of their specialized areas, there have been key personnel changes that have altered the structure. It is not always easy, but there is room to maneuver. Advancement is based on a combination of factors: the publisher's favorable opinion, for one; merit; and the term of employment (few have stayed longer than five years). The situation is the same for men as for women—whose ideas and abilities are usually credited in-house.

The staff does not suffer from abundant company restrictions. Dress is not subject to regulation; jeans are often the uniform for staff members in their more casual moods. Lateness does not generally incur penalties for those who have difficulty getting up in the morning. If it does not incur rewards, it does not, at least, interfere with advancement.

As term employees, women working at Avon are not subject to and do not participate in a sex-based competition with their male colleagues. The staff works on a basis of equality and there is both rapport with and respect for individuals. (No one worries about who has an office with a view since there is nothing to see outside the Avon offices.) Women need have no fear of being patronized for their ideas or initiatives—they are given the same support as men's. This may, of course, mean no support at all.

Avon absorbs from its employees a mixture of their emotional and professional resources (and pretends to give in return heady psychic wages). Do women suffer more from this drain? You'll have to find out for yourself.

The Tender Trap

BANTAM BOOKS

Bantam is owned by a "leisure-time" conglomerate portentously named National General, which also goes in for movie distribution, life insurance, and Southern-fried-chicken franchises—all in readiness for the three-day work week. Meantime, National General keeps pretty much to itself on the West Coast, leaving Bantam's president, Oscar Dystel, to run two floors of 666 Fifth Avenue in the manner of a close-knit family business.

The distinguishing feature of this patriarchy is that daughters are nearly as favored as sons, and in some ways may have even more freedom of movement, if not more pay. (A bright daughter, after all, more easily fits the requirements of family solidarity and gratitude; an ambitious son is always a subtle threat.) True, the Bantam hierarchy can talk a fair sexist line on occasion, but a good deal of this stays at the level of fantasy. In actual practice, many of the men from Dystel on down (1) *like* working with women, (2) do not stereotype competence and assertiveness as "unfeminine" qualities, and (3) seem genuinely interested in developing female talent. Think of the kind of father who boasts to the neighbors about his daughter, the tennis champ and class valedictorian (she's a *nice* girl, too), and you'll have the dynamics about right.

Of editors above associate rank, three out of eight are women. Executive Editor Grace Bechtold has been with the company longer—and probably brought in more money--than anyone else in the department. With Publicity and Public-Relations Vice President Esther Margolis, Subsidiary Rights Manager Mildred Hird, and School- and College-Marketing Manager Gloria Steinberg, the biweekly editorial board meeting shows a female majority. Publishing decisions are nominally made in this committee, although Editorial Director/Vice President Marc Jaffe has the first and last word. The women have had some success in promoting feminist books but almost none in shouting down juicy and salable sexist tracts. Esther Margolis is the only woman among eleven vice-presidents; the big-money management—and hence the top-salary level—is strictly male.

That women fare as well as they do psychologically is probably directly attributable to Dystel's respect for ideas—commercial ones, that is. While he is utterly merciless with mealy-mouthing and half-baked reasoning—male or female—he will listen to and be persuaded by anyone, of whatever sex or rank, who makes sense. ("Listen to her!" he shouted at some inattentive salesmen in a recent meeting. "She's saying something *important!*") This attitude filters down through the company in a general policy of recognizing effort and giving it public notice. If an assistant does a good editing job on a manuscript, this will be duly noted in an editorial meeting—almost as in a formal laying on of hands.

Bantam also has a stated policy of promotion within the company, and there is more than the usual horizontal movement among departments to fit individuals to jobs (a woman production assistant becomes a copywriter, a publicity assistant, an assistant editor). Promotion can come rapidly (for one woman, four years from assistant to senior editor, accompanied by a more than doubled salary). High visibility to the powers that be is the essential ingredient here; enthusiasm and demonstrable loyalty are the winning combination. It helps to have looks *and* brains, but in the crunch, brains come out first every time.

Tops for visibility and mobility is the second-assistant's desk in the president's office, where scheduling is coordinated. This is a nerve-shattering and thankless job, at which most women last no more than a year. However, within recent memory, those women who did not leave town immediately have become cover-copy chief, assistant managing editor, and head of the Bantam Lecture Bureau. This is a better record than for editorial assistants, only one of whom, in the past three years, has been promoted to her boss's job when he left. Other individual supervisors differ sharply in the degree to which they encourage development on their staff; the best way to learn about mobility of a particular job is to find out what has become of the last three people who held it.

Personnel Manager Frances Cameola does preliminary screening for most entry-level editorial and sales jobs, hiring from agencies that service publishing and also off the street. Typing tests are not given for most secretarial-assistant jobs, and only a few of these require shorthand. At least two current editorial secretaries are not college graduates. There is *no standard wage scale*. The personnel office insists that "secretarial" work varies markedly and adjusts the salary to the individual job; the real variation is more likely to be in the status of the supervisor. However, the starting salary is uniformly unlivable at about $110 to $115 a week. A new employee who is "working out" may be raised $10 to $15 after six months. Thereafter, salaries are reviewed once a year. On the higher levels, there is so much variation among titles and experience within ranks that parity comparisons among salaries are nearly impossible. What every woman knows is that a man to replace her would come a good deal higher.

You have to put in an antediluvian six years in order to get a three-week vacation with pay. (Two weeks after one year, another two days after five.) Other benefits, however, are good. Life insurance, Blue Cross, extra medical, convalescent and maternity allowances are completely paid for by Bantam. There is no specified sick leave, but the company has a good record on holding jobs and continuing to pay partial salaries through serious, months-long illnesses. (Obviously, all this flexibility and individuality—as opposed to union-type standardization—is on the old, paternalistic mode. Humanely exercised here, but deadly in the wrong hands.)

The most effective device ever invented for keeping down salary demands is the atmosphere of the Bantam office. Even cynical veterans of the New York publishing merry-go-round admit that it's a nice place to work. Women seem particularly susceptible. (Where else could the editorial director's secretary bring in her cairn terrier to snooze under her desk?) One recent college graduate turned down two higher-paying offers because she thought the Bantam job would be "more fun."

Both protocol and office politics are at a minimum, although some male vice-presidents still freak out when secretaries, whom they call by their first names, use first names back. Amenities such as window offices, expense accounts, and credit cards go by rank, not sex. This means that most assistants sit in the interior open spaces of the office; but so do the male production assistant and low-ranking men in the Sales Department, while many women enjoy the view from the twenty-fifth floor. Marc Jaffe *is* keen to see people at their desks at 9:00 A.M. and makes sporadic efforts to organize lunch hours, but supervision is generally relaxed. The assumption is that Bantam employees are dedicated, hardworking types, who take reading home. If you're not, they'd rather fire than harass you. (All of this applies mainly on the editorial floor. The women who fill the Accounting and Bookkeeping Departments on the twenty-fourth floor are far more closely supervised.)

The main problem Bantam employees have is in breaking free from this cozy spell. There are people who have been moaning for years that their personal development depends on getting out—but they stay and stay. We all know how hard it is to leave home.

Friendly and Frugal

BOBBS-MERRILL

Bobbs-Merrill is no worse for women than the average publishing company. For one thing, the New York office is small, which helps create a friendly feeling among the workers. (Bobbs-Merrill is based in Indianapolis.)

The New York office is made up of the Adult Trade Division (sixteen people) and part of the College Division (two people). Four of these eighteen people are men; the editor-in-chief (naturally), one adult editor, one salesman who is out of the office most of the time, and the mail clerk. The balance—two adult editors, the juvenile editor, her assistant and secretary, the publicity director and her assistant, the production manager, and the secretaries—are female.

Salaries are very low, even by publishing standards. Myth has it that this is so because the wage scale is established in Indianapolis, where the cost of living is much lower than in New York. Whatever the reason, the effect is that everyone here, from a secretary on up, makes less than they might in other publishing companies. And that's obviously the reason there are fewer men here.

Bobbs-Merrill is a good place to work if you want a "beginning" job where you can learn a lot and do a lot, but don't expect to get promoted from within; it almost never happens. Editorial assistants/secretaries write some flap and catalog copy if they want to, look over copy-edited manuscripts, compose their own letters, read manuscripts, suggest book ideas, and do just about everything an editor does—except get paid for it.

The company is also a good place for experienced women looking for an editorial job, although openings are infrequent because the house is so small.

There is change in the air, however: the editor-in-chief who has been largely responsible for this liberal policy toward women has just announced his resignation. We are keeping our fingers crossed that his successor will be as enlightened as he was.

Double Duties

DOUBLEDAY*

PICTURE QUIZ

Check One: The good-looking girl above ordering two coffees regular is: (1) picking up her boss's coffee and her own, (2) being treated to coffee by her boss, a junior editor three years older than she, (3) ordering for her boss and his visitor, (4) an editor herself, ordering for her secretary.

Answer: Sure. Any one of the above, 1, 2, or 3; (4 is just a matter of good conditioning in her own years as a secretary).

Second Question: (*For rumination only*): How often does a senior editor or even a young editor (male) appear on the coffee line?

Doubleday is no exception to this syndrome, although changes favoring women's status here have seemingly eased the atmosphere just a bit. How much is hard to tell yet. Clearly women want the kind of equality that will mean hiring five male for every five female secretaries as well as promoting equally talented associate editors, one male, one female, to full editorial positions after approximately the same length of time on the job. This is not yet the rule.

Women at Doubleday do get promotions and salary raises, but it takes them longer than men. Both raises and advancement generally mean that the woman worked much harder and much longer. However, it cannot be denied that good female employees are rewarded with respect, meeting-attendance, party invitations, salary, and promotions. Their contribution to the company is as wide and large as they wish it to be. *But it all takes longer.* An

* See Preface.

example: one girl replaced a man when he left. A very responsible job. He had a secretary, and so does she, but she still handles many of the secretarial duties (telephone answering, etc.). Her "accompanying" raise occurred *one full year* after the promotion, and even then her salary was considerably less than her predecessor's.

Of thirty-nine editors, seventeen are women, less than half the total. One of those women is editorial director, which is a marvelous position, but nonetheless, she reports to the publisher (male), director of sales (male), director of marketing (male), and five vice presidents, all male. There are now three female department heads who work alone—that is without a male codepartment head. Doubleday had no female department heads until 1971. The majority of women in the company are secretaries.

At these lower-salary rungs of the ladder, new trainees are now hired on a more nearly equal basis than, let's say, in 1967 when women were paid $85 per week and men $120 for the same work. The present male and female trainees (it's not specified whether these are editorial or secretarial trainees—their fate is left to subsequent placement) are paid a starting salary of $105 per week. It would be nice to think that ability alone would determine their "rise."

At the top, our president, vice presidents, treasurer, and all others on the executive level are men. There are no women. At present, the ceiling position for women is "senior editor." Those women got there because they are excellent editors. Flirting, sleeping around, thigh exposure, etc., play absolutely no part here. Responsibilities are too great to let a wiggly ass have the job. The same is true for assistants.

Our maternity benefits should be better. They have improved in recent years in response to numerous complaints and some legal action taken against Doubleday by several women employees, but they are still inadequate. More argument forced the beginnings of medical coverage for abortions. Maternity costs are covered—up to 80 percent of the total bill if a woman puts her husband on her insurance policy (at $7 per month for Blue Cross benefits). If the husband is not covered, the returns are zero. Until the fall of 1970, a woman was forced to quit work when she became pregnant. That is no longer true. Because of insurance requirements (or so we are told), you must leave work at the end of the sixth month and you cannot return until the baby is one month old. However, you may stay out as long as three months after the birth. After that three-month period, you return at full pay with full privileges. If you do not return after three months, you are "let go." Doubleday has no day-care or child-care services at all. (Parenthetically, when marriage between coworkers occurs, "house" rules decree that one partner leave the company.)

There are problems harder to put a finger on: vague titles disguise hard-core secretarial work, and suggestions initiated by a woman are listened to, but always a bit more reluctantly than those initiated by a man. People, sure, will listen, but we are not urged to suggest. Women, very simply, are not actively encouraged to develop.

On the plus side, the atmosphere at Doubleday is more relaxed than in most large companies. Long peasant skirts and casual slacks are commonly seen on women workers. Hair length for males is not an issue at all: ponytails aren't unusual. Friendliness and humor are valued and they keep the Doubleday vibrations good. If Doubleday women could feel confident that ability would always be rewarded fairly, a very necessary corporate strength would, I think, unfold naturally.

Flunkies by Any Other Name . . .

E. P. DUTTON

Approximately 50 percent of the employees at Dutton are women. Whether in editorial, promotion, or accounting, the women work as appendages to men in higher positions. This of course is true not only at Dutton, but of the entire publishing industry.

There are also many men with menial jobs, but they are not usually of more-than-average intelligence or college-educated as many of the secretaries are. Women who are above the secretarial rank handle permissions, magazine serial rights, or foreign rights, assist in the art department, copy-edit—but these are all glorified secretarial jobs in one way or another—and the pay does not come near that of an executive secretary in a business corporation.

The myth that publishing is not a big business, but a higher calling, is a pernicious one that enables publishers to keep the salaries of women (and men) below those of other industries. The standard: *"We are here because we love books"* has very little to do with the harsh profit-motive reality of the publishing industry.

Women at Dutton who want to advance faster than the average secretary in an editorial department might try the Children's Book Department, where all the editors are women, or the Publicity Department, which is headed by a woman. But both these departments are extremely small.

Most people perform their jobs feeling cut off from a sense of participation in a publishing company. They are removed from what they do and from each other. There is virtually no dialogue between the men who make the important decisions and the rest of the people in the company. As a result there is a lot of bitterness, resentment, and suppressed rage.

Several of the women who are secretaries are very bright, but they are likely to remain secretaries as long as they stay at Dutton. Women who are editors are limited in that they cannot achieve much autonomy or power. The only woman editor at Dutton who ever had any real power was fired after being there for over ten years.

The tendency is for women who have some kind of status positions themselves to feel just as threatened by younger women as the men do. Publishing is an industry of young vs. old, beautiful vs. ugly, hip vs. conservative, men vs. women. Dutton is just a microcosm of that industry and of the larger society of which it is a part.

The atmosphere at Dutton: restrained, workmanlike, a bit deathlike.

Women editors are paid less than men; they also perform functions that men in similar positions would not be asked to do—a little female cleaning up every now and then. Advancement is practically nonexistent, job security another useless myth. There is no way upward but out.

Benevolent Chauvinism

FARRAR, STRAUS & GIROUX

If the physical appearance of the offices of Farrar, Straus & Giroux and its location (Union Square) bother you, you would be wise to look elsewhere for a job. This is a publishing house without glamour and without the finer things of life, such as heat on wintry Mondays, working elevators, spacious offices, a lounge, carpets, coffee breaks, and drapes. However, if you are willing to give up a midtown office and all that goes with it, life at FS&G can be pleasant.

The company is small and still functions as one big family. Dress is casual to the point of slovenliness. Dingy offices do have a certain panache. The location is bearable. (May's and Klein's begin to look good on the salary they give you.) Eating places do exist: Greek, Szechuan, health food, Max's Kansas City, Luchow's, and, of course, the Dardanelles, an Armenian restaurant that functions as company lunchroom. And you can always walk to the Village on your lunch hour.

FS&G has five book divisions: trade; juvenile (staff of three); Noonday paperbacks; Octagon Books (scholarly reprint, staff of two); and a new addition, Hill & Wang, which is owned by FS&G but operates independently. The total number of employees, excluding Hill & Wang's, is about fifty-five (sixteen men and thirty-nine women). All but four of the men are heads of departments or are in decision-making positions. (Two of these four are the mailboys.) Only thirteen out of the thirty-nine women are in decision-making positions, and of these only three are in editorial (two in the Juvenile Department). The rest of the higher-ranking women work in the Production, Copyrights-and-Permissions, Subsidiary-Rights, copy-editing and billing departments.

An editorial assistant (there are five) starts at $115 to $120 per week. A woman with ten years' experience may get up to $150 a week as an assistant.

There are only two women who have worked their way up in the Editorial Department: One has a knowledge of five languages and is working toward a Ph.D. in Greek and Roman art. She first came to work at FS&G as a secretary from a job at Doubleday. After two years she became editorial assistant to the managing editor, and after another year she became an assistant editor. Two years later she became an associate editor at a salary of $165 a week.

The other, with an M.A. from New York University, came to work at FS&G direct from Cornell and the Radcliffe publishing course. She first worked as assistant to the heads of Library Services and the Juvenile Department. Two years later she became an assistant editor in the Juvenile Department, and now, after five years with the company, she makes $150 a week.

Salaries are low, but the company does provide excellent benefits: a $5,000 life-insurance policy, Blue Cross-Blue Shield, and major medical ($100 deductible). Vacations are far from liberal: two weeks for the first four years, three weeks for years five through nine, and four weeks each year thereafter. Holidays are the usual, and the company allows two hours off on election day.

Up to the seventh month of pregnancy, you may work with permission from your doctor. (All this applies only if you have had at least two years of employment.) Company payments to Blue Cross and Blue Shield are continued through pregnancy and for three months after the infant is born. However, "The time, terms and conditions of return to work are wholly at the option of FS&G." This last rule has never been tested.

FS&G is known as an editor's house, and the editors are some of the best. Bob Giroux is editor-in-chief and handles the more literary authors. Henry Robbins is the editor for Didion, Wolfe, Walker Percy, Walter Goodman, et al. The bright and shining hopes for the company's future are Michael di Capua (who now does picture books), Hermann Hesse, and Larry Woiwode. Because it is an editor's house, and because the editors are all different, an assistant's job varies according to whom she works with and how well editor and assistant get along.

Some reasons for *not* working at FS&G: low salaries, with little hope for improvement. (Being a small company, FS&G can plead poverty rather persuasively. The general feeling is: if you want money, go elsewhere.) There is a high turnover rate among assistants, mostly because there is no room to move up in the company. Despite the company's liberal persuasion (warmth toward the blacks in South Africa, Publishers for Peace, the migrant farm workers) it has so far failed—by way of salaries, positions, and general attitude—to acknowledge women as equal to men.

It is a hardworking office, from Roger Straus on down. A natural result of working in a small office is that you do things you weren't hired to do. This is called "learning the ropes" although it is understood that the ropes lead to nowhere. There are no real office parties. They tried one once. It lasted forty-five minutes, after which everyone compulsively went back to work.

There is a mistaken belief that office politics can be played only in large offices. Politics in small offices is a much more subtle and insidious game and, once it becomes apparent, also more noticeable. Office affairs are the same way; in a small office, there is no such thing as a little affair.

The reason for considering FS&G at all? It is one of the last independent, family publishing houses. With women's lib, unionization, mergers, recessions, and so on all around, there's no telling how much longer it will stay that way.

Will It Sell?

FAWCETT PAPERBACKS

The book department at Fawcett is *very* small. There are three lines: Crest, a reprints-only line, reprinting hardcover best sellers, both fiction and nonfiction; Gold Medal, a paperback-original line, mostly fiction (today's answer to yesterday's pulp fiction); Premier, primarily a nonfiction school-oriented line.

Almost every decision is based on two questions: Will it sell? And is it worth the money? Men *and* women are hired for fairly low salaries with (usually) the carrot of possible promotion and, in fact, it *is* a place where you can work your way up.

The editors of two of the three lines were, until recently, both women (Gold Medal has a male editor). Pay is slight, but if you know your own worth, you can get paid accordingly—if you ask.

The vice president, Ralph Daigh, who approves all hiring in the department, is always on the lookout for men to work there because he feels surrounded by too many women, but—for the money the company is willing to pay—he has trouble finding men as well-qualified for individual jobs as are the women who apply.

The top management of the company is *not* liberated. Their idea of a liberated woman is Clare Boothe Luce, and those who have heard of Gloria Steinem think she is "probably a lesbian"— that sort of thing. To introduce any young or with-it idea requires an indirect approach, and if you can use numbers or statistics that show a possible market, you can often win your point. But the wind may just as easily shift in another direction after a new idea has had too short a time to be tested, because the top people tend not to be in tune with the New Woman either.

Fringe benefits are almost nil, and the atmosphere is not particularly loyalty-inducing either, though 'it is fairly relaxed. There's a strong feeling about your arriving on time in the morning, but lunch hours are leisurely, and there's no slavish after-five working—when you're finished you're finished—unless you are a reader or an editor, and then you feel you *have* to do reading at home.

Expense accounts are quite liberal and no different for women than for men. And as soon as you have a job with any authority, you are *urged* to have a secretary type for you—you have to battle for your right to do your own typing if that's your style—though the last I heard the secretaries were all women. (Incidentally, there aren't too many black faces around, and those there are all female.)

Fawcett tends to be a sexist company—remember it publishes *Woman's Day*—but the editors of Crest and *Woman's Day* were recently made vice presidents of the company, and within its limits, I'd say it's a good place to work—if you like the product.

Much Sound and Fury Signifying Little

HARPER & ROW

When you walk into the Trade Editorial Department on the seventh floor of Harper & Row's elegant, expensive new building on East Fifty-third Street, you may be struck by the number of female editorial faces. The thought may even occur to you that Harper's (as those with a sense of history still call the company) is not at all averse to hiring or advancing women into editorial positions. Of a total of fifteen trade editors, seven are women. It should be noted, however, that females are not recruited outright for an editor's job, nor deliberately trained and advanced for one, although some *have* moved up from lesser positions. In one case, it took eighteen years. One brilliant woman was moved over from advertising when her unique editorial talents proved too valuable to be ignored. Women editors—women anything—earn less at Harper's than the men. (This refrain will be repeated.) It should be acknowledged that there are just not enough creative jobs in publishing for everyone who wants or deserves to get one. But if an editor's job were to open up at Harper's, management would in all probability recruit male talent from the outside.

It is necessary to add that the Board of Directors is almost entirely male (one woman), and that of the twelve officers, only two are women. If it is true that one intelligence is a majority, then two should easily solve all women's difficulties at Harper's. What this means in real life, however, is that decisions are male territory.

There has been a tradition dripping with maleness at Harper's since 1817—primarily nonethnic or WASP maleness. This tradition has had its effect on the non-WASPs who have managed to make it in the company—they are indistinguishable from the home-grown product.

A consulting firm was hired two years ago to conduct a survey among women employees. Answers to the questionnaires bore out (surprise!) the suspicion that women in the house are underpaid and their opportunities to advance are negligible. One result of the survey was the formation of a women's group that has so far met a number of times, and is now in the process of drawing up proposals to present to management. (These things take *time*.)

Some direct quotes from the report growing out of the survey:

"Men are often directly contacted by Harper; women rarely are." "Men more often get jobs which require a college degree; women, even with college degrees, more often get jobs for which typing is the major requirement." "Three-quarters of the men, but less than half of the women, were offered jobs described as growth positions that could lead to greater responsibilities." And, of course, the ever-popular "Women are not paid as much as men in comparable positions."

Openings for all positions are, theoretically, posted on house bulletin boards, but those for supervisory positions come up so rarely that the women have grave suspicions that such matters are settled behind the scenes. Such is the atmosphere, in fact, that when the bulletin boards were moved from the kitchenettes to the rest rooms, several women were heard to mutter darkly that this was no doubt to make sure that some juicy jobs would never see the light of day in the Ladies'.

Opportunities for women in the College and Religious Departments are even fewer than in Trade. The Paperback Department is generous toward women.

In Sales, opportunities of any sort are nonexistent. Moreover, the male chauvinism seems more pronounced, which may be due to the clubbiness of the three male chiefs. If you enjoy the atmosphere of a Cornell Smoker, try Sales. The all-female subordinate cast performs well in spite of it all, and a few of the more courageous ones have even been seen to smile. In Advertising and Publicity, women hold all the key jobs under the lone male of any prominence in the department, the director . . . a club unto himself. (See Sales.) The women who have responsibility here are allowed a certain latitude but the possibility of any female's rising from assistant or secretary to one of these jobs is academic.

There was a woman salesman (sales "person" sounds asinine) who did receive a good deal of encouragement. She has left the company and there are now no women salesmen. The reason there are so few women "college travelers," we are informed, is that the professors don't want to talk to women—"they feel insulted." Go fight the system.

Although there is a lot of foot-dragging, some changes have been made. Two male editorial assistants have been hired. One seems to be moving forward (up?) rapidly. Watching his progress dizzies the eye. That, however, is largely because the male editor for whom he works gives him a lot of responsibility and opportunities to learn. Since there are no formal guidelines for training or advancement, what you learn depends on whom you work for. That young man is lucky. And who is to fault that editor for doing what comes naturally to him—*helping a young man get ahead?* Most editors, including the women, unfortunately, do not delegate so much. For editorial assistants, the work is largely monotonous. Coupled with a starting salary range of from $125 to $160, this has led to a high turnover.

The traditional women's jobs in publishing—juvenile books, subsidiary and foreign rights, the head of copy-editing—are held by women. Even most of the designers are women. The heads of Trade and College Production are male, as is the art director.

However, working for Harper's, one of the most highly (and rightly so) regarded houses in publishing, can be a stepping stone to better jobs in other companies. You can always *lie* about the extent of your creative responsibility.

The company is also struggling with a policy of hiring more members of minorities for meaningful positions, and of offering learning programs to those holding nonwhite-collar jobs. A few *have* trickled into white-collar jobs, but in general the minority woman gets the double-whammy. One of them is prettily show-cased as the manager of the bookstore, but all the directives regarding decisions on the bookstore come from a higher floor.

There is a union, the Association of Harper & Row Employees, which handles grievances and has been valuable in obtaining benefits, including cost-of-living increases. Its effectiveness in cases of discrimination—sexist, racial, or monetary—has been minimal. These are high-risk issues, unpopular with management. Some of the more militant union workers, feeling discouraged, are phasing themselves out of these voluntary positions. The union is about to affiliate with a larger union, probably the Newspaper Guild.

Benefits at Harper's are among the best. If you are content with nice surroundings and reasonably congenial coworkers, you may not notice that today you are fifty years old and still typing labels. But if you're hooked on gentle care through the years, this is your outfit.

Although there are interesting and creative people around, Harper's is not your swinging house. Do not come here if you're looking for the romance of the year (. . . or the week). The few affairs that go on are subtle, discreet, and uninspiring to the naked eye.

Amid the sound and fury of the survey, the women's group, and the long-awaited proposals to management, one has the feeling that male management devoutly hopes none of this will get off the ground, though a good many smiles are bestowed on the strugglers. (Perhaps God also smiled on Sisyphus.) But at least there *is* a sound and a fury, so, if you're young enough . . .

As this book goes to press, history has at last caught up with Harper & Row. The Association of Harper & Row Employees voted to strike and walked out on June 17, 1974, over the issue of money as set out in the conservative and retrogressive contract (in the eyes of the Association) that was offered to replace the three-year agreement with management that expired May 1. The strikers, showing a totally unexpected unity, stayed out for two and one-half weeks, picketing the offices at 10 East 53rd Street, singing labor songs, and booing scabs—a new and enlightening experience for both sides.

The strike was, of course, significant to women in publishing. It should surprise no one that women comprise most of the membership in a union that excludes all "hire-and-fire" supervisory personnel.

Moral and financial support poured in from larger unions, individuals from other publishing houses, passers-by, and one elderly lady who handed her $5 contribution to a picket because her granddaughter worked for a publisher and was "living from hand-to-mouth, poor thing."

The new agreement does not bring Harper & Row into line with other industries, nor is it a great deal better than the old one, since most of the fight was over benefits already won in previous negotiations. But it does now bear some relevance to financial reality for the next three years. Management's negotiating attitudes and methods bore out the feeling that brass knuckles were concealed under the velvet glove and the warm smiles of the normal business day. And it should be heartening for men and women in the rank-and-file of all publishing to know that progress can be made once the worker learns not to confuse the special quality of personal relationships with the special issue of survival.

Promises, Promises

HOLT, RINEHART & WINSTON

Holt, Rinehart & Winston has no female corporate executives and no male secretaries. In this regard it is typical of publishing houses in general. But within the last few years, there has been a change in the attitudes of the Columbia Broadcasting System,

Holt's parent company, which could bode well for the future of women at HRW. CBS has ostensibly committed itself to equalizing opportunities for women throughout the corporation in ways ranging from establishing consciousness-raising groups for male managers, to upgrading the job of secretary, to guaranteeing "the principle of equal pay for equal work."

The change in attitudes at CBS has many sources, not the least of which are the women's movement in general and the determination of a group of women at CBS to have their grievances heard. In 1973 an ad hoc women's committee made up of representatives from CBS's New York offices, including HRW, met with Arthur Taylor, president of CBS, to discuss specific changes that might be made in the treatment of women throughout the corporation. At the first meeting, during the summer of 1973, Taylor told the committee that it was his wish that CBS "become known throughout the country for its forward-looking policy . . . because it is the right thing to do as well as making sound business sense."

For the moment, the position of women at Holt is not dramatically different from what it was before the advent of the women's committee. There are signs, however, that improvements are gradually on the way. The management of HRW asserts that it wants to find women to fill jobs in sales, accounting, computer-programming, and other formerly male provinces, and that it will try to promote women from within the company before recruiting from outside. Holt, along with the other subsidiaries of CBS, has been provided with a women's counselor, whose job it is to act as a channel for communication between the women at Holt and the management.

Over at "Black Rock" (the dark stone building that houses CBS headquarters in New York), Holt is known as CEP and is itself a small conglomerate. Its components are: Popular Library, a mass-market paperback house; a magazine division that publishes *Field and Stream, Epicure,* and *World Tennis,* among other things; a group of paraprofessional schools; a film division that produces films, tapes, loops, and other educational devices; and Holt, Rinehart & Winston, publishers. The traditional book-publishing branch of Holt, Rinehart & Winston, Inc., roughly comprises a School Division, a College Department, and a Trade (General) Book Department. Since Holt, Rinehart & Winston, the book publisher, is actually quite separate from the rest of the CEP group, it can and should be discussed separately.

A walk around the stark cubicles of HRW's midtown Madison-Avenue offices reveals nothing very surprising. In School, College, and Trade, young women—many of them college graduates, some with advanced degrees—work as low-paid secretaries. Occasionally, they are graced with the title of "assistant" or "editorial assistant." Women have a smaller percentage of cubicles with wooden (as opposed to metal) desks, doors, carpets, and windows, all symbols of status and power. Promotion for women throughout publishing has almost invariably been from a secretarial to an executive-level job, while men have begun their careers as junior executives. Holt is no exception. But women do get promoted from time to time. In the Trade Department within the last few years, one woman was promoted to an assistant editorship, another was made an assistant juvenile editor, and a third was appointed publicity assistant. All three had been secretaries.

As in most publishing houses, also, salary discrimination is often hard to pinpoint. For example, there are seven editors in the Trade Department with a total of six different titles. A small staff with a hierarchical series of titles masks salary differences between male and female members of the department. Although CBS has fixed salaries for each job category throughout the entire corporation, it is easy enough to side-step this rule and pay women less than men simply by putting women at lower job levels.

Holt's College Department has the distinction of having been among the first in the industry to make use of women acquiring-editors. While women have acted as acquiring-editors in Trade

Departments for years, they have worked mainly as in-house editors (and, needless to say, at less prestigious jobs) in College Departments. One of the reasons for this is that acquiring-editors gain their experience from stints as traveling sales*men*. In the very recent past, it was almost inconceivable that a woman should go out on the road alone. This notion has slowly given way before the insistence of women; Holt now has two women acquiring-editors (representing about five percent of the college-sales force).

The School Department has a scattering of women in middle-level positions, mainly—and predictably—in the editorial end.

In such matters as hours, dress, benefits, and so on, HRW fits the publishing norm. There is virtually no such thing as overtime, although secretaries have recently asked for and won the right to compensatory time. Thus, if they stay one or two hours after five to work, they can theoretically arrive one or two hours late another day. Dress is considered a personal matter and there are no rules. Most women dress fairly conservatively in pants or dresses, but jeans are not frowned on.

HRW has the same benefit package as CBS. Its health insurance does not cover psychotherapy, dental care, abortions for either married or unmarried women, nor—for executive women—maternity care. The last is provided for women in jobs below the executive level (secretaries and others), and CBS has said that it will try to get maternity benefits for all of its female employees, if this can be worked out with its insurers.

Women are seeking to extend health coverage to abortions. The attitude of CBS toward maternity leaves is: "The woman employee [CBS does not take paternal child-rearing into account] is given a reasonable leave of absence and assurance that the interruption of service will not prejudice her career opportunities."

(Note: All quotations in this article are taken from "CBS and Its Women: A Dialogue," a special supplement to *Columbine,* the CBS house organ, in its September 1973 issue.)

In Mailer's Wake

GROSSET & DUNLAP

Grosset & Dunlap, the home of childhood heroes and heroines—Nancy Drew, the Hardy Boys, Thornton Burgess, Ernest Thompson Seton, the Bobbseys, and miles of other children's favorites—stepped into fashionable trade publishing with *Marilyn* by Norman Mailer. *The* book of its year capped earlier announcements that Grosset, who's been doing grown-up books all along, was going to take a more aggressive posture in adult publishing. It would be like your Doubleday, your Simon and Schuster. Guess what? It would be male chauvinist in the same old way. A glance at the *Literary Market Place* shows both the firm's abundance of male vp's (nine of them) and its paucity of female management (one only).

However, it's some comfort that Grosset's chauvinism is the result of history rather than malice. There's a quaint, old-fashioned quality to it—women are treated with courtesy, even gallantry. Also disdain.

The background of the seventy-seven-year-old company explains this. From the beginning Grosset addressed itself to selling masses of books to masses of people. In addition to the kiddie books and an endless series of how-to's, and long before the paperback revolution, Grosset was the famous publisher of millions of cheap hardcover editions of other publishers' works. (Bantam Books was born here, and now both companies are subsidiaries of a large insurance-based conglomerate.) This goal ordained that Grosset would be sales-centered rather than the editorial-centered operation most "trade" (as opposed to textbook) houses are. The huge printings required to keep list prices low simply precluded any other judgment. You had to be sure you could sell a lot, so books weren't selected because they brought messages to a waiting world, but because, to Grosset's army of sales experts, men to a man, they looked like merchandise that would have wide appeal; that, in other words, would move.

The system certainly worked, and is certainly the basis for the chauvinism. Women, dear reader, didn't go into sales. They wanted to be editors. Grosset was sales-dominated; it was male-dominated. Q.E.D.

It still is, admittedly so, as the management set-up shows. It's sort of a men's club, plus one, consisting of the various vp's and department heads, and run by the dynamic president, who, not at all incidentally, used to be sales manager. The delineation of vp's mirrors the contributions their functions make to the throbbing sales machine: no less than five are sales-related; two are package-related (production and art); and two are editorial (adult and children's books). You guessed it. The "plus one" woman vp is the head of children's books.

The sales orientation also shows in the tone of the place, which is full of the delights and drawbacks of old-fashioned Music-Man-flavored paternalism. Beautiful modern quarters overlook both the Hudson and East rivers from high in the New York Life Building, hard by the wholesale toy center, far from the temptations of Publishers' Row. Inside, 250 workers toil to produce 300 books a year, roughly half children's and half adults'. Many of the employees have been with Grosset twenty years or more. Most seem content in their jobs. Hard work is expected and pretty faithfully performed by all. The savagery and backbiting often found in corporate corridors are barely evident. Promotions are from within. Salaries are fair-to-good. Benefits are good. First names are used. There is sometimes a bonus, and always a party, at Christmas time.

The dark side of all this wonderful hominess is that women and other editors aren't taken seriously. Business is men's work. Because women have not traditionally been in sales and merchandising, most of the management class at Grosset has had little or no experience in dealing with women as equals; and, in any case, they don't seem to like the idea much. They have wives, they have daughters. They may even have girl friends, though to Grosset's credit, there's less of that than in high-rise literary factories, where taking advantage of the female help is literally and figuratively the rule. No, these men have secretaries, to whom they seem universally courteous and thoughtful. But secretaries don't make decisions, and it hasn't occurred to these men that women can—or even should—"do much" in business. And after all, why should it? They've done just fine so far without women messing around in things.

Men, on the other hand, are serious about their jobs. They are treated seriously. They are trained. They are promoted.

This is not to say there's not a female to be found in the place without a steno pad. Change does loom on the horizon, and there are already a number of women in the rank between vp and assistant-something around the company. Half the adult trade editors are women (two of them having risen from within); two senior designers are women; the chief editor of a paperback line is a woman; there are women in responsible roles in data processing, subsidiary rights, contracts, and so on.

But it *is* to say that old habits die hard. None of these women are decision-makers as men in comparable positions seem to be. Few, if any, have any idea where the company is going, or why, or how it might expect to get there. It is probably assumed they're not interested, and they may very well not be.

To discuss the one area where women might have made a dent—editorial—is to repeat the theme. Since this area never blossomed at Grosset, the company never attracted (nor therefore exploited) the waves of editor-eager coeds who've been the staple slob-work force of other houses. Who needed them anyway? There was no pretty correspondence in the Max Perkins manner. There were orders to be filled! A good editor was one who could produce for sales needs: "Dog books are doing well—get more dog books!" "More cookbooks!" "More diet books!"

Editors still haven't gotten very far in the brave new world of Grosset, despite *Marilyn*. Yes *Marilyn* was an editorial concept, but one that fitted perfectly into the proven Grosset sales/package formula. Editors on the whole are still assumed to know little of sales, less about design, and least about manufacture, i.e., the important things at Grosset. They have no voice in the disposition of their books in these areas. Books are often brought in by executives and passed along to editors for follow-up, and all new book ideas are submitted to a panel of executives (almost all from sales) for review. There's an advantage to this—everyone has had ideas he's lucky to have been saved from—but it can take weeks to get a decision.

As to design, if it's a jacket that works for sales, it's a jacket that stays on the book. And a jacket that works for sales is clear, nongimmicky, precise, nondaring.

Some of this will never change. Why change a formula if it works? But some of it inevitably will. First, good ideas are at a premium, and as Grosset's classical resistance to editorial-(v. sales-) originated ideas breaks down, as it is slowly beginning to do, the flow of ideas will increase and some of them are bound to be promising. Second, because more talented women are becoming available in *many* areas, not just editorial, to turn away from talent—even female talent—would be impractical. Not good business. So, in the end, good business and practicality should win the day at Grosset as they always have. (Not without some kicking and screaming, mind you.)

Ladies-in-Waiting

LIPPINCOTT*

None of the usual criteria seem to apply to Lippincott. Their logo is "Good Books Since 1792." To this should be added, "1792 was a good year for the family, so why change anything?" The aura of devotion to procedure, memorandums written in inexplicable prose, "certain standards," and the Lippincotts themselves overshadow product, pragmatism, and justice.

Lippincott is perfectly preserved, a museum piece among publishing houses. The fifth generation of Lippincotts, in the person of J. W. Lippincott, Jr., is now serving as president of the company.

A nod was made in the direction of the twentieth century when, at its inception, the Lippincotts erected a new building on East Washington Square in Philadelphia. The fact that some important publishing must occur outside of Philadelphia was acknowledged when the New York office was opened in the late 1940s. Currently, that office houses the Adult and Juvenile Editorial Trade Departments and the Publicity and Subsidiary-Rights Departments. Sales, Management, Production, Promotion, and copy-editing are in Philadelphia. `

A feeling of gentleman's agreement pervades the atmosphere, and an almost pathological attention is paid to treating everyone the same. This is the tip-off that many are privately considered inferior, but, publicly, devotion to government regulations and legislated justice prevails. Those who get anything done at J.B.L. do so because they seem to have forgotten to ask permission.

How do women fit into this tidy arrangement? Neatly and in their place. Lippincott, not inconsistently, has an inordinate num-

* See Preface.

ber of women employees. They are economical and more easily managed, it would seem. The Children's-Books staff is entirely female. The general manager is a man, with a female staff. The advertising and promotion manager (male) has eight women reporting to him, including the staffs of the Publicity and Library-Promotion Departments. Production, Art and copy-editing are all headed by men with female staffs. Subsidiary Rights is run by a woman with two women and one man reporting to her. So the men have all the power. The gents run the place, and they run almost exclusively female departments. They retire to the men's room to consult.

There is one flaming exception, and that is the oft-quoted and much-publicized Genevieve Young. Ms. Young was lured from Harper & Row to the specially created position of executive editor. Equipped with the classically lethal combination of brains, ability, riveting good looks, and a strong will, she seems to have been let alone to do what she wants to while they figure out what to do with her.

The following situations are more typical: The personnel director is a woman. As personnel director, she is the assistant to the executive vice-president. In this capacity she also has the privilege of typing the confidential letters for the v.p., answering the phone, and opening and sorting the mail for the chairman of the board. These honors are hers in addition to directing personnel.

A lady department head of no small ability recently asked for a raise. The opening reply to her request was, "What do you need all that money for? You are single and have no obligations."

Lippincott hires very competent women. It is a matter of pride. A woman there with a master's degree and heavy secretarial experience works as a secretary for not one, but two editors.

If you are a woman and work for Lippincott, you can be sure that you could comfortably remain there for the rest of your working days, as long as you don't make waves. You will always be treated with the utmost courtesy.

E Pluribus Unum

MACMILLAN

Macmillan is a vast corporation that owns an international collection of subsidiary companies. Besides Macmillan Publishing Inc. of New York and its various divisions, there are Collier-Macmillan of London, the parent company, and Collier-Macmillan of Mexico and Canada. Other interesting subsidiaries include Berlitz, Brentano's, and G. Schirmer.

The modern Macmillan building at 866 Third Avenue houses all the divisions of Macmillan of New York, as well as The Free Press, Hafner Press, Macmillan Information, and a few other divisions. Dictionaries and encyclopedias are written here, and Macmillan's Text, Trade and Juvenile Departments are here. The Adult Trade Department and the Juvenile Department share the fifth floor.

The fifth-floor plan economically boxes all personnel into offices or cubicles. Thus, the setting is orderly, if somewhat dehumanized. A sense of physical isolation subdues the social instinct and nourishes a kind of myopic intensity. However, on the bright side, the people themselves are most refreshing. Many of one's fellow employees, on all levels, are quite engaging and interesting in their own right. There are, of course, those that one could do very well without, but "those" would be defined differently by different people at different times. The turnover is heavy, and if one is considering working here, it sometimes helps to be known, to know someone, or to know someone who knows someone.

Women are vitally, steadily, and sometimes forcefully active in the company. While the Juvenile Department is headed by a female vice president and is staffed almost entirely by women, the Trade Department is headed by a man, a senior vice president, and is staffed with both men and women. Recently, two women in the Adult Trade Department, the manager of subsidiary-rights and the director of publicity, were named assistant vice presidents. Rumor has it that they were only minimally compensated for their new responsibilities. One of them has remained quiet since her promotion, but the other has assumed a very active role, overseeing jacket copy and art, and circulating conspicuously among the troops. Although some feel that her language is a bit too spicy for comfort, she does seem to be making a sincere effort to use her new influence to improve the package of the Macmillan book. The other woman has remained a gentle but shrewd businesswoman within her sphere. The talk is that both women were named assistant vice presidents chiefly in recognition of their fine work on *Jonathan Livingston Seagull.*

Jonathan Livingston Seagull, the best seller that has now been made into a movie, was acquired by one of Macmillan's women editors. Apparently, the editor was quite insistent that the book be published, despite the skepticism of her bosses. *Seagull* has been a financial boon to the company at a time when all publishing companies are in need of funds.

Macmillan has a number of women who are filling positions of some responsibility. Half of the Adult Trade editors are women, as are nearly all of the Juvenile editors. There is only one woman in the Art-and-Design Department of Adult Trade, but in Juvenile, the art director and her entire staff are women. A woman heads copy-editing for Adult Trade, and approximately half of her staff is female. There are two production managers for Macmillan hardcover and paperback trade books. Both are women.

But the company is headed by men. The chairman of the board is a man and the president is a man. Throughout the Trade Division the leadership positions are filled by men. Male power is often exercised in unconfronting ways: edicts filter down to the staff; paternalism is practiced. Some of the men in controlling positions have a tendency to pat their women colleagues on the head. To be fair, I think that at least some of them are blissfully unaware of the fact that head-patting can be a very demoralizing gesture, and that it can elicit anything but the best response from a woman employee. Certainly, a professional woman who has been given a serious job is not a teddy bear. She deserves to be taken seriously. Still, there are a number of men on all levels who relate very constructively and professionally to women employees.

At Macmillan, as elsewhere, the upper echelon makes considerably more money than the underlings, and the upper echelon is predominantly male.

Is there equal pay for equal work? In two specific jobs that I checked, a relatively inexperienced woman and a relatively inexperienced man were receiving the same pay. In two other jobs, a more experienced woman was receiving higher pay than a less experienced man. But my sampling was not extensive enough to draw any firm conclusions.

I hope that I have been fair to Macmillan. I *would* recommend it to women as a place to work. Although women do not hold the top positions, we are definitely making significant contributions through the opportunities given us in the company.

They Love the Dear Silver

MCGRAW-HILL*

Mother McGraw, as she is affectionately known to some of the inmates, is too enormous to engage in petty thievery. In civil-service style, each job has a graded level and within that level there is a salary range. It appears to work rather well, and you can be fairly certain that men and women performing the same job for the

* See Preface.

same amount of time are being paid approximately the same wage. The grading system holds true right down to the size and location of the offices or desks, and it does keep questions concerning status at a zero level. You know exactly what your position is by your grade level as well as where you sit (should you ever be in doubt).

In the General Books Division there are a fair number of women in nonfigurehead positions. The breakdown is as follows: The editors-in-chief of both American Heritage and Junior Books are women, the subsidiary-rights manager was rewarded for her supercompetence with the additional work load and title of executive editor (rumor has it that she also got a lot more money). Of the three senior editors in Trade, two are women, and I have known secretaries who have become assistant editors of some responsibility, and women who started as assistants who are now department heads.

Making money is the corporate objective and the best-seller-oriented atmosphere is tense and very high-pressure. Life at McGraw is generally strictly business and most people are too busy and harried to indulge in petty discrimination. Whatever problems women have here usually result from the attitudes of the immediate superior and are never matters of subtle and unspoken policy. Middle management has many women. Top management is something else again. There is one corporate vice-president of Management Informations Systems who is a woman. There are no general female managers of any of the book-company divisions.

It has been rumored that the above rather benign report would not hold true for the College Division, which has always been somehow more politically aggressive than the other book divisions. Several years ago a Ms. Davis claimed she was axed because of her political activism. McGraw said not so—she was axed because she was spreading the word on company time and company property.

All the usual signs of condescending behavior are missing at McGraw-Hill. Nobody asks you to pour coffee; you are lucky if they tell you where to go get it yourself. No doors are held open. Men and women eat together in the company cafeteria and there is a good deal of intra-gender joshing and jostling for position.

Pride and Prejudice

W. W. NORTON

It isn't that W. W. Norton is run by an evil administration. The worst that can be said of the company is that it's a deliberately unenlightened one.

Norton likes to remember that Warden Norton, its founder, was from the same intellectual environment and of the same gentlemanly, though businesslike, ilk that produced Alfred Knopf and D. W. Huebsch. As a result, the firm has about it the air of an old family estate—a house in which intelligence, aristocracy, and moneyed gentility are not only respected but consciously exhibited. Along with this air of gentility comes conservatism and oppressive paternalism.

The Norton "family" of employees is, on the whole, treated well. An excellent pension plan exists; major-medical and hospitalization insurance is extensive and paid for; Christmas bonuses are generous and rise handsomely with years of service; stock options become available to longtime employees; profit sharing goes to all (when the board of directors so directs). But an aristocracy, even a benevolent one, is inherently stifling in that it requires a carefully constructed hierarchy with everyone fitting—and remaining—neatly in his appointed station.

Because of this rigid structure, Norton denies to many of its employees the things they want most: recognition and reward for their individual talents. This is true of management's treatment of all workers. Accountants have never been made editors; order-takers rarely become office managers; mailroom workers never take on managerial positions; and, of course, women keep *their* place. Because the environment is genteel, women are treated kindly and courteously, but because it is aristocratic, there seems to be an unspoken consensus that ladies—who are not really cut out for the rugged business world—should never rise above a certain level . . . and no woman ever has.

The Trade Department now consists of five editors: three men and two women. (The president of the company also acquires book manuscripts, so he could be counted as the sixth Trade editor.)

Until recently the Trade Publicity Department was headed by a young woman who had succeeded in rising from the secretarial ranks of Norton to what could have been—and is in many houses—a powerful and lucrative position. Given Norton's genteel aversion to publicity, anyone on her job would have been selectively ignored. Given also that she was a woman—and a young woman at that—she was completely stymied. She left. Whatever the official reasons for her departure, more private reasons hovered in the "once-a-secretary-always-a-secretary" syndrome. She felt that she would forever be treated as the "girl" who had, by accident or indiscretion, been given a man's job which she would never be allowed—or encouraged—to handle properly. She was not given the salary the position deserved, and at the end, I fear, had begun to think that maybe the job was, in fact, too big for her. Such is the self-fulfillment of responsibility withheld. The administration thinks itself safe from censure on this score, however, since they hired a woman, with many years of publicity experience, to replace her. This woman seems to have gained the respect and power needed to operate her department successfully. Good. But, she had never been a secretary at Norton.

The College Department seems to have an even more oppressive attitude toward women. Women employees there are "girls" who "belong" to the editor for whom they work. Upward mobility in the secretarial ranks (secretaries at Norton are called "assistants"—a euphemism that salves our souls until one of the editors forgets and calls us secretaries again) is rare—once you work "for" a man, it seems that some mystical (sexual?) bond incapacitates you from ever working "for" another man. Movement from secretarial into editorial ranks is unheard of. (Exception: one young woman, a Phi Beta Kappa graduate from Smith College, was made a copy editor after she had done time for a year as a secretary.)

Here the picture becomes clouded by the "travelers." The College Department maintains some sixteen or seventeen young men (they have interviewed, but never hired a woman) who are salesmen-*cum*-manuscript scouts circulating around college campuses. Traditionally, editors and the college-department administrative staff are pulled from these ranks. This "tradition" exists, however, only in the rosy "ought-to-be" corner of the administration's collective mind. Neither the English editor nor the music editor nor the associate music editor (a woman brought in from the outside) were ever travelers. Yet, because we have all been told it's a "tradition," it's very easy to keep secretaries out of those jobs "destined" to be filled by travelers.

The future of the traveler and the future of the assistant are evident from their respective starting salaries. A June college graduate starts traveling in September with a salary around $8,000, plus expense account and car, admittedly necessary for his job. An assistant, *no matter what her educational and work experiences have been,* starts at $125 to $135 a week (that's $6,500–$7,000 a year). If she starts at $120 a week, she might be making $130 in eight months. If she starts at $135 a week, she won't see a raise for at least a year—perhaps longer. After two or two and a half years, she will be making $150 to $155 a week. After all,

women have no wives to support or future careers to bother themselves with. They'll all probably get married and drop out of the
work force anyway. Right?

But these are sad commonplaces in all industry. There is
much specific evidence to drag across the Norton College Department stage: the fact that no assistants and all travelers go to the
College-sales conference for what is, in the words of one of the
editors, a glorious stag party; the fact that *all* the travelers and
none of the assistants call the head of the College Department by
his first name; the fact that the College-Department office manager, a woman, has been with the company longer than the head of
the department; the fact that the president's secretary, a Norton
employee for over twenty years, still calls him *Mr.* Brockway; the
fact that no woman—except the former Mrs. Norton—sits on the
board of directors; the fact that women's-lib posters and articles
are immediately removed from the College Department's public
bulletin board.

In short, the administration hasn't yet realized—though mild
lip service is paid to their supposed newly acquired awareness—
that women don't want to be treated like little girls. By not paying
us salaries that are competitive with men's salaries, by not increasing the responsibilities of obviously capable women (and men,
though I am consciously avoiding what is—and should be—a
problem larger than just the women's issue), they keep us professionally un-adult, unchallenged, and unsatisfied.

Some of us have left, believing the world must hold something
more. Others of us have stayed, knowing that Norton—with all its
faults—*is* a pleasant, genteel place to work—a place where thinking people do cross your path—a place that, perhaps, thinking
people will some day change.

Post-Prussian Progress

PRAEGER

Praeger isn't everybody's cup of tea, but I don't think the tea is much sweeter for men than for women. To take the negative first:

The work load is unbelievable. So-called assistants "assist" two editors apiece—and at Praeger that's at least a double load. Most editors do acquisitions as well as pencil-editing, and they are supposed to do about twelve books a year—also at least a double load. So it goes, all through the house. The pay scale is on the low side, especially (but not only) at the bottom. And the offices are as far from posh and well-located as Twelfth Street is from Fifty-third and Klein's from Bloomies. Nor is the company prestigious—although it's getting there.

The positives: it's a fantastic learning opportunity, simply because everyone *is* overworked; people at the bottom get to do a lot of things their counterparts at less-berserk places don't do. Promotion isn't especially rapid, and it's certainly not automatic, but it does happen: the place is small enough so that talent is readily recognizable, and sometimes it's even recognized. The atmosphere ("call me Dave") and the dress code are extremely informal; assistants can and do wear jeans, and most female editors wear pants (not necessarily pantsuits) most of the time. And the place is on the rise—which is kind of fun to watch.

Praeger was founded by Frederick Praeger, who was succeeded in the presidency by George Aldor when the firm was sold to Encyclopaedia Britannica. Aldor was an old friend of Praeger and continued the Prussian tradition FAP began.

But under the new, "American," regime, that tradition has been modified: the boss's door is always open, and at least nominal democracy prevails in other ways. As far as women are concerned, however, management's attitude is still generally patronizing, if not so obviously patriarchal as it used to be. And the long arm of Encyclopaedia Britannica, which interferes not at all with editorial policy, has a good deal to do, none of it really good, with women's place at Praeger. What benefits there are are discriminatory. For instance, under the health-insurance program, a man's wife is covered; a woman worker at the same salary level pays the same premium, but her husband is not covered. Aside from this, the medical policy isn't bad—but in order to get it, employees must also accept, and pay for, a life-insurance policy. Further, they must take a policy of which the size is dictated by their salaries. This despite the fact that in most cases single women, and some married women as well, don't want or need life insurance; they'd rather have the $20 or so it costs per month. But no life insurance, no health insurance. That's EB.

Again on the positive side, the firm's output is changing, and this may affect its treatment of at least some women. Once a kind of backwater, semisubsidized, university-press-type operation, Praeger now has aspirations to becoming a hot trade house, with a profitable college list as well. It has, in fact, already had a couple of best sellers. The need for product, and the highly competitive directions the firm is taking mean that anyone who can produce can probably dictate terms—even if the anyone is female. This situation may have favorable effects on daily life for women at Praeger, but it will take more than this to change the views of the parent company.

The typical entry job at Praeger is as an "assistant"—to an editor, to the subsidiary-rights manager, to the promotion director, or whoever. At present there are equal numbers of male and female assistants—they were hired on the basis of the same criteria, and they are paid equally. Two assistants—one male and one female—have just been promoted to junior editors. Top administrative jobs are held by men, but there is one very highly placed woman (a senior editor and head of the Washington office), who also sits on the executive committee, and two of the other three senior editors are women. The promotion manager, subsidiary-rights manager, high-school and library-sales manager, and head of the International Department are all women in jobs that are commonly held by men in other houses. The current managing editor is male, with a female assistant, but his job was held at least once by a woman.

The assistants do all the standard secretarial garbage, but occasionally—if they are bright and aggressive, and the work habits of the people they assist are congenial—they get to do a lot more. Most Praeger editors do the whole job on their books, from inventing projects to reading submissions, negotiating contract terms, proposing the books to the editorial board, text editing, writing flap copy, approving jacket and interior designs, presenting the books at sales conferences, and representing the firm at conventions of academics, booksellers, and so on. With some exceptions, editors are generally only too happy to permit (or even require) their assistants to take over any or all of these jobs—but only if the mountains of scutwork are done first.

Various other personnel—advertising copywriter, art director, production assistant, advertising and publicity people, copy editor—are also overloaded and underpaid, but there seems to be no sex discrimination. The same is true of the various clerical workers in the College Department. (That department was headed by a female at one time, but the current head, a male, has expanded the job's functions in such a way as to change its requirements. It is now much less likely to be filled by a woman, largely because it requires extensive experience as a college traveler. At present all the college travelers are men. One of the college clericals, a woman, was promoted to traveler and held the post briefly, but quit.)

Of the editors who don't do the whole job themselves, the one who does *only* acquisitions is male; the two in-house editors (who do no acquisitions) are female. This is a common division of functions among publishers, as is the fact that college travelers are generally male. This may stem from the fact that women, for one reason or another, are usually reluctant to be away from home very much, or from the patriarchal tradition that discourages publishers from sending women out of town alone. (For their safety or because they might misbehave and give their employer a bad name?) For whatever reason, the tendency is still to keep women in jobs that tie them to the office and to let the men go off to the hinterlands—but there are a few signs (e.g., the short-lived career of the lone woman traveler) that Praeger is willing to unbend.

In short, Praeger has its charms for one who is eager to learn, and it seems ripe for a breakthrough—as far as opportunities for women are concerned.

Girl Scout Cookies

PUTNAM-COWARD-McCANN & GEOGHEGAN*

Besides sharing the same corporate umbrella, Putnam's and Coward-McCann & Geoghegan share an archaic view of women's position in business. That view results in an underutilization of available resources and in a corporate image that smacks of male chauvinism.

Putnam's Adult Trade editorial staff consists of six male editors and one female. That lone female has as her primary responsibility mystery and suspense titles, an area that rarely (if ever) affords her the opportunity to acquire or work on a potential best seller. Additionally, she serves as the back-up editor for both the publisher and the editor-in-chief.

* See Preface.

While Putnam and CMG seem to have accepted the credibility of the presence of women in quasi-executive editorial positions, it is a grudging acceptance, born of a fill-up-the-gaps-with-the-existing-staff policy, rather than from a conscientious effort to find the best available person for a given position. This means that women arrive at the executive level through the back door rather than through a fair initial evaluation of their abilities.

Promotion and publicity are among the traditional female jobs in book publishing, and Putnam and CMG dutifully fill these positions with women. Yet their meager salaries and authority belie the magnitude of their contribution to the total effort. Their work is closely supervised and regulated by male bosses (either the publishers or the directors of advertising or sales) and they are rarely given the credit they are due: the credit for the genesis of an idea that results in a coup is always taken by one of the men.

Subsidiary rights is an area in trade publishing that has the potential for supplying a major portion of the income that keeps a firm in business. It is a position that requires a well-organized, quick-thinking, and shrewd person. However, neither Putnam nor CMG has enough confidence in a woman to let her use her own head in making crucial decisions; all rights sales have to be approved by one of the men—publisher, editor, or sales manager. Because of this policy and other more insidious kinds of supervision (e.g., checking on submissions, reviewing letters before they are sent out, double-checking with clients, etc.), a woman's effectiveness in this job is minimized. At the present time, while the subsidiary-rights director is a woman, a man (and a former director of rights for the company) has been hired to oversee the department.

There is an all-pervasive feeling that there must be something wrong with women who have chosen business careers instead of traditional roles, whether they are married, divorced, or single. This defect, while never explicitly described or defined, makes a woman's ambitions, achievements, and overt qualifications suspect. Witness that with the one exception cited above, no woman has ever been promoted to an executive capacity from within the ranks. No matter what a job actually entails—in terms of responsibilities, qualifications, or quantity of work—women working under this corporate umbrella are all lumped into the "drone" category of second-class employees. At any time they can be, and frequently are, called upon to fill in at secretarial chores. This attitude on the part of management carries over into salary considerations. Women are rarely given legitimate merit increases, their current salaries usually being considered "good enough for a woman." And it is a fact that their salary scales are not competitive with those of men in equivalent positions.

Finally, there is a tacit conspiracy against accepting the female point of view in business dealings. Women are not as precipitate in their judgment; they give more time and consideration to details; and they frequently develop more viable solutions to crises than men do, yet they are not credited with having business acumen. In this specific corporate setup, a woman's opinions and/or suggestions are given second thoughts or periodic serious consideration only when no man has come up with a solution to a pending problem.

Let My People Grow

PYRAMID PUBLICATIONS

While Pyramid is not the best of all possible media worlds, it is certainly not the worst. The consensus among women here is that the attitude of management is changing considerably—that the women's-lib thing has finally hit them and they are becoming aware of women as a source of human potential. Although the overall ratio of women to men in executive positions and as heads of departments is two to nine, a great percentage of editorial and production responsibility falls to women.

There are four main editorial departments: Pyramid softcover books; religious, inspirational, and health books; the men's magazine division; and the women's magazine division. All but one are directed by men. Carol Plaine heads—what else?—the women's magazine division.

Only four of the seven women editors and associate editors seem to earn close to a "masculine" wage. (One woman holding an editorial position said a male in her job would make $3,000 a year more than she does.) Of the four-best-paid female editors, one has been with the company a number of years (I believe more than ten), and heads her own department. She is also the daughter of one of the former owners of Pyramid.

The two women in executive positions (a third, Miriam Helfgott, heads the Foreign Rights and Permissions Department) have been with the company almost from the beginning. This is not to reflect on their individual abilities but does give a fair idea of management's promotion policy to date.

You need not necessarily know someone to get hired. Many of the women answered want ads or came through agencies; some came directly from other publishing houses. If you have experience in the field for which you are being hired, no trainee program is inflicted, but a typing test is always given to those applying for secretarial positions.

A few women who started as secretaries have moved up to editorial positions through hard work and, sometimes, luck. One of them moved up because the two editors in her department left simultaneously. Having been there long enough to know the routine, she was moved into the vacant slot. Luck. Quite obviously, she is capable or she wouldn't have retained the job. Which poses an interesting question: How many women working as secretaries are overqualified for that position?

An interesting and frustrating point: It seems that secretaries can earn higher salaries than women coming in as associate editors. I know of a case where the secretary of a department head was making $45 a week more than the woman associate editor.

(The male associate editor was making $80 more than the woman with the same title.)

A secretary can move up to associate editor and even to editor, but she is seldom allowed to forget she *started* as a secretary. (The boss of one of the associate editors who started as a secretary has his calls put through on her phone when his secretary is out, but he doesn't subject the women who came in as editors to this indignity.) The men also remember that you can type and file and take shorthand, so when you get bogged down, it's a hassle to get an assistant or temp to do that typing, filing, etc. And in some cases, when a temp is brought in for *you,* HE snows her under with a mountain of work he has just discovered.

Here is some advice given by a number of women editors: DON'T LET THEM KNOW YOU CAN TYPE! Or, let it be known that you can type with two fingers, *very* slowly. And avoid other little gems like: "Oh, I know how to work a duplicating machine" or "Oh, let me type that up for you!" (when his secretary is out) or, "I can replace that typewriter ribbon for you" or "I can take shorthand. . . ."

DON'T be too obvious about how much you know about literature (most employers are not interested) or that you want to learn a lot about editorial work—"they" usually get nervous.

Most often letting "them" know how much you know (because you want to be indispensable) will backfire on you. You'll find extra responsibilities falling on your head, bit by bit, with little or no money falling into your pocket. Occasionally, there is an out-and-out promotion with title and money, but many times responsibilities are increased with no title, no money—or, a title and no money. What you make depends on how loud your "boss" stamps his feet. For example, the all-encompassing title of associate editor carries with it the following salary disparity: from $6,240 to $12,600—same general title, same amount of responsibility.

Currently, budgetary problems are plaguing most businesses, and it is felt by some that in certain departments at Pyramid more promotions would be forthcoming if the money was there.

One of the most blatant examples of discrimination at Pyramid is the "problem of the switchboard." *All* of the *women* (except the two department heads and one executive assistant) were *ordered* to learn the operation of the switchboard, in case the operator was out or had to be periodically relieved. For some reason, the sane suggestion that a temp operator be brought in on the rare occasions when our operator might be ill was ill-received by management. So one by one the women learned, except for a few stout-hearted souls who absolutely refused and triumphed on the strength of their position.

When asked why the men did not have to participate, management's totally honest, serious, and candid reply was: "It doesn't sound *right* for a man to be answering a switchboard!"

Other not-so-blatant forms of discrimination exist, as would be expected. Bad vibes come from many of the men if: (1) you are a woman (2) you are ambitious (3) and/or you are young. Resentment seems to be strongest from the males in their forties and up, due certainly to encroaching feelings of insecurity which seem to be concomitant, in the business world, with the aging process.

Some women feel the best way to get along with the men is to "act dumb"—ask their advice when you don't really need or want it—just to make them feel secure. One of the women editors feels that the male head of one of the departments would still be in the secretarial pool if he were a female. And a few sense condescension from some of the women in "higher" positions.

Getting credit for your own ideas depends on the size of the ego you work for. Some women are given due credit, some have to remind Him it was her idea, and some get absolutely no recognition. One of the women who doesn't get credit from her boss says she won't fight for it; she prefers to avoid nastiness in working conditions. In other words, she'd rather keep the peace than get the credit.

On the opposite end of the spectrum, another editor feels that her boss's attitude is healthy—unique—almost asexual—that he thinks in terms of productivity and contribution to the total operation. He not only sees that his women are credited, she says, but expresses his appreciation toward them.

Management's attitude regarding women in responsible positions is changing. Not long ago, women were not included in the editorial meetings. That policy has changed. And they are now also included in the sales meetings as a result of the efforts of the editorial director of the softcover department. The women editors make presentations at the editorial meetings, and, for the first time *ever*, present books they will be selling to the salesmen at sales meetings. The women editors who have expense accounts have them on an unlimited basis.

As to benefits and penalties, I do not know of an instance when anyone was docked for being late. Although I was threatened with it, the threat was never carried out; but guilt resulted and I would rather have lost the money! Within the company, I believe my case to be an exception. On the other hand, speaking of guilt again, no limit on sick days is officially set, but a large percentage of the women have been made to feel guilty at one time or another for having been out sick. Two reported that their bosses made it a practice, for a while, to call them at home to make sure they were indeed there.

There are no maternity benefits if you have conceived before being hired. And since the company has its own medical plan, Blue Cross is not paid for by them. The dressing code is quite liberal now—but only after a bitter fight. I was among the first to try to break it, and the attitudes we pioneers had to combat were infuriating. For example, when I asked why *not* slacks, the answer was, "Women are *supposed* to wear dresses and skirts!" (Be my guest! The Scots do—are they uptight about *their* manhood?)

". . . besides, I like to look at your legs!" (and my ass, no doubt, when I have to bend over for the packages of books which have been delivered on the floor near my desk, and which you, if you were a gentleman would pick up for me, a dress-wearing lady, since you want to talk about roles!)

Freelance opportunities at Pyramid are fair. Editors hire on the basis of résumé and brief phone conversations, or recommendation. In sending in a résumé, the covering letter is, of course, the most important element.

Like I said, it's not the worst . . .

Payment: Peanuts and Prestige

RANDOM HOUSE AND KNOPF

At Random House there are approximately twenty-two women in a Trade Editorial Department of about thirty, from the editor-in-chief through the secretaries. Of this number, all the men are in senior positions with the exception of one young man hired directly out of college as an assistant to an editor (the editor already had a secretary). The women are in senior, associate, assistant, and secretarial positions. They either began as secretaries and were advanced or came in with previous experience on a higher level. The publicity department relies on ten women.

Most women seem to feel that they are somewhat better off at Random House than they might be elsewhere. And there is a degree of camaraderie among them. Even those most bitter about their own situations are more concerned about a general restructuring than about their own specific salary or position. Money and power are the two foremost issues in discussion.

While a few women in senior positions say there are no problems, or that those that exist are not based on sex, many more feel there is discrimination. Among women who have risen within the company, there is a particular feeling of frustration. They know that coming up through the ranks is very difficult and they admit to psychological barriers—it is difficult for a one-time secretary to assume command within the same company. Women feel especially guilty about demands for more money. These requests are met with excuses, with pointed reminders that "performance is rewarded," or strong hints that one should use one's expense account more freely to "make up" for the salary deficiency. Some feel that the only way to make it is to find another job.

One senior editor has suggested that both men and women executives are unconscious sexists because the women who made their way in the sixties did so by adapting to the system. It worked for them—so it should for others; ambition and talent will win out. When sexism is unconscious, the problem is *not* that the one who harbors it refuses to be outspoken, but that the idea never occurs. Men are used by women in this situation too—as tools and as a means for advancement and security.

Other women who have not achieved their goal feel trapped. Having gained a small title, an expense account, a job in a good firm with "glamour," they are expected to be content. "They're lucky to be there at twenty-five." But the fact remains that executive secretaries are better-paid than are those holding most "glamour" jobs here. Many women feel that they have no recourse but to quit. They are quite aware that Random House can easily replace them and will not make it worth their while to stay. Women in the middle, trying to get a track record, are vulnerable and frustrated. Assistant editors need to acquire authors—and the women complain that the lines to do so are wired against them.

The only possible solution they see is unionization because the facts remain that women *will* work for less money, that they *are* afraid to make demands, and that some still feel that they can make it in the old system. In the meanwhile, the opportunities for women to achieve authority are severely limited, and those that are given some responsibility are often underpaid. All in all, it is fair to say that women at Random House do have legitimate complaints, but that unconscious attitudes among both men and women—among the haves and the have-nots—exacerbate the problems on both sides.

At Knopf, women are constantly subjected to overriding male decisions. Executives of the corporation, sales personnel, and most senior editors are men. Women at the editorial level are given a certain amount of freedom and respect, but they are never allowed to forget where the power lies.

Salaries are low (secretaries make $105 per week; very few associate editors make $10,000 or better—one associate with six years' experience makes less than $10,000). There has been no need to attract men to the lower editorial levels when women with low salary and promotion expectations are had so easily.

The job ladder goes from secretary to editorial assistant (a move few secretaries are able to make; one secretary of two years who was doing copy-editing and other editorial functions begged for at least the title "editorial assistant," if not the salary increase, and was refused) and from there to assistant editor to associate editor . . . well, for most women, it stops there.

A recent change in benefits makes it possible for women employees to take maternity leaves and be reasonably sure of keeping their jobs. A number of women have taken this opportunity and have returned to work full or part time.

Pluses at Knopf, for women willing to work for peanuts with little hope for advancement in a male-dominated company, include a pleasant atmosphere, the company of a surplus of other bright young women, many of them feminists, and association with a prestige publishing house. But don't expect excitement.

"For God's sake," said one associate editor, "even the parts of my job that are supposed to be glamorous—the lunches with writers and such—usually turn out to be a drag."

The Short, Happy Career of One Girl with a
Good Education

SCRIBNER'S

Anyone familiar with the tone and atmosphere of Mary McCarthy's "Rogue's Gallery" in *The Company She Keeps* ("an extract from memoirs by the heroine") or the personae of the employees and the Victorian decor in Melville's "Bartleby" will recognize the outer trappings of my first real encounter with the book world. From the moment an intense, bespectacled reference-book editor read my employment form and murmured "Good education. Now let's see what you can *do*," to the moment of my exit as an assistant editor in the College Department, I found Charles Scribner's Sons (established 1846) interesting, humane, indefatigable, somewhat unpredictable.

My entrance and my first days on the job were spent on a typing test: the fascinating brief biography of Dorothea Dix. My initial assignment was to type the edited manuscript of the *Concise Dictionary of American Biography* for the copy editor, a project continually in flux for about four years. Happily, there also were such pleasant tasks as proofreading the galleys of the *Concise Dictionary of American History, Dictionary of American History,* supplement one; trade and college manuscript reports; library and picture research—a notable job was selecting a panel, "Marmion" in Virginia, at the Metropolitan Museum of Art—for *Arts in America, The Colonial Period.*

Still a fledgling in the four-person editorial wing of the then "Subscription Department," surrounded by workers in the business end and by wrought-iron railings, I was attempting to create layouts for the revised edition of the *Album of American History,* volume one, *The Colonial Period.* Mr. Scribner passed by and casually inquired, "Knitting?"

"I do feel like Madame Defarge," I cheerfully replied.

He complimented me warmly on my work—my boss had kindly reported that I was a great help in producing project "Chartres"—and thus began my admiration for Mr. Scribner, classics scholar, potential university professor, a man who taught himself physics in the navy, and a lover of science (manifested in his own creation, the many-volumed *Dictionary of Scientific Biography*—"to leave footprints in the sands of time" and to fortify one of the few, small family-owned publishing houses left).

It might seem that the character of the once-famous trade publisher boasting Maxwell Perkins, Hemingway, Fitzgerald, Wolfe, and such prominent theologians and philosophers as Reinhold Niebuhr, Jacques Maritain, Susanne K. Langer, and Martin Buber has been altered. But, of course, the Scribner Library's paperback series, among others, keeps the works of such writers alive.

After publication of the *CDAB,* with my name on the contributor's page ("in case you want to teach some day"), it must have seemed logical to assign me to the *DSB* because of my previous experience in Dictaphone-typing the *CDAB,* editing a volume, critically proofreading it in galleys and page proofs, and doing the necessary research.

However, the jobs and interest in subject matter, as witness the lives or the scientific careers of people from the ancients to the moderns, do not always coincide. The meetings of a highly selective editorial board to choose candidates for the *DSB,* who would submit typical articles, formulate policy, and consider translations were stimulating, but my real interests were in the humanities and the social sciences. Mr. Scribner became aware of that fact. Fortunately, there was an editorial position open in the College Department and I made an appointment to see Mr. Scribner, who generously regarded my request as "courageous."

In the College Department I copy-edited and proofread textbooks and text revisions of both college and trade books on literature, history, and sociology. Author contact, picture research, departmental discussion groups, and a spirited, workmanlike atmosphere contributed to many productive days. But the College Department (reduced from approximately twenty-five men and women to three women) has now "merged" with the Trade Department. For some of us, including the heads of small family-owned book companies and bookstores, "these are the days that try men's souls."

I have always been naïve about salaries; with a good deal of embarrassment, I can recall a surprise telephone call from my father to my boss, followed by an immediate raise.

My generous profit-sharing money and my severance pay have stood me in good stead. I am grateful for what I learned at Scribner's about editing books, for the company of the gracious and talented people I worked with, for the close friends I made, and for the volumes I added to my home library. (Imagine owning the New York Edition of Henry James!)

But what do I do now?

Getting Fired with Ambition

SIMON AND SCHUSTER

What can you say about a brilliant, eager, well-educated girl whose ambition slowly atrophied? Chances are she worked for Simon and Schuster. At this marvelous house, inequality reigns, while bright young women are harassed by hunger pangs.

Not so for the bright young man, especially one who happened to graduate from the publisher's alma mater. One day, as Peter Swede was sentimentally perusing the *Princeton History Review,* he came upon a well-written article by a senior. Within an incredibly short period of time, that young fellow—that erstwhile senior in New Jersey—found himself editing in New York.

In the old days it was the tradition at Simon and Schuster to hire only girls with outstanding typing ability, skill in steno—and B.A.'s in English from the Seven-Sisters schools. Today there are very few of these package deals floating around, so the requirements for an editorial secretary have dropped sharply. But it is still a must to be able to type and to have parents rich enough to support you.

Salaries, which have risen considerably in the past few years, start in the region of $115 a week, with a $5 raise every six months. Operating on an inverse-value system, Simon and Schuster does not give raises on the basis of merit. The merit system is still an unknown quantity in this house, where it is a proven fact that the harder a woman works, the more she deserves the right to stay in the same place. Even two years' editorial experience and a master's degree in English are useless in elevating her from the position of starving secretary if she is also unfortunate enough to be a quick, accurate typist. Such was the case of an extremely intelligent young woman, who not only possessed all of these attributes, but also had to her credit some exceptional editorial work, plus the discovery of what turned out to be a very successful unagented manuscript. Her reward was the happy news that she would soon become secretary to *two* editors instead of to just one—at, of course, the same salary.

Yet it will not do to despair, for where there is time there is hope. For instance, there is the example of the woman who was a member of MENSA with a master's degree in French literature and some brilliant translating work behind her. After thirteen years as a secretary, she became subsidiary-rights director and now brings in the money that pays everyone's salary. On the other hand, it took the former assistant advertising manager only ten years as the publisher's secretary before she rose to that position, and from there, only five more years before she could become an in-house editor and from there, only a year before she was fired because the publisher didn't like her personality.

One cannot end this discussion of the opportunities available for, and the instances of, female mobility without mentioning a woman who has an honored place in Simon and Schuster history as the true symbol of ascension. In less than one year this aggressive young woman defied tradition, became an editor, and set herself up to the rest of the downtrodden forces as an example of the power of feminine will. How did she do it? It was quite simple, actually. She couldn't type.

As far as such things as the editorial board go, there are, of course, no women members. And although Simon and Schuster has more vice presidents than the East Village has cockroaches, only one of them is a woman.

As a final comment, it is a perverse point of interest to note that Michael V. Korda, the "egalitarian" editor-in-chief who is author of the highly successful *Male Chauvinism,* was once overheard issuing the following edict: "Please don't send me any more bright girls. I only want to see girls who smoke pot and don't want to go anywhere!"

Without a doubt, the greatest career opportunity that can befall a woman at Simon and Schuster is to get fired. This, as a rule, is very difficult to achieve, since all types of delinquent, lax, and antisocial behavior are accepted, condoned, or even encouraged—anything to make a secretary stay a secretary. But it's worth a try, because even if a woman leaves to become a secretary in another company, the worst that can happen is that she will finally be able to earn a livable wage.

Many people today make livable salaries. Many people take them for granted. That is something Simon and Schuster women can never do, because the cherished dream of one day being able to support herself with at least minimum comfort is an unattainable fantasy for her. In another setting, the dream may suddenly become reality.

After all, when you're at the bottom, any step is a step up.

She Asked for Bread and Got Stoned

STRAIGHT ARROW BOOKS

by Barbara Kelman- Burgower

Straight Arrow Books is the book division of Rolling Stone, that million-reader miracle rag which has dispelled the rumor that rock is dead and that the under-thirty population has no political consciousness. At its inception, Straight Arrow was a small company (staff of four) dedicated to publishing for what some call the counterculture. I guess you could say I grew up with Straight Arrow, and it was horrible and wonderful, as adolescence often is.

I came to Straight Arrow as the general editorial assistant shitworker and coffee gofer despite my Barnard B.A. and seven years in publishing (Praeger, Pyramid, and Canfield Press, Harper & Row's San Francisco-based junior-college text division), with a commune, a pornographic movie, and some PR work scattered in-between. I was wooed away from Canfield (where A-S-S-I-S-T-A-N-T is pronounced secretary but where a bearded sociology grad student "manned" the phones during my tenure) by an impressive salary offer and the understanding that the company was growing and there was no end to the possibilities for future advancement.

Though the immediate attraction of a high salary is obvious, and though my ego certainly responded to the prospect of working with the great and near-great at Rolling Stone, what finally (after about three seconds actually) persuaded me to take the chance and leave my cozy but dead-end job at Canfield was the last promise. My previous experience had led me to believe that a young lady seeking a career in publishing could expect a very long apprenticeship at the Selectric, with vague promises of dubious rewards. Somehow, my being a superior secretary, a devoted laborer, and an unstintingly loyal employee had always queered my chances to move ahead.

Life at Canfield had been a most discouraging repetition of that pattern. On my arrival there, I had been encouraged by the fact that all the production editors were women. (They had some men there, called THE EDITORS, who made more money, to be sure, but as far as I could tell, they were glorified salesmen.) "Ah ha!" thought I, "I'll show them how talented and hardworking I am and within six months I'll trade my battleship-gray desk and egg-salad sandwich for one of those lovely Parsons tables and an expense account." Well I showed them, and within *three* months I was promoted. No longer secretary—I mean assistant—to a mere editor, I was now same for the editor-in-chief. No raise, no new desk. The only change in my status was that it fell to me to oversee the other assistants and make sure they didn't spend too much time in the ladies' room. As one of the editors so pungently described me, I had now become super-cunt.

So on to Straight Arrow. First the good news; the titles were exciting, and I was suddenly able to work on books that I would have read anyway, perhaps even have bought. And work on them I did. Because the Editorial Department was essentially a one-man operation, and because Alan Rinzler is a fair and prudent man, he tossed me into the deep waters and encouraged me to swim. Within another three months I was managing editor as well as the putative "other editor." I signed up some projects, including one everyone was opposed to but was willing to give a chance since I seemed so enthusiastic; I got to actually edit a number of books, blue pencil in high hand; I oversaw the whole list, hired freelance copy editors, and yelled at the production department; stuck my finger in the subsidiary rights pie; wrote catalog and press-release copy (which I hated but unfortunately had a talent for—one particularly dazzling hype for a less than dazzling title was given the Nina Bourne Dynocosmic Trash Award by my giddy coworkers); and I was forced, not merely permitted, to study and understand the budgets and financial statements—though I suspect that last privilege had more to do with squelching my constant pleadings for a raise than anything else.

But I had complaints and I believe most of them to have been valid—they were in the end fatal. And, alas, it was in that area that I was considered a kvetching she-bitch rather than the respected colleague I had otherwise been led to believe I was. The lofty salary that lured me there didn't keep up with the cost of living, or with the salaries of some later importees from the Big Apple. Nor did my status as managing editor entitle me to a secretary. Indeed I served in that senior capacity for a full year before I was even relieved of my secretarial duties to the president-editor-in-chief-executive-vice-president of Rolling Stone, all wrapped up in one adrenaline-propelled package. The conflict, unfortunately, was not easily expressed in terms of the Equal-Rights Amendment or any classic male-chauvinist-pig syndrome I'd heard of. Because I loved my work and I liked my boss and fellow workers and I cared a lot about the company and was a sucker for subsuming my own needs to the commonwealth.

There are a lot of nasty things to be said about working for a large publishing house whose president you've never met and whose editor-in-chief calls you by your first name while he's Mister Someone to you. But the hole-in-the-wall and struggling independent house, San Francisco superstars notwithstanding, is a thorny bed of roses at best. There's no better place to learn the ropes, to get close to the whole process and ask your stupid questions and make your ghastly mistakes amidst people who know and maybe even love you. And the sense of being at some sort of frontier—we used to call it the Edge in our more paranoid moments—is truly exhilarating.

But emotionally it can be hell, like asking your father for a bigger allowance when you know the mortgage is killing him, or whining to your mother that your brother's room is nicer and brighter and bigger when you know he's older and your own time will come. Or not wanting to help with the dishes or mow the lawn or clean up your room or wear your older sister's hand-me-downs . . .

I'm doing something now that is very personally satisfying—freelancing. Which means I'm my own boss (and the income is still lousy!) and the absence of all that paperwork, ringing phones, and endless useless editorial meetings doesn't keep me from doing the most nearly perfect job possible on the work at hand. Sometimes I wish I belonged to the family whose book it is, but, on balance, it seems worth it not to be involved in the family fights.

And Straight Arrow has grown: there are secretaries and assistants and executives galore, and the books are getting more ambitious and more "grown-up." And, I'm told, the atmosphere is more professional. I doubt that it's a New-York-type house yet, or that it ever will be, but we've both gotten through our growing pains and things are calmer, tidier, and perhaps a bit more boring.

Caution: Men Working!

TIME-LIFE BOOKS

The Book Division of Time Inc. emerged almost unscathed from the tempestuous legal action in which the women employees charged the company with discrimination against them (see page 278). Perhaps because it is a younger, less tradition-bound off-spring of *Time,* Time-Life Books has never been as ruthless about keeping women in their place, that is, a secretarial chair or a researcher's corner. And since the conciliatory agreement was signed, Jerry Korn, the managing editor, and Bea Dobie, chief of research, have faithfully carried out their pledge to "actively pursue hiring and promoting policies designed to place women in categories now filled mainly or exclusively by men, and vice versa . . . women and men are to be considered on an equal basis for all positions at all levels."

None of us are naïve enough to think that subliminal discrimination can be stomped out by a decree from the attorney general's office, but we do believe that our management has been acting in good faith. Highly qualified young men have been hired as researchers and copy readers; male and female researchers have been accepted as writer trainees; a number of female researchers have been made writers and editors; and even the hitherto sacrosanct profession of designer has now been entered by a woman. Although the women's movement here can't claim any credit for it, a new series of books is headed by a woman editor for the first time, and two women are in line to direct new projects. The publisher is a woman as well (even though she has been signing herself J. D. Manley).

Time-Life Books differs from many other companies in that it is perhaps overly optimistic of an inexperienced, ambitious woman to accept a job such as editorial clerk or secretary here in the hope of moving ahead. If by some miracle this does happen, it could be at the expense of her youth and as the result of expending all of her energies. There are job opportunities here for women with talent and provocative résumés as text or picture researchers, picture editors, and even writer trainees. Personnel, with the prodding of the government, no longer operates on the principle that women are willy-nilly researchers and that any man out of college is an instant writer. But it is still helpful to have an introduction to the managing editor or chief of research. It is too early yet to judge whether more experienced women will be hired as writers or editors, but the climate is certainly more favorable today than ever before. But although the older women who have worked for the company for many years are not at all discriminated against—in fact, they are often cosseted—it is questionable whether many older women would ever be hired from the outside.

Salary levels are generally equitable. The minimum wage scales for each editorial category have been established by the Newspaper Guild, but once you've passed the minimum, you're on your own—and management is still believed to be more sympathetic to a man's plea for money. Fringe benefits in Books are identical to those elsewhere in Time Inc.—profitsharing plan, good medical insurance, including psychiatric and dental assistance partially paid for by Time Inc. There are also good vacations and educational assistance—and a one-year maternity leave!

The hours are humane—10:00 to 6:00—and lunch hours are flexible. But working wives, mothers, and women with active social lives should be warned that the publishing schedules are more similar to those of monthly magazines than of books, and that there can be a great deal of pressure and overtime.

To sum it up—Time-Life Books is far in advance of the rest of the company and of much of the publishing industry in its attitude toward women on the job.

Moving Up Is Moving Out

VIKING PRESS

The Viking Press is a middle-sized publishing house, not a book factory. It is independently owned and thus editorially autonomous, so it can afford to base publishing decisions on a book's quality, first and foremost.

Viking is a cheerful, close-knit house, staffed by congenial people. Because of the male/female ratio on the senior editorial level, for example, Viking is notorious as a good place for women to work. Out of six senior trade editors, three are women.

The secretarial dilemma is probably less acute than elsewhere; there are no unsung martyrs on that level doing the real work while the editor cuts a flashy figure in literary circles and cops the glory. But like most other publishers, Viking hires women just out of college for their brains and enthusiasm, not their Kate Gibbs stenographic skills, so the frustration of remaining "just a secretary" sets in for them almost as soon as they learn the ropes.

The discontent is usually mitigated by the free-and-easy office atmosphere and by the fact that secretaries are given a wide variety of responsibilities that teach them a lot about the publishing business. But, in a place as small as Viking, it's clear from the outset how entrenched the people already there are in their jobs and how minute the possibilities are for an opening. So newcomers learn fast that moving out is usually the best way to move up. In fact, the relaxed friendliness of the place and its high status in the trade have been known to lull young women into staying on long after they should have progressed to bigger things.

Editorial and executive pay varies with seniority, not sex. At the secretarial level, salaries start between $100 and $125 a week. Nice as they are, Viking will take you for as little as they can get you for, so negotiate. Salaries should be automatically reviewed after three months, and there is a liberal health-insurance policy with provisions for dentistry, psychiatry, and paid maternity leave.

5

WIDE-ANGLE VIEWS

A Greener Field

SELLING PERIPHERAL RIGHTS

While it's fairly obvious from the foregoing that discrimination against women varies from house to house only in its degree of blatancy, it should be remembered that the most obvious (and in many ways the most explicable) discrimination exists in the editorial area. "Publishing" to most jobseekers is synonymous with editing—and this is the first mistake. Every English major who makes it to New York thinks "editor"—and discrimination or no, there aren't enough of those jobs to go around.

Of the other doors that exist, subsidiary rights provides one of the best entrées into publishing. There has recently been a recognition of the fact that most companies' profits are equal to their rights income. The old feelings that "rights will take care of themselves" has pretty much faded, and rights directors are recognized as important executives in their houses. This is an area where many women are well established (Milly Marmru, Leila Karpf, Beverly Loo)—and well paid. Salaries are not yet commensurate with the contribution of rights to corporate profits—but this is a problem faced by male as well as female executives.

Rights jobs have another great plus—they're fun. Matching up books with potential buyers, conveying the hardcover publisher's enthusiasm for new books and authors, assessing the market for various categories of books—all those things require ingenuity and are highly rewarding when you see tangible results.

A job as an assistant to the director of rights gives a beginner all the on-the-job training necessary for a crack at the bigger job.

A year's experience as an assistant gives insight into the basic procedures, as well as an acquaintance with the appropriate contacts at book clubs and reprint houses. Once you've gotten a grasp of how rights are sold and have established contact with editors, you're ready to move up. And in the continual game of musical chairs that's played in publishing, you shouldn't have to wait long for an opportunity.

As for those suppressed editorial longings, in most houses, rights people have editorial privilege. After all, who knows better than the Rights Department what a book's hard-cash potential is? Many books are bought primarily for their resale value—and it's usually your option whether you wish to edit the manuscripts you acquire or simply turn them over to an in-house editor.

A great many publishers are now extensively involved in copublishing ventures with foreign publishers or in originating projects in which they retain all-language rights. Establishing and maintaining contact with foreign publishers is an important function of the rights director—and the obvious fringe benefit of travel is included. Putting together a big multi-language deal on a property has to be one of the great highs of publishing.

Because sooner or later it's all measured in dollars, the Rights Department is one of the best places to be. Your contribution is a highly visible one—and your arguments for your own advancement are easily documented when you're doing a good job.

Preparing the Book

PRODUCTION

When I began considering a career in publishing five years ago, production was about as far from my thoughts as anything could have been. To me, publishing was synonymous with editing, and I thought nothing could deter me. It was only after I'd been turned away from more doors than I care to remember, lacking as I was in both office experience and typing skills, and after the urging of three employment agencies, that I accepted the fact that my career could not be successfully launched until I had learned to type. Enrolled in a standard course, I was in good company. My classmates included women whose degrees were more impressive than mine, among them two Ph.D.'s. But there was a noticeable absence of men in the class, and I have never been able to convince myself that the male of the species has an innate knowledge of typing and can adapt more readily to an office environment than a female.

My course completed, I once more made the rounds of the employment agencies and publishing houses—this time making it past one outer office only to sit before the personnel manager of one of New York's larger publishing concerns to be asked the usual question: What was I looking for? Somewhat naïvely I related my editorial aspirations for the umpteenth time. After listening tolerantly, if impatiently, the man offered me a job as a secretary in production—there were no openings in editorial. If I hadn't been through three such interviews already, I would have believed my interviewer to be stone deaf. But after a thirty-second survey of my financial situation, I accepted the job figuring that (1) it meant that some money would be coming in for a change, and (2) as an insider I would be given an opportunity to move into the first available editorial spot more readily than an outsider.

With the detachment that hindsight affords, I can vouch for the fact that a secretarial job can easily be turned to one's advantage. While gradually becoming acclimated to an office atmosphere, one can pick up the terminology of a given field and get a firsthand view of the specific functions of the various departments that make up a publishing house.

The women that I first encountered in production were a far cry from the young, vital women of today I expected to find. Except for a few, these women had been at their present posts for more than fifteen years. They had earned their stripes at a time when women were rare in offices—outside the secretarial pool—and I imagine they must have had quite a struggle in the climb up. As a consequence, they guarded their knowledge like food in a famine, fearing that even the smallest leak would diminish the supply to fatal levels. People who feel threatened by those under them try to hold them back, thus creating an even greater feeling of job insecurity for themselves. They miss opportunities because they can never let go of the reins in their hands long enough to take hold of a stronger pair.

But the men I worked with were only too happy to launch into lengthy dissertations in answer to questions so basic as to seem inane, and readily handed out endless reading matter—which was most gratefully received. The difference in attitude may have been due to the fact that to men a secretary is not considered a threat, though from the experience of some of my female friends who began as secretaries, the men might do well to think twice.

Before long I was moved up to "production scheduler" as vacancies in the editorial department came and went unnoticed. My direction was determined in spite of myself.

Currently the production manager for the trade division of a small publishing house, I must admit that my success owes a lot to my predecessor who, at the time of my interview two years ago, frightened me into taking the job, and with it the responsibility. He told me to consider the job carefully, and to refuse it if I thought I couldn't handle it, otherwise I would be doing us both a disservice. If I did decide to take it, I would have all the responsibility I could carry.

I worked for him for a year and a half before he left for a better job, and I was promoted into his. During that time he made it a point to help me grow along with him, passing on all new information as it came his way, often going out of his way to do so. Unlike the women I had known in production, he recognized the true value of a strong backup in enabling him to move up, to let go of current responsibilities and take on more important ones. He was also the first boss I had who understood that production is an exciting field for both men and women; that to hire a woman for production work is not synonymous with hiring the handicapped. All that he taught me has proved invaluable in and out of the office, and I have tried to pass it on to those working for me.

The Production Department of a publishing house forms the nerve center around which all other departments revolve, but, as such, it is prey to relentless pressure, both physical and intellectual, stemming partially from a constant race against time. Manuscript schedules are, more often than not, tight, even before the copy reaches production, but production remains responsible overall for the bound-book date, regardless of where the delays have taken place.

In a large publishing house, there are numerous subdivisions within Production: estimating, scheduling, composition, paper, jacket manufacturing, printing and binding, and each is in the charge of a different group of people. In a small house, all of these jobs are performed by the production manager and his staff. But along with the pressures must go the benefits—for one can learn more about publishing in general, and production in particular, in one year in a small house than in five years in a large one.

Aside from the technical knowledge of book manufacturing needed, Production must have a thorough understanding of the functions of the other departments in the house, yet it is astounding how little, in turn, is known of production proceedings outside of that department.

Certainly, for a woman in production, there are various pitfalls that a man is never threatened by, such as the occasional salesman who refers to her as "the broad," or others who on first contact feel obliged to test her technical knowledge, doubtful that a woman could comprehend a machine. But these are pitfalls that no doubt gape before women in many other fields.

The compensations for working in production are obvious—

production offers tangible rewards in the form of bound books. Looking at the numbers on a sheet of paper does not afford the same exhilaration as thumbing through a book one has worked on, knowing that it has received the best possible production job.

Production still remains a field primarily staffed by men, but this is rapidly changing. For me personally, it has been overwhelmingly rewarding, as well as taxing, and from the production seat I think I have gained a better insight into all facets of publishing than I could have from any other vantage point.

The Selling of a Publishing House

ADVERTISING, PUBLICITY, LIBRARY PROMOTION

In a book publishing house, if you are not involved in the editing or the production of a book, you are involved in selling it. Although almost all sales managers are men (their clerical staffs are made up of women), the people involved in promotion are often women. Advertising managers and publicity and promotion managers are frequently women. The prejudice against women administrators is less here because promotion departments are service departments and require less administrative ability than good old-fashioned razzmatazz. Also, originally, the work involved a lot of entertaining and women were considered less expensive and better suited to ordering canapés.

As publishing involves more and more money, however, more and more men are to be found running service departments in the large publishing corporations. Harper & Row, Doubleday, Simon and Schuster, and McGraw-Hill all have men doing advertising and publicity. Although vital to a publisher's success, service departments are rarely part of the ladder leading to corporate management jobs for either men or women; an exception was

Esther Margolis of Bantam, who was recently named vice president and had to find a replacement for her old job as publicity director.

General books, adult and juvenile, have two major markets: the general public, and public and school libraries. Selling books to these markets involves advertising and sales promotion, publicity and public relations, and school and library promotion. All these jobs require the ability to write decent copy, a talent for organization, a certain glibness, and a quick wit. The pressure is often nearly intolerable, the work load is always killing, and the salaries are usually commensurate with those in other areas of publishing—that is, low. The job mortality rate and turnover are fairly high. The only place the beginner can start is as a secretary, but it is not unusual for a woman to move from secretary to department head within three to five years.

An advertising job in a publishing house is not the same as one in an advertising agency. It isn't glamorous or creative. It means schedules, budgets, percentages, and constant pressure from editors who want to know what is being done for their books. Advertising layout and copy are prepared by whatever agency has the publishing firm's account, while catalog and direct-mail copy and production are usually done in the firm's own advertising department. The manager decides what money is going to be spent where and how and on what. As a secretary in a department, you will spend your life keeping track of everything; as an assistant you will be keeping track of money and supervising production.

Depending upon the size of the publisher, "school and library services" can mean selling to anyone—corporate educational programs, loving-hands-at-home, librarians. It always means working in a department that prepares catalogs, curriculum-related mailing pieces, and conventions, and conventions, and more conventions—books are promoted to schools and libraries by showing them at national and regional meetings of educators and librarians. It involves a good deal of contact with educators and librarians on various levels. It involves writing a lot of cozy letters and arranging a lot of meals and getting to know all the people who are part of the educational establishment. It also involves a good bit of politicking for awards and prizes.

Publicity is the most unstructured and the fastest moving of the promotion departments. Theoretically, publicity is free, so the entire concentrated effort of the department is directed toward getting someone to do something for a book for no more than a telephone call or a free lunch. Publicity is nothing if not contact work—radio, television, newspapers, magazines, reviewers, columnists, awards committees. The rest of the time goes to writing releases and seeing that everyone who could conceivably do anything for a book gets a copy of it. The details of list-maintenance, mailings, photos, etc., are endless. Almost always, publicity develops specialists: writers, print media, radio, and television. In publicity, too, there is a great amount of contact with the author, who is always waiting to be sent on a cross-country media blitz.

Compared to the rest of publishing, service departments are good places to rise quickly. They are good places for a woman to escape being buried as a secretary forever. But they are also the most high-pressure jobs in publishing.

People, People Everywhere

SALES DEPARTMENT

by Wendy Jaeger
Assistant to the Vice-President, Marketing
(*Real Job: Assistant Sales Manager*)

Women who are new to the industry almost always start as secretaries and usually enter the editorial or publicity end of a company because these are said to be the glamour spots. From the aspect of advancement, this may be true: in sales and related administrative departments, there are rarely any jobs other than secretarial available for women; thus there is no incentive. An exception is school and library sales, which, in many cases, are handled by women.

It may not be as difficult as is imagined for a woman to get a job in sales. In fact, it may even be easier. The qualifications for a male applicant usually include a college degree and some selling experience. Most in-office applicants have been book salesmen. A woman, however, can be promoted from secretary. One does not need a specialized academic background in order to be promoted, which would probably not be true in other areas of publishing. Of course, it is always helpful to have a college degree, but not really necessary, because the sales and marketing aspects of book publishing mainly require time, experience, and common sense.

The standard problem, however, persists. A woman usually will receive less money for the same job, the standard excuse being that salary is commensurate with experience. But which kind of experience is more important? Experience in running an office and people, or experience in selling books?

One question frequently arises, "How does a female in a management or administrative role deal with male salesmen?" The answer is simple: Sales management should not imply "managing salesmen" but serving the salesman by giving him the best possible selling tools to enable him to increase his sales. In this way, if a salesman fails, he cannot rightfully curse the woman whose job it is to fire him; he has only himself to blame.

The work in a sales department is quite diversified and is often a springboard to better things. How many presidents of companies were formerly heads of sales departments? It is easy to run a company when you know how to sell its products. It is also fun. It might entail:

(1) Handling customer phone and mail inquiries.

(2) Overseeing printing of catalogs and order forms (ensuring that prices, trim, and titles are correct).

(3) Checking and approving expense reports, free-book requisitions, etc.

(4) Making sales conference arrangements—preparing salesmen's kits, programs, etc.

(5) Corresponding with salesmen—sending them books, bulletins, supplies, press releases, reviews, etc.

(6) Coordinating conventions and exhibits.

(7) Coordinating autographing parties with an author at a bookstore.

(8) Selling co-op ads.

(9) Coordinating with other departments (production, editorial, subsidiary rights, etc.) and attending meetings and conventions.

One should never fear being one of only a few women in a predominantly male-managed company. It's really quite easy if one thought is kept in mind, "Never try to assume a male role in a man's world; be a woman and you may be successful."

I believe the publishing industry in general is fairer to women than most industries. Granted we have a long way to go, but at least there is a beginning. In most publishing offices, women can wear pants or other fairly casual clothes. (Don't forget, most men are still bound by the custom of wearing a tie!)

The Matchmakers

WOMEN AS AGENTS

The successful agent generally has a healthy ego, a matchmaker's instinct, and the ability to say innocently "Who, me?" while wielding enormous power. Many agents are women; many are in business for themselves; and most got there via the yellow-brick road.

There is absolutely no set way to become an agent. Some

agents were editors in publishing houses and jumped straight into agenting; others started as secretaries either in publishing houses or in agencies themselves.

The agent is basically an author's business manager, handling anything that has to do with money or contracts. They function as the intermediary between author and publisher.

The editorial role that an agent plays is an individual matter. She really has two jobs: the first is defined by the nature of her relationship with the client, and the second by her work with the house. To an author the agent is generally not only a business manager, but also lay analyst, confidante, mother, social worker, friend. The agent's job is to sell the author's work to a book or magazine publisher who will do personal and professional justice to the author. She also can serve as a real catalyst in the career of a writer. It is the agent's business to see as many editors and purchasers of writing as possible and, when necessary, to match a writer and a project. Frequently it is up to the agent to make subsidiary-rights sales of an author's works.

On the other side, once a book is published an agent must do follow-up to ensure that the publishers are meeting their responsibilities toward the book in the areas of accounting, advertising, publicity, and distribution. The agent is frequently caught in the middle and given the author's dirty work to do. She becomes the buffer between the author and the publishing world.

If you have been a secretary in a book agency for more than five years, the chances are that you are in the wrong place (assuming you are competent). You might try agenting. Many have built a list of clients by reading the trade magazines, by going to "pub" parties, and by writers' sending their writing friends. The process is relatively simple.

Most agents work for a salary, and the 10 percent commission goes to the agency. The money isn't terrific. Sometimes an agent who has a moneymaking list discovers the agency is making far more on commissions from her list than she is earning in salary. When this happens, she often starts her own agency. The list of one-woman agencies is long. (So is the list of one-man agencies.) Agency exploitation seems to be evenly distributed between men and women.

Women are enjoying an equal role in agencies these days. Money, as usual, is the determining factor. Those who produce for the agency move up, those who don't leave. This was not always true, but such well-known agents as Candida Donadio, Elizabeth McKee, Phyllis Jackson, Helen Brown, and Martha Winston fought the good fight with extraordinary competence—and now female agents are numerous. In the large agencies, it is not uncommon, however, to find a male-owned management with an exclusively female staff. The problem may then be who is going to handle the writers who have clout. (I'm not sure that this is as much sexist as it is a part of the corporate syndrome.)

The agent is powerful. A good agent serves as a check on the publishing industry, and a rather cordial hostility exists between publishers and agents. Agents imply that most publishers will screw an author if given half a chance, and publishers feel that most agents are unreasonable, greedy, and ignorant of a publisher's problems. It's a hairy business, strenuous, gregarious, sometimes nasty, often creative. Those who do it, love it—they have to or they would expire.

Mss. Welcome

PAPERBACKS

In addition to increased original publishing, the paperback houses compiled an impressive list of innovations and experiments in the past year, indicating that this aspect of the publishing industry, at least, is vital, young, alive, and kicking. Tradition has not yet entrenched itself in this ever-expanding business; standard operating procedure is still to be established. New imprints, new formats, experiments with graphics and type, covers and sidelines marked the year in bold high points, possibly some low ones (not reported) and certainly an acceleration of adrenaline through the business at every level.

Publishers Weekly
February 7, 1972

There is a latent snobbism in the publishing world that implies, "Better a secretary at Random House than an associate editor at Pocket Books." Forget it. If you are looking for independence and a chance to find out what you can do, don't pass up the paperback houses.

Paperback firms offer a relatively open field to women because, as *Publishers Weekly* points out, they are almost all younger than the establishment hardcover houses, and tradition does not weigh so heavily on them. All are still running to catch up with the "paperback revolution" and the changing nature of the book market; they know they need new blood. Here, the status game works in your favor, drawing men with editorial ambitions to the hardcover publishers and leaving a vacuum into which you can rush.

Paperback houses often pay women better than hardcover houses (but it's still publishing and you're still underpaid). Paperback firms are notoriously overgenerous with titles; an "assistant managing editor" may find herself numbering the pages of manuscripts. Associate and even senior editorships often do not represent anything like the time and heartbreak they do at a hardcover house, and anyone reading your résumé will know it. On the other hand, many of these jobs do allow you to make publishing decisions, spend money, work on original manuscripts, take authors to lunch, and generally try your strength.

What kind of books will you be working with? For your parents, paperback may still equal "porn," and they will react to your new job as if you had sold yourself into white slavery. Without question, the mass-market houses continue to grind out enormous quantities of schlock, much of it reprinted from series done by those classy hardcover firms, sometimes without even being read by the paperback editor. As the Wonder-Bread-and-butter of the American reading public, this kind of publishing has its own gritty fascination. But the better houses balance this with high (if commercial) standards and some sense of social responsibility in other areas, and even the second-stringers are now rushing to put out "quality" higher-priced lines.

Some of the best paperback publishing never hits the drugstore racks but is done primarily for the school market. These "curriculum-related" materials represent a huge future growth area, as do general trade books for adolescents and children, which are only just beginning to get a major run in the bookstores.

The already strong trend toward original publishing in paperback can only increase, with paperback houses often reversing the standard process and selling hardcover reprint rights for prior publication. (Hardcover books still attract more review attention and publicity, though this, too, is changing.) Reprint sales, in either direction, represent the financial cream of publishing, and the paperback people are tired of paying out all the time. In addition, many hardcover houses are developing their own paperback lines, which effectively throws the paperback houses back on their own resources. Finally, some books simply are paperbacks by nature—handbooks for the counterculture, for example—and will never appear in hardcover at all.

In addition to this changing editorial climate, the growing school-sales departments of the major houses may provide alternatives to traditional jobs-of-entry for women. (Most male staff in publishing apprentices in sales as a matter of course, and trade-sales departments are still cigar-reeking masculine preserves.) There is room here especially for ex-teachers. Avon has twice recently hired young, relatively inexperienced women to head its school sales, and the equivalent Bantam department is headed and almost entirely staffed by women. Some houses have even experimented with women as educational area representatives; loneliness and the predations of fellow (male) travelers make for hardship duty, however.

Given this highly fluid situation, you must sometimes exert considerable ingenuity to find out what kind of house you are confronted with before you take a job. Check their product in the bookstore first; ask for a catalog and/or backlist order sheet when you go for the interview; and then ask what they have under contract for the next year (as a new line). Also find out as much as you can about where the firm's capitalization comes from, who controls it and whether this has changed in recent months. Such details can make the difference between a dead-end job and what, in the good old days, was called an opportunity.

More Women TK

THE NEWSPAPER COPY DESK

Listen, there was a little old lady—or big old lady, I don't know which because she died before I was born—who used to cover religion for an English-language morning newspaper. She existed—I've seen her clippings in the morgue. And this woman, so the story goes, rushed across the city room one afternoon shouting: "Hold it! Hold it! I just got a hot insert from the Bishop!"

Isn't that a swell story? The only one I like better is the one about the woman publisher—you probably know it. Mrs. Reid comes down to her copy desk and says imperiously: "Mr. Holcombe, who edited *this* story?" Her tone makes it clear that *this* is a disaster. Mr. Holcombe, faithful to the code of the head of the desk, replies: "Mrs. Reid, I can't tell you." Mrs. Reid, eyes narrow, says: "Well, I'll find out anyway. I already know his initials—HTK!" This is a real knee-slapper for copy editors, all of whom mark their copy HTK—Hed To Kum—when they intend to send the headline along later. And I really love it, whether it's told about Mrs. Reid, Mrs. Sulzberger, Mrs. Graham, or Mrs. Schiff.

And the lesson of those two stories is clear: Women get no place in the newsroom because they don't know anything. Every time I hear these stories, I know the lesson I am getting from my male copy-desk colleagues. Women get no place in the newsroom because they're dumb. To their credit, or to the credit of women's liberation, I haven't heard them much lately.

Many men do not like women on their desk. It is to these men an invasion of a place akin to the bathroom, the squash court, or the men's bar, or a combination of all three. Every woman who sits down at a copy desk goes through the ritual fandango. Can she be made a pet of? Can she be reduced to helplessness? She will be. Is she naïve or has she somehow missed one of the ten thousand potential double entendres that can find their way into headlines? She will be laughed at. Is she attractive and agreeable? She made it on her back. Is she dirty-mouthed and overtly tough? She will be told—indirectly—not to wear her skirts short because her balls will show. Does she shudder at foul language? Her life will be wretched.

But if she wants a good job and can survive the initiation, the desk is ideal. The salary is excellent, and on any newspaper with a Newspaper Guild contract, equal pay is protected. The work is indoors and sitting down, so pregnancy is not a physical problem. The hours and days are somewhat more regular than reporters'.

But there aren't many women on copy desks at newspapers. Young women interested in editing apparently gravitate toward magazines or books, even though in my experience, they are paid less and are given less responsibility. Women who are potential newspaper editors probably constitute a "discouraged group," in the phrase now being used by the women's law groups: they don't apply at newspapers because they assume they aren't wanted. I think this was true twenty years ago—there were plenty of reporters with tired legs, a number of castoffs, and a number of dedicated men to fill the rim of the copy desk. But the situation has changed—television is only part of it—and now there is a national shortage of copy editors and a great deal of piracy among newspapers. It is a gross oversimplification, but I would say that a woman with editing experience, knowledge of editors' marks, grammar and stylistic requirements who applied herself to a textbook and to reading her local paper for a couple of months could probably equip herself to take a stab at copy-editing.

After that, the picture is not so rosy: the road upward from the desk at a newspaper is by and large as grim as the road upward for women everywhere else. There is little pretense about it. A ranking editor at a notable American paper said to a new employee: "You'll be fortunate to be working with Miss Z—a really fine editor and person. We're lucky to have her on our desk—she'd be news editor if she weren't a woman." The number of women who have burst through this barrier is infinitesimal; it's really easier to own your own paper. Changes in state laws are having an impact, however small, on this problem. Previously a woman denied a promotion on the grounds of incapacity by reason of her sex had no recourse. Now she looks like a potential lawsuit, and management may think twice before passing her over simply because she is a woman.

There is another factor, probably more important: the heightened consciousness brought on by women's liberation in all its aspects. For years I toiled my solitary way, feeling that the problems I faced were individual and probably freakish. I now learn that I was never alone, but only felt alone. Now the newspaper sisters discuss their problems, solutions, and challenges, and we all derive great help and support from this. There is a growth through solidarity that is not imaginable until you've tried it. A woman who is in a situation where she's oppressed feels ashamed and downhearted. When she learns that the woman next to her feels just the same, her shame passes and the two of them can at a minimum laugh and, better, take action. A comparison of attempts by men to co-opt militant women is also beneficial—one learns how cheaply men think we can be bought.

There is a particular large challenge that I hope will bring more women onto copy desks: as long as papers in this country are mostly edited by men, the kinds of stories that make women cringe will not be shut off permanently. The subconscious orientation of editors remains male, and white. (See an excellent essay called "They Still Write It White," by Robert Smith, in a collection called *Our Troubled Press,* published by Little, Brown.) It will take a steady number of us to alter the consciousness of the papers. Sisters, are there takers?

Running the Boston Marathon

TEXTBOOK PUBLISHING

by Cushman Miller

A few women enter the Boston Marathon every year; but most of them drop out before the finish.

An Onlooker

"My dearr-r girl," the voice fluttered over the telephone. "These girls will do *any*thing just to see the inside of a publishing house! That's what we do—take them on tours!"

My informant was the well-known director of the Radcliffe Publishing Course, Boston's traditional means of access to the private ear of publishers. Advertised as a six-week seminar which will supply the know-how necessary to land a job straight from

English-major naïveté, it is in fact an established clearing house for "contacts"—of course, the only *real* way to editorship.

But for the bright-eyed young woman who turns over her savings for the chance at creative work, the course can also be an introduction to sex discrimination. For the Radcliffe Publishing Course is, naturally, coeducational, and the young men are courted and groomed for careers while the young women are steered toward their dead-end niches as publishing secretaries and editorial assistants.

Boston is a textbook town. Job opportunities for female novices in the two major trade houses in town—Little, Brown and Houghton Mifflin—are few and far between in any area, and depend to a large extent on social contacts.

Textbooks for elementary and high schools are produced under the supervision of an army of former teachers—mostly women, a large number of them supervised, in turn, by men. In college publishing, the system of holding women down to lower, supportive positions is imposed with even greater unconcern by the men who run it. The world of college textbooks, gathering its writing talent as it does from the college campus, revolves around the traveling representative, the man who sells books and recruits manuscripts.

"We will never hire a woman as a traveler," the vice president of one textbook house told a group at the Radcliffe course. "They don't have the physical stamina." Again and again, from marketing managers and from college travelers, I have heard the same sentiment.

One can only laugh. With their feet up on the desks of the editors' offices in Boston sit the soft, overweight men who were travelers a short time earlier. Exposed like a bad joke is the system that effectively keeps women from the top jobs: to be an editor, "marketing experience" is required. A few years as a campus representative qualifies almost any young man for the position. Yet the women who do the editors' jobs for them, who organize their lives and know their files inside out, the women who take over smoothly when an editor leaves—*until* a new man can be found, the women with superb educations who look with growing dismay at the sloppy thinking and blatant prejudice that appear in the textbooks acquired by men who never read them—these women are derided for applying for editors' jobs when they have no sales experience.

The "physical-stamina" objection is obviously farcical; to drive the company car around the campuses and have a few drinks before dinner with the textbook authors of America require little more endurance than the average housewife expends every day. Yet there are other stops to pull as Boston shows itself to be unprepared for the liberated woman.

"Honey," a Prentice-Hall interviewer told me ingratiatingly over the telephone, "this job requires up to fifty percent overnights—why, your husband wouldn't stand for that!" To my husband, calling under an assumed name five minutes later to apply for the same job, marriage was mentioned only as a desirable stabilizing factor.

By far the most well-traveled route to editorship, then, is closed to the woman as the car door slams in her face. No matter what her education or qualifications, she is pointed toward secretarial duties as a way to get in on the ground floor of book publishing. Whether her position is titled editorial assistant or secretary, it involves enough supportive, behind-the-scenes work to ensure that she will become indispensable, and thus immovable. No man will let his right-hand girl go.

"All these girls *need* is $65 to $85 a week," said the president of a large and prestigious Boston house in an overheard statement that was to bring down the wrath of the Massachusetts Commission Against Discrimination. "Why, I look on this company as a finishing school for young ladies between college and marriage." Cost of living? "Don't they all live at home with their parents?"

That situation was righted under pressure. But for women,

$14,000 to $15,000 is considered a very high, almost ceiling, annual wage, while male executives tower above them in salaries by a good $10,000 to $12,000 more.

The positions of influence, then—those that confer the power to decide what books to publish and when—go almost exclusively to men in educational publishing. The number of female acquiring-editors can be counted on one hand. The illusion of successful women in publishing is perpetuated, nonetheless, by the many intelligent—if not ambitious—women who make the actual production of books their business. "Publishing is good to women," the production manager of one textbook house remarked; and his department was indeed filled with female production editors and designers with intelligence and good taste. But those women could copy-edit and design a book until they were blue in the face and still have no power to stop publication of a book if even the most rigorous editing could not disguise its vapidity. A woman who has been a successful production editor, moreover, holds no key to a good job in an acquisitions department—she still lacks the prerequisite marketing experience.

Advertising departments of book publishers will hire women as copywriters and even as directors because advertising is a traditional field for educated women. The knowledge of "the market" which is gained in a job of this sort, however, is rarely considered marketable when it comes to an influential editorial job. We are enjoined once more, "Know your place, woman."

There seems to be no out. Young men in the Radcliffe Publishing Course walk away with assistant editorships ("the assistant editor takes his job home with him") and equally well-qualified women "start out" typing—and end up typing. But for women of pluck and cunning, the marathon can be endured, and there are prizes of a sort, at the finish.

When you apply for the job you want, tell the interviewer about the outrageous discriminatory experiences you have had, or have heard of. Nobody wants to be the bad guy, and more and more companies are hiring token women as college representatives, for example. If you show that you are aware of the system men have set up against women, you just may unnerve the interviewer sufficiently to get the job.

Use your supportive role to its full capacity—the more you know about the top jobs, the more easily you will be able to land them. Apply for jobs with more responsibility elsewhere, and write your own job description of the work you have been doing. Detail exactly what you *did,* not merely what you were supposed to do.

Better, use your imagination to invent new jobs—some with no sex stereotypes pre-attached. In a company with no market research group, suggest one, and put yourself in a position to gain the marketing experience you are not likely to get elsewhere.

In a town as hidebound with tradition as Boston, it will be difficult. But we can always use the old guerrilla strategy, and we should remember the success of a few poorly armed colonists fighting a staff and formidable red-coated army. They won, and so can we.

Liberty shall not be banned in Boston!

WOMEN ON THE AIR[1]

by Helen Epstein

In 1970–71 women tripled their previous representation at Hastings Law School in San Francisco; passed 35 percent of the bad checks in Raleigh, North Carolina; were legally recognized as qualified to deliver newspapers by the New York State Legislature; and held a National Women's Political Caucus in the nation's capital. New and angry books, headed by Germaine Greer's *The Female Eunuch* and Kate Millett's *Sexual Politics,* hit the bestseller lists as well as the consciousness of American women.

The broadcasting industry did not remain unscathed. In

[1] © 1971 The Trustees of Columbia University in the City of New York. Reprinted, with permission, from "Survey of Broadcast Journalism 1970–1971" (Grosset & Dunlap, New York, N.Y.).

August the American Civil Liberties Union brought charges against ABC News for alleged "unlawful discrimination against women." According to the ACLU, less than one-fifth of the division's 250 employees were female; of these, 33 were secretaries, 7 were researchers, 2 were assistants to a male producer, 1 was assistant to a male director, 1 was assistant to a male film editor, and only 4 held independent positions. In March three women's groups filed charges with the FCC, the Equal Employment Opportunity Commission, and the Office of Federal Court Compliance of the Department of Labor against WRC Radio and Television, an NBC owned-and-operated station in Washington, D.C. As in the complaint against ABC News, the charges were that women at WRC had been overwhelmingly restricted to secretarial jobs and low pay. That left CBS, notoriously conservative in employing women. In May William S. Paley presented his network's case: although no women sat on the network's fifteen-man board of directors, 42 percent of the CBS work force was female and 13 percent of its executives were women.

Protestations of this sort were plentiful this year, and, in many cases, deceptive. The juiciest jobs in the industry—the on-air network newscasters—have been given to few women. NBC, by far the most progressive network in gauging the aptitude of women, lists only five of a total of fifty-six persons designated correspondent. ABC lists two of forty-two. CBS and Group W list none. "I have the strong feeling," Reuven Frank, president of NBC told *Newsweek,* this year, "that audiences are less prepared to accept news from a woman's voice than from a man's."[2]

While 94 percent of those television news directors (all male) who responded to a recent survey conducted by Irving Fang of the University of Minnesota's Journalism Department indicated their readiness to hire qualified women reporters, only 45 percent could say there was, in fact, even one woman reporter working at their

[2] Women's voices seem to be authoritative enough off camera. Several distinguished network producers and producers of Du Pont award-winning documentaries are women.

station. Twenty years ago, when Pauline Frederick, an M.A. in International Law and an experienced international affairs reporter, asked her boss why she was kept off the air, the ABC News executive informed her that "women's voices lack authority." This year, an Ohio radio station manager refused to hire a female newscaster on the grounds that "news coming from a woman sounds like gossip."

This persistent prejudice has kept women off the air since the inception of television and has carried over into management, where women in other than secretarial positions are conspicuously absent from board rooms and executive suites. "Women need help breaking thru the ordinary low- and middle-level broadcast positions to upper-level status," contends Maureen Bunyon of Boston's WGBH. "In the Bay area," writes KRON's Valerie Coleman, "I know of none." There will be no real equality for women reporters and news personnel, they say, until women move into management. The 1971 radio and television volume of *The Working Press of the Nation,* which includes a majority of television stations in the U.S., lists only twenty-one female newscasters on locally originated newscasts, as compared with over six hundred men. The reason for this, small stations claim, is that women cannot be expected to carry heavy equipment, although lighter equipment and gamer women are rapidly rendering that argument obsolete. No such obstacle, moreover, exists for the radio reporter, an almost exclusively male job category, except when a woman is called in to moderate a panel on "How to Catch a Husband" or to interview the wife of a man-in-the-news.

Radio discrimination against women transcends both political stance and style: it is found in liberal and conservative managements, on rock and on classical music stations, on all-news formats, and on mixed programming. There are, however, three radio stations in the country run by women. The oldest, WHER Memphis, is sixteen years old, and hired its first *male* announcer last year. One radio station that has created a new series of programs specifically aimed at the intelligent and liberation-conscious woman is WBAI, the Pacifica station in New York City. At this writing, WBAI carries three programs especially addressed to women: "Womankind," a weekly series comprised of discussions and commentary from the feminist community; "Consciousness-Raising," an on-the-air group session which has dealt with masturbation, marriage, and puberty among other subjects; and "Electra Rewired," an all-night talk show hosted by a woman. The need for this kind of broadcasting was underscored as soon as the three programs were instituted; after the first broadcast of "Consciousness-Raising," WBAI received more listener mail than for any other first broadcast in its history.

Unfortunately, WBAI's programming is the exception which highlights the rule. While many radio stations prefer to ignore women entirely, 207 local television stations across the country employ special women's editors or women's directors who deal exclusively with what is felt to be "women's news." Eleven are men.

As might be expected, there is a direct correlation between women reporters, large news staff, and metropolitan centers. Washington and New York both feature more than ten on-the-air women reporters, whereas there are none in places such as Sioux Falls or Fort Wayne. "We have wanted to have a woman on the news staff for quite some time," writes Bonnie Libhart, talk show hostess at KAIT-TV Jonesboro, Arkansas. "To no avail. When a position was vacated recently, it was given to a man less qualified than myself."

Tokenism, however, is a pattern which appears throughout the country. Although the last year has witnessed a spurt of hiring, the overall picture indicates only superficial change. In Peoria, Illinois, all three local television stations employ women, but Sally Larvick of WMBD reports she is the only female on a news staff of fourteen. At WIIC Pittsburgh, Pat Kiely is one woman working with nine men; in Oklahoma City, WKY's Pat Shockey is a part-time one of eight; and in Atlanta, black reporter Jaci Hayward is one of two women on WAGA's news staff of seventeen.

Another pattern that has emerged from the hiring spree, and one that reinforces the first, is the hiring of black women. Both of Denver's female broadcasters are blacks, three of Cleveland's five are blacks, as is one of Detroit's two women. In New York, there are seven women in the employ of the three network affiliates: five are black, one is Puerto Rican, and one, Pia Lindstrom, is white.

The promotion of Pia Lindstrom is characteristic of the way women, black or white, are packaged by station publicity departments once the news departments have agreed to hire them. *"News isn't always glamorous,"* reads the logo WCBS placed beside a subtly-shaded photo of Miss Lindstrom in *TV Guide. "But Pia is. Pia brings her own special qualities to every story she covers. Be it a subway evacuation. The arrival of the circus. Or interviewing unusual New Yorkers."* Lest the implicit condescension elude the male reader, he has only to apply the formula to, say, John Chancellor; *"News isn't always attractive,"* this ad would read, next to a smoky snapshot of NBC's top correspondent. *"But John is."* Needless to say, John would not be covering the arrival of a circus, or interviewing "unusual" New Yorkers.

Marlene Sanders of ABC was the first woman on any network to be permitted, albeit briefly, to anchor a nationwide evening news program when she filled in for an ailing anchorman in 1964. "I am still subject to the prejudices of particular assignment editors and the producers of the evening news, who have, on occasion, kept me off sports subjects and riots even though I've covered Vietnam and the Columbia riots. Many men are emotionally unable to accept the fact that a woman doesn't need to be 'protected' and doesn't want to be." In Oklahoma City, Pat Shockey has been restricted entirely to fashion reporting except when she fills in for someone who is sick. "Personally," she says, "I would hope that my six years of reporting would fit me for more meaningful work."

Concomitant with the policy of assigning only "ladies' stories" to female reporters is the practice of hiring former models, receptionists, and secretaries whose faces and figures count for more than their résumés. The biography of Jeanne Parr, former WCBS weather girl now at KNXT Los Angeles, provides a typical history of the Aspiring Girl Reporter. "Blonde, statuesque," reads her bio, "News Correspondent Jeanne Parr has been whistled at (by boys of almost any age) and shot at (by a sniper . . .). The very next day, she interviewed the King and Queen of Nepal at a posh affair, dressed in a stylish gown, in contrast to the steel helmet and old slicker she wore the night before." Miss Parr began her career, like many of the women now on the air, interviewing other women in Madison, Wisconsin. Later, during the 1963 New York newspaper strike, she appeared on "The Midday News" with Harry Reasoner, "Interviewing prominent women, attending Broadway and motion picture openings, commenting on fashions, and visiting the kitchens of famous restaurants." Eight years later, she and Ruth Ashton Taylor are KNXT's only women reporters.

The prime examples of discriminatory employment practices, however, are the weather girls, often the first women employees a station allows on the air. Apparently hired for their skill at projecting mindlessness, weather girls are often nothing more than clothes horses for the local department store.

The most blatant case of sexual exploitation this year occurred at WSNS Chicago, which produces a news program entitled "Heart of the News." Linda Fuoco, a recent graduate of the University of Illinois, delivered the headlines each midnight from her sponsor's product, a heart-shaped bed. That a programming gimmick as degrading as this could gain air time is an illustration of the power that an all-male management has to determine which women are hired, what image they present, and what events they are suited to report.

Such control is frequently exercised with regard to male appearance, too, but not to the extent demonstrated at WABC New York in June, when Melba Tolliver, the station's black reporter, changed her hair style. The management asserted its right to determine Miss Tolliver's image and kept her away from in-studio work—until a leak to the press produced poor publicity for the station, whereupon the reporter was speedily returned to her usual routine. "The problem," maintains Geraldine Lange, public affairs director of WBHK San Francisco, "is to be able to project yourself as you really are—not as someone thinks you ought to be."

An all-male management also decides what news goes on the air, whether it be in prime time (when only 32 percent of the adult audience is male) or in daytime (when a mere 17 percent of the viewers are grown men). The Du Pont Survey, in conjunction with the YWCA, this year, questioned women throughout the country about their satisfaction with television coverage of women. Sixteen percent replied that they found it excellent, 22 percent said it was adequate, 43 percent said it was inadequate, and 19 percent termed it "bad."

Flint, Michigan: "No coverage on facilities, on child care, abortion, family planning. Equal pay, equal work? Not in a G.M. Town!"

Rochester, New York: "I can't remember a time when a women's lib rally or any activist meeting run by women has been covered by any of the TV or radio stations."

Indianapolis, Indiana: "There has been little effort to program around the day-to-day concerns of women from diverse backgrounds."

Salt Lake City, Utah: "In our city, one rarely ever even hears any discussion on the subject."

Berkeley, California: "Not enough unless it's a sensational or humorous story of a 'liberated' restaurant, club, etc."

Johnstown, Pennsylvania: "If anything, the humorous approach has increased due to women's lib."

Mason City, Iowa: "The local news media do not appear to be aware there is a women's liberation movement."

Charleston, West Virginia: "One station is 'trying out weather girls'—and this only as a result of other TV stations having had a weather girl for some time."

Sixty-five percent of the YWCA women surveyed said there had been no improvement in television's attitude toward women; the other 35 percent said it had been slight. When questioned specifically about daytime television, the Du Pont correspondent in Los Angeles (female) replied that local programming "presupposes an audience of women who have given up on intelligence"; the Du Pont correspondent in Honolulu (female) was unable to watch the entire day, concluding that daytime television is aimed at "morons—male or female"; in Chicago, the Du Pont correspondent (male) begged off with the concession that on television "women are to be manipulated or ignored."

There have been scattered instances of improved coverage this year: KWYO Sheridan, Wyoming, reportedly promotes a day care center for working mothers and announces women's meetings over the air free of charge. In Miami and San Francisco, the educational stations have developed new and better ways of presenting news of interest to women as dispassionately as anything else they feature. In Salt Lake City, KSL-TV produced a five-part series on women convicts in one of the few programs to recognize their existence. Television and radio stations cross country have programmed a special or two on abortion and women's liberation this year. KYW Philadelphia has advised its staff to avoid presenting stereotypes of women; KAUM Houston was the only station in the country to broadcast this year's Chicana Conferencia. Several stations preempted regular formats and programming for a day August 26, 1970, when women rallied to observe the fiftieth anniversary of women's voting rights, and substituted all-women newscasts and specials on women. The inadequacy of *year-round* coverage, however, was made clear to KQV Pittsburgh when an irate women's group pelted the building housing their studios with fresh eggs.

Inequities in job opportunities for women are not restricted to television and radio news departments. In public affairs departments, the situation is hardly better, and on the talk shows, which are increasingly oriented toward public affairs, it is worse. There are four major television talk shows broadcast nightly in the United States; all four have male hosts. During the day, when there are several syndicated talk shows as well as hundreds of locally originated programs, male hosts are consistently given "serious" formats, while hostesses are hired to chat, cook, garden, or exercise. "The Phil Donahue Show," syndicated in forty-two markets across the country, regularly invites distinguished journalists, politicians, ecologists, and other specialists who participate in intelligent discussion. In May 1971, for example, Donahue was host to the Last Poets, politician Lester Maddox, journalist Seymour Hersh, psychologist Arthur Janov, and journalist Charles Silberman. In addition, a doctor discussed families with drug problems, a sociologist discussed sex roles as they are taught to children, and a gynecologist reported on the newest method of sterilization.

"The Dinah Shore Show," shown over 187 NBC-affiliated stations, is, by comparison, almost a caricature of programming. Heralded as "a potpourri of entertainment, information, conversation, and demonstrations of particular interest to today's woman," the program plan for the third week in January 1971 read:

January 18: Carol Burnett instructs Dinah in the comedienne's slimming exercises.

January 19: Gardening expert Jerry Baker shows how to grow spring flowers in cake pans during the winter.

January 20: David Frost chats with Dinah and samples her maple-nut ice cream.

January 21: Myrna Loy talks about her career and helps Dinah fill lunch boxes. Dinah sings, "I've Been Workin' on the Railroad."

For the daytime viewer who finds this tame fare, Virginia Graham, television's Mistress Chatter, is syndicated in sixty-one markets, drawing vistors of distinction into vapid conversation around her pet subjects, sex and marriage.

Virginia Graham is, however, one of the few women who has

insisted upon and has been granted control of the production staff of her show. Usually it is an all-male management which creates a show, decides its tone and character, and hires the host or hostess. In most cases, the production staff surrounding the talk show hostess is also all-male, as is the programming department which conceives and advertises it.

A unique and extremely successful example of an alternate approach to daytime programming should be noted at WBZ-TV Boston. There hostess Sonya Hamlin and her cohost Jack Cole appear on "For Women Today," a show whose production staff consists entirely of women and whose programs enjoy a reputation for relevance and depth. At WLWC-TV Columbus, Ohio, Ann Walker produces and hosts a weekly public affairs series, "Focus on Columbus," which in June investigated Model Cities, prostitution, and hunger in Columbus. Another instance of apt selection of both hostess and format is evinced in the now midday talk show "Straight Talk" on WOR-TV New York.

"Straight Talk" hostesses Carol Jenkins, a young black, and Elinor Guggenheimer, an older white, now provides the only serious public affairs daytime program seen on the city's six commercial stations aside from Aline Saarinen's "For Women Only." In June, Miss Saarinen left the program to become network television's first female overseas bureau chief.[3] She was replaced at home by Barbara Walters, perhaps television's most successful woman. Since her arrival as a writer for the "Today" show in 1961, Miss Walters has transformed the role of "Today" hostess from that of pleasant mannequin to full participant, an achievement capped by her exclusive interview with President Nixon last March. On the West Coast, much of the innovative investigative reporting at KRON-TV San Francisco has been the work of Myra Scott, whose "Myra Scott's Predicament" is a daily feature of the station's news program.

It is significant that, except for rarities like Saarinen and

[3] Editor's Note: Aline Saarinen died July 13, 1972.

Walters, reporters and hostesses complain of, or suspect, a salary differential between themselves and their male counterparts. While it is difficult to ascertain comparable salaries (due to variable schedules, in-studio versus field reporting, and popularity of the individual newscasters), it is clear that many women receive far less money for their work than men. "I am earning on a par with my male counterparts for the first time in twenty years," reports Virginia Graham. "My salary wasn't on a par with the men's until I put a stop to it," concurs Sonya Hamlin. "I'll guess that I am paid less," agrees June Miller, hostess at WSPD-TV Toledo.

Bonnie Libhart, women's editor and hostess for KAIT-TV Jonesboro, Arkansas, discovered that men were being paid *five* times the amount she was receiving per guest, and her work securing talent and researching background material remains without compensation. In Bakersfield, California, KERO-TV's Sunny Scofield says that her cameraman (who until two years ago was her prop boy) now makes almost double her salary. In Atlanta, where the city's three network affiliates now employ six female reporters and three talk show hostesses, news executives claim no differential in salaries between men and women. The women disagree. "Once when I asked for a raise," one of the nine told *Atlanta* Magazine, "I was told 'We can't give you one. What would the other girls think?' The 'other girls' were secretaries, for heaven's sake!"

Women are now visibly present at the majority of television stations throughout the country. Yet any gains they have made in broadcasting this year fall entirely within the realm of tokenism, and prospects for their full integration into television and radio journalism look bleak indeed. Traditionally, the television newscaster has been a man, and also traditionally, he has landed his job through his prototypically American looks rather than through his sagacity as a newsman. In the visual medium the cultural model he represents counts for more than any writing, reading, or analytical skill he may possess. Thus even those women who have had successful careers in the medium are pessimistic about the possibility that women will truly integrate its work force. "As far as I know," says Pauline Frederick with a smile, "no woman was even *considered* for the position vacated by Chet Huntley on NBC's evening news."

No Happy Medium

oPRESSion

by Marian Ellias

John Doe, slim, attractive, but complex executive editor of a leading newspaper, is 41 years old today, but he doesn't look it.

How does he manage to combine a successful career with this happy home life he has created in his gracious Georgetown home?

In an interview today, pert, vivacious Mr. Doe revealed his secret. He relaxes after a day of whirlwind activity of the newspaper world by whomping up a batch of his favorite pecan-sauerbraten cookies for his thriving family.

Sound familiar? The above is an excerpt from a parody written by *Washington Post* women. Substitute Brenda for John and *she* for *he* and you've seen the cliché-packed item hundreds of times in newspapers and magazines.

Many women feel that the item is a typical example of the derogatory image of women presented by the press. Although advertising and TV are, perhaps, more obvious offenders, these women say something should also be done about the press.

Here are some of the ways the press puts down women as shown in the item:

The use of adjectives, which one woman called "gratuitous" and another termed "vulgar personal assessments." A reference to youth, which is a way of keeping women "in their place" and of suggesting that they are mindless, inconsequential creatures. And no matter what her career is, stories about a woman usually include the information that she runs a home (even if she really doesn't) and a recipe (even if she couldn't care beans about cooking). But perhaps most important, there is a patronizing attitude not found in stories about men.

Observers of the press—women readers, newspaperwomen, magazine employees, and feminists—have a number of other gripes. They object to:

The use of the husband's name to identify the woman. Feminists are urging the use of *Ms.,* rather than *Miss* or *Mrs.* A woman's marital status is always an issue; she often remains a "divorcee" for life, for example.

The use of cheesecake photos and obscene camera angles.

The use of "woman" as an adjective, as in "Woman Panther Returned to Jail." Feminist Mary Phillips says the above headline shows that the press assumes a person to be a man unless otherwise noted.

In a word, the observers find the press sexist.[1]

One newspaperwoman said that papers use words such as "shapely blonde" to attract attention to the stories, and some writers, including a number of women, feel that such descriptions are essential to the story. One suggested solution was to at least get rid of the stereotypes and demeaning characterizations.

A pet hate is the women's section of newspapers. Women's pages are "repositories of trivia, advertisers' propaganda, and so-called society news," said a report by Cleveland newswomen. The implication seems to be that women aren't interested in the rest of the paper. It has been said that women's pages resulted from the feeling (by male editors) that women had to be lured to their own section.

[1] The *Columbia Journalism Review* awarded a "dart" to AP for this lead on a battlefront story, October 29, 1973: "TEL AVIV—Premier Golda Meir of Israel, wearing a beige dress and packing a white handbag, visited Israeli troops in Egypt. . . ."

At a conference of women's editors, Colleen Dishon, president of *Features and News, Inc.,* Chicago, said that the men who control newspapers are not ready to change women's pages because managements need to cling to an image of an impossibly ideal woman and because top editors need to be accepted socially in the communities.

Although that may be true, a nationwide survey of 100 women's-page editors showed that many of them are modifying or abandoning some traditional practices to make news stories and features more relevant to their readers. Some papers don't call it women's news anymore. The Grand Rapids *Press* has a "Flair" section and the Chicago *Daily News* calls its section "Everyday/ for and about people."

Magazines also have received a lot of criticism. "Women have been put down in women's magazines for years," said freelance writer Sandie North. "It may be more subtle than in newspapers, but it's there." She said that men who work for women's magazines have the best jobs but still feel denigrated. "They don't want to rock the money boat, so they never publish any disturbing ideas."

Betty Friedan, who writes a column for *McCall's,* has, in the past, been highly critical of the role American magazines have had in shaping the standard view of women. She said that after 1949, when women were no longer needed as wartime workers, the magazines' main idea was that "fulfillment as a woman had only one definition—the housewife-mother." She emphasized that magazine editors are "less interested in ideas . . . than in selling the things that interest advertisers."

Two magazines especially devoted to the married woman, the *Ladies' Home Journal* and *McCall's,* "seem out of touch with the younger generation," according to A. Kent MacDougall in the *Wall Street Journal.* "Some industry executives say that unless the two magazines start wooing and winning younger readers, one or both could be in serious trouble."

In March 1970, recognizing that the *Ladies' Home Journal* had not been wooing them, 100 women occupied the *Journal* offices for a day. Their list of demands included employment of more black staff members, higher pay for secretaries, a day care center, and the ouster of editor-publisher, John Mack Carter.

Trucia Kushner, a participant in the protest, said in *Women's Wear Daily* that the women had picked the *Ladies' Home Journal* "because it so typifies the demeaning paternal and sentimental attitude that women's magazines take toward their underestimated readership."

Another invader remembered that when they entered the offices, one woman editor kept telling them to stop being so shrill. "Carter started out being very patronizing," she said. "The *Journal* features the line: 'The magazine women believe in.' We told them we didn't believe.

"Male staffers wouldn't let us in the ladies' room, so we liberated the men's john for a while. The press had been coming in and out, and then a TV reporter came in with a lot of equipment. He knocked into one woman who said: 'Watch that mother-fucking equipment.' He told *her* to watch it. Then we jumped him and all of the women in the room yelled, 'Out, out, out,' and we shoved them out and they left without their story."

What resulted from the confrontation was an agreement by the editors to publish a special eight-page section. Written and edited by feminists, it ran in August of 1970. As for the other demands? Dick Kaplan, a managing editor, said there has been "massive disinterest" by *Journal* women in such items as day care. In addition, he said that he believed it would be an "enormous expense" and that there was a zoning problem.

However, Kaplan said the invasion had led the editors, "to take younger women staff members a little more seriously and to bring them into the process more." He said that his secretary now edits some manuscripts.

The magazine received 2,000 letters on the women's lib

supplement and Kaplan called it a "substantial" amount, but not a record. About 34 percent liked the section, 46 percent attacked it, and 20 percent had mixed feelings.

Carter later said: "Some of the complaints made about our magazine by Women's Lib types were right. There has been a lot of silliness cranked out to sell products and life-styles to women, but it will never happen in this magazine again."

Newsweek has reported that most women's magazines are "as yet unsure how to deal with new challenges presented by the Women's Liberation movement," but are "hurriedly changing in taste and tone as they strive to keep pace with changing times." However, the magazines "hesitate to move too far for fear of losing millions of readers who still rate house and family above a campaign for equal status with men."

Although there have been numerous articles on women's liberation, most feminists and some other observers feel that it has had a bad press. Ben Malkin, an editorial writer for the Ottawa *Citizen,* told an editorial writers' convention in Boston that comments about bra burners, the use of obscene language, and the invasion of men's bars were fringe stuff that "has been vulgarly and mistakenly emphasized by the press to the neglect of the movement's more important targets."

Another man who objects to the media's treatment of women is Jim Gash, local-news reporter of WNEW, a New York radio station. Gash, in a letter to *Women's Wear Daily,* said its coverage of the August 26, 1970, Strike for Equality was "snide, bigoted, juvenile, embarrassing, and most important—totally unprofessional." The *Chicago Journalism Review* called coverage of the August 26th demonstration "a media circus."

Representative Martha Griffiths (D.–Mich.) said that editors did not take the day seriously.

Because of the media's treatment of women's rights subjects, some feminist groups have refused to deal with the press or will talk only to women. Other feminists feel that the only answer is to control their own publications. Among publications no longer run by men is Atlanta's *Great Speckled Bird.*

For those feminists who will talk to the press, KNOW of Pittsburgh publishes a list of "reporters you can trust."

Some editors do not trust feminists to cover women's rights news because they feel they will be biased. "This is like saying a Republican shouldn't be allowed to cover Nixon," one newspaperwoman said. "It's a question of our professionalism." Of course a major reason that women are treated poorly in the press is that there are few women executives who have the power to keep out offensive images.

Typical of the situation women journalists encounter is the one described in the *Chicago Journalism Review* by *Chicago Daily News* reporter Diane Monk. "There isn't one woman managing editor, city editor, or staff photographer on any of the four major Chicago newspapers. Rewritemen, as the name implies, also are all men." Only 12 percent of the editorial jobs at the *Chicago Sun-Times* are filled by women. A *New York Times* survey showed that only 82 of 700 employees in writing and editing jobs were women.

As for salaries, 25 of the Newspaper Guild's 134 contracts do not include parity for women. In these contracts, the publishers "still couldn't bring themselves to agree that reporting women's news was reporting, period," commented the Guild.

But women throughout the United States and Canada have been doing something about their oppression by the press.

Cosmopolitan, a favorite feminist target, has been picketed and boycotted. Stating that the magazine was "geared to selling women as sexual objects," one group charged that *Cosmopolitan* exploited "sexual differences" and fostered anxiety among its readers about their ability to attract men. Editor Helen Gurley Brown replied that *Cosmopolitan* was "very pro-women's lib" and that she thought it was wonderful that a woman was "sexually desirable."

Newswomen at the *New Orleans States-Item* ran engagement

announcements with pictures of the prospective grooms rather than the brides-to-be.

In Atlanta, women reporters presented the publisher of the *Constitution Journal* with a petition demanding equality in assignments.

Women reporters at the *Delaware County Times* in Chester, Pennsylvania, wore signs stating: "Don't Tread on Me! Women Are People."

A group visited the *New York Times* to discuss issues that newswomen throughout the country have been complaining about —hiring and promotion of women, the women's page, and sexism. Abe Rosenthal, *Times* managing editor, said he would ask the editors "to try harder to avoid the quick stereotypes such as 'the blonde divorced grandmother.'" The next week a *Times* bulletin said in part: "A few things have cropped up that suggest we have not always given women the equal status they seek and deserve. Look, for instance, at this passage: 'Now 18 years old, tall and pretty, she won a tuition scholarship . . .' And look at this one: 'Mrs. Jones, a lively blonde, worked with the group's women growing food . . .' Would similar phrases have suggested themselves if the subjects had been men? Probably not."

Despite the *Times*'s suggestion to its staff, demeaning images sometimes still appear. A sports story about a race at Le Mans concluded with: "Tradition is being flaunted [*sic*] also by Marie-Claude Beaumont, a 29-year-old blonde French pin-up, who will be the first woman pilot here in 20 years. Miss Beaumont . . . is an expert rallyist. She'd also look very good in the back seat of a car."

Sometimes even when feminists cover women's-rights activities, strange things happen to their stories.

Maryanne McNellis and Ellen Fleysher were assigned by the New York *Daily News* to cover a feminist event. It was agreed that they, not a rewriteman, would write the stories. But early on the day of the event, McNellis phoned in and was told to give her information to an experienced rewriteman. "The first thing that struck us was the breach of the promise that we could write it ourselves," said Fleysher. The two felt that the story was well written, with a few exceptions. The story said: "only a few thousand strong," describing the attendance. " 'Only' degraded the day," Fleysher said.

What they really objected to were the headlines, captions, and choice of photographs. One picture showed a woman in a ribbed sweater wearing a Marine cap. The caption: "She's got a Marine cap . . . now how about a boot?" "A boot in the ass, maybe?" asked Fleysher.

The two women took their complaints on the handling of the story to the metropolitan editor. Soon there were seven male editors in the room.

"Your front-page headline, 'Gals Unbutton Their Lib,' was pure sexist," Fleysher said. "If this had been a civil rights demonstration . . . your headline is comparable to 'Blacks Go Cotton-Pickin' Down Fifth Avenue.' "

The managing editor admitted that the women might have a point.

Two other New York reporters, Lindsy Van Gelder and Bryna Taubman, then of the *New York Post,* also decided to confront their editors. Their action began when Van Gelder, a self-proclaimed baseball nut, was assigned a story on Nancy Seaver, wife of Mets' pitcher Tom Seaver. When she turned the story in she said she didn't want a by-line. That created a flurry, so she finally agreed to permitting a by-line on that story if she got no more such assignments.

The next day she was assigned a story on Joan Hodges, wife of then Mets' manager, Gil Hodges. She objected and Taubman supported her. They sent a memo to the city editor citing the clause in the Newspaper Guild contract stating that a reporter's by-line may not be used if he or she objects. Their memo said: "Our political belief in the equality of all people demands that we refuse by-lines on stories . . . which recognize women in ways that the *Post* does not recognize men. One example of this is stories about women whose news value is based on their husbands' accomplishments. We are convinced that there are many women in this city who have achieved success without the aid of a marriage contract and are more deserving of recognition."

They were fired for "gross insubordination."

The Guild interceded and the two were eventually rehired after three-fourths of the reporters sent in memos saying they were refusing by-lines until further notice.

"Our decision not to do this type of story was not something personal against the women involved," Van Gelder said. "We don't want to imply that being a housewife is an easy job. But we don't think papers should glorify being a wife."

Separate classified ads have disturbed a number of feminists. The American Newspaper Publishers Association disagreed, and went to court to oppose an Equal Employment Opportunity Commission edict requiring the elimination of segregated ads. Later the ANPA decided the suit was unnecessary because two court decisions had held that newspapers did not have to screen ads. However, a number of publishers have desegregated ads voluntarily or to avoid litigation under regulations issued by state agencies.

Male-only press clubs also have come under attack. The Gridiron Club dinners in Washington and the San Francisco Press Club have been picketed. The Milwaukee Press Club was sued by several members of a journalism society. Some clubs, however, have decided to admit women, among them the National Press Club in the District of Columbia.

Women reporters have also complained about being kept from private clubs and sports press boxes. One of the exceptions is Washington's RFK Stadium, which recently allowed a woman television reporter on the field, in the press box, and in the clubhouse.

The Washington newswomen have been very active in organizing to secure better treatment for themselves and for women who become news subjects. The newswomen drew up a list of grievances. It said in part: "Newspapers must purge themselves of the sexual stereotypes if the climate of the society is to change in the area of women's rights." The statement was presented to editors at the *Post* and the *Star*. Ben Bradlee, the *Post's* executive editor, agreed with it and issued a memo to the staff, stating: "The meaningful equality and dignity of women is properly under scrutiny today . . . because this equality has been less than meaningful and the dignity is not always free of stereotype or condescension." In the news columns, "discrimination against women is generally unconscious but nonetheless offensive.

"Words like 'divorcee, grandmother, blonde' (or 'brunette'), or 'housewife' should be avoided in all stories where, if a man were involved, the words 'divorcé,' 'grandfather,' 'blond,' or 'householder' would be inapplicable. In other words, they should be avoided. Stories involving the achievement of women are often implicitly condescending. They imply 'pretty good for a woman.'"

The day after Bradlee's directive, Charles Seib, managing editor of the *Star,* issued a similar memo.

The Washington women say that they have to keep reminding the copy desk to make sure that the directives are followed. *Time* Magazine had a brief story about the Bradlee memo and noted that a post-directive story described Leonore Romney, a Senate nominee, as a "60-year-old grandmother." *Time's* headline: "Grandmothers Die Hard."

The Dallas *Times-Herald* has liberated "Mrs." and "Miss" in its women's news coverage. It also now uses "Grace Smith" rather than "Mrs. George Smith" when marital status is not pertinent to the story.

One of the most significant actions occurred at Time Inc., where 147 women employees, most of them researchers, accused the company of "keeping women in the lower echelons" of its staffs.[2] The group was the largest up to that time to charge an em-

[2] See articles herein on Time Inc. publications and related material in Appendix.

ployer with sex discrimination. The New York State Division of Human Rights found "probable cause" for the complaint. The outcome was that Time Inc., said it would "actively" integrate all jobs and pay and promote employees without regard to sex or marital status. The company is required to report quarterly to the Human Rights Division.

At *Newsweek* a somewhat similar situation exists.[3]

The Newspaper Guild decided that its major effort one year would be directed toward obtaining full equality and opportunity for women and minorities in the newspaper industry. A conference was held on the industry's discrimination against women, attended by 97 women and 20 men. The conference stated that unequal treatment would "no longer be tolerated" and called upon the Guild to take steps to eliminate it.

The Women's Rights Committee of the Cleveland Guild studied the situation at the *Press* and *Plain Dealer* and met with both managements. The women also attacked the stereotypes, saying: "How many times must we be told that Golda Meir is a grandmother?" The *Press* agreed to avoid stereotyping.

A similar committee collected information about the Indianapolis *Star* and *News*. The group compiled a file of "demeaning, condescending, and patronizing" news stories and ads for a "manifesto" to management.

Lindsy Van Gelder has neatly disposed of the media bosses' principal defense against charges of sexist bias: namely, that they are only reflecting the prejudices of our society. Van Gelder noted that when she first began reporting for New York newspapers, the media identified "Negroes" in crime stories, and "practically the only time blacks got mentioned in the paper was when they held up a candy store, unless they were Pearl Bailey or Willy Mays. Then newspapers took the lead in wiping out this type of discrimination. If they have a precedent . . . then they can do it again."

[3] See article on *Newsweek,* page 56.

Still the Second Sex

NEWSPAPER REPORTING

by Nancy Borman

In·March 1970 when I was writing for the *Long Island Press*'s "For and About Women" section, I was assigned to do a feature on Letty Cottin Pogrebin, author of *How to Make It in a Man's World*. Not that the *Press* actually wanted women to make anything (beyond pumpkin-raisin muffins) in a man's world, but Ms. Pogrebin had grown up in Jamaica, Queens, part of the paper's circulation area, and that qualified her as a subject for discussion. So, after reading Ms. Pogrebin's slick little opus, I visited her in her carpeted office at Geis Publishing.

Midway through the interview, Letty turned the tables on me. "Take yourself," she challenged me, "are you paid the same as the male reporters on your newspaper?"

Notebook in one hand and pencil in the other, I looked that woman straight in the eye and said, "No, but that's because I'm an editorial assistant."

"See?" she concluded triumphantly. And I forgot what I was going to ask her.

After that, I did see. Not only that I myself was underpaid by about $50 per week and that the women around me who did deskman work were getting reporter's pay.[1] I saw, too, that we were quite complacent—even defensive—about it all.

Women in journalism are like the happy darkies down on the plantation. We have been sold the sequel to Bullfinch's. We've sat at our typewriters batting out weddings and engagements, believing all the while that the reason we're "social assistants," or whatever, after thirteen years in the business, while former copyboys have become assistant managing editors, is that we simply don't try hard

---

[1] Reporter is a lower job category than deskman on a newspaper.

enough. Our tough old sisters who have made it tell us that we want it too easy. What they are really saying is that if they had to be twice as good as a man to get where they are, then we too should have to be more than equally qualified.

And more than that is gumming up our typewriter keys. Too many of us fell for the Brenda Starr or the Lois Lane myth. Like most comic strip readers, we grew up believing that journalism is an exception to the patterns of sex discrimination rampant in other fields—that the door is wide open for the girl child who would be a "girl reporter."

Actually, newspapers were among the first male fortresses ever breached by the few uppity females of the nineteenth century. The gates did give way, if only to token numbers of women, and even if they didn't have it easy. During John Quincy Adams's administration, journalist Anne Royall tracked the president to the Potomac, where he was in the habit of taking swims at daybreak, and sat on his clothes until he granted her an interview. Abolitionist editor Jane Swisshelm raised holy hell until she gained admittance to the Senate press box in 1850. And in 1887, would-be muckraker Nelly Bly had to get herself committed to an insane asylum (for an exposé article, of course) before the *New York World* would put her on staff. Getting into the reporter training program at the New York *Daily News,* for example, is elementary by comparison. But only by comparison.

The fact is, sex discrimination still flourishes in the newspaper world. Real-life Lois Lanes are treated like second-class Jimmy Olsens.

Equal Employment Opportunity Commission tables compiled for 1969 show that on the 573 newspapers filing reports that year, men outnumbered women by 77.2 to 22.8.

In the upper levels, things were bleakest of all. Nationally, only 6.4 percent of officials and managers were female. In New York the figure was 5.8 percent.

In the category of "professionals" (where employers listed reporters and editors), the national proportion of women was 22.4

percent, and for New York State, 21.1 percent. The only category in which women dominated was office and clerical workers, where they made up a whopping 67.9 percent nationally and 63.1 percent statewide.

Even these figures for the upper levels may be deceptively high in that they do not take into account the sex stereotyping that goes on within the categories.

For example, not long ago a very capable and experienced classified-ad saleswoman at the *New York Times* asked to be admitted to the paper's training program for outside-ad salesman, a high-commission job. She was turned down, but again and again the *Times* brought in young men fresh out of college to fill openings in the program. EEOC tables indicate only that women are 23.9 percent of all "sales" workers. A private survey conducted by the Newspaper Guild, the leading union organizing editorial workers in the United States and Canada, shows that almost all the women in the sales category are confined to low-paying inside-advertising sales jobs.

The Guild survey, which covered more than half the union's locals throughout the country, was conducted in preparation for the Guild-sponsored Women's Conference held in November of 1970. It was on the basis of the results of that survey that the conference report opened with the statement, "Discrimination is an inherent and all-pervasive reality in the journalistic profession."

Among the patterns revealed by the survey were:

(1) Newspaper employers tended to consider certain jobs "male" and others "female," as shown in their advertising of job openings and in informal conversations on the subject.

(2) The female jobs were those of women's page reporters, morgue librarians, editorial clerks, and, inevitably, secretaries.

(3) Jobs considered male-only were outside circulation jobs, outside ad sales, most news-reporting jobs, and the entire sports department.

(4) Most employers were at a loss to defend this policy.

Their excuses were lame: "It's just the way we've been doing it." "Women are interested only in temporary work." "Women are not ambitious." "Women's records show excessive absenteeism." "Women with children aren't interested in added job responsibilities." "Men are better suited."

The Guild's Women's Conference resulted in the creation of a women's rights committee coordinated by the Guild vice presidents Eleanor Dunn of Ottawa and Dorothy Sain of Cleveland. The women are tackling two main areas of discrimination on newspapers: the female ghettoes of classified ads and of women's news.

There seems to be an unwritten law on newspapers stipulating that all female applications be kept in mothballs until an opening occurs in the lowest slot on the women's news desk. If all women can no longer be kept in the home, those that are not can at least be confined to writing for those that are. Food, fashion, furnishings—all are assumed to be the natural interests of women, including women who are journalists.

The women's page—or the Family Section, Leisure, Living, Everyday, or whatever the euphemism—is the stepchild on any newspaper. Here's where they dump you if you're sick, old, feeble-minded, neurotic, incompetent, illiterate . . . or female.

Whether they do this consciously or unconsciously, management avoids the place like the plague. They blame its staff problems on the sex of the staff. They hand out few raises, no merit pay, and negligible promotions. (When you switch from reporting to deskman work, they raise you from clerk to "social assistant" or something similar. Progressive papers pay women's-news deskmen—female—reporter's pay.)

Nicholas Von Hoffman, whose column appears in the women's pages of the *Washington Post,* says that one of the most frequent questions he gets is, "Don't you resent being put on the women's page?" He doesn't, because, he says, it's one of the best-read parts of the paper.

In an article in the *Columbia Journalism Review* July/August

1971, Von Hoffman observes, "The rules for journalism are upside down on the women's page." What he means is that while all your training in journalism school taught you to expand a press release—get another side to the story, use an imaginative lead—the people in the women's section are encouraged to do just the opposite. Press releases, including blatant puffs, are rehashed uncritically. Sometimes the paper's advertisers are handled with suspicious solicitude; public-relations people tell the editor what to do, not always in vain.

As soon as she catches on, the first impulse of a young reporter in the women's section is to leave as rapidly as possible. But the plus side of this department must not be overlooked: here the rigidity of the inverted-pyramid writing style of city-side reporting is escaped completely. A gutsy women's page editor willing to buck management can resocialize the reader to consumerism, ecology protection, feminism, new lifestyles.

The woman headliner of recipes and writer of golden-wedding announcements who asks to be transferred to a police beat might as well announce her intention of first going to Denmark over the weekend to have her sex changed. Management suddenly becomes concerned about her physical safety and her possible exposure to naughty language and gory sights. They would never worry about you like that if you were a male. False whiskers, anyone?

On some papers such a woman is regarded as an uppity nigger, a troublemaker to be gotten rid of. On a rare few, she gets the transfer. But God help the woman who wants to break into the sacred temple of masculinity that is the sports desk.

At this end of the ballpark, women are so scarce that those who do make it are often written up in Newspaper Guild publications. The chief problem of the female sportswriter seems to be getting press passes to the various stadiums. Some women reporters and photographers have been denied credentials on the pretense of protecting them from the kind of language used in the press box; they have been chased off the field while their male colleagues were permitted the privilege of that vantage point. Unfortunately, the best interviews still come out of the team's locker room and we all know who that's off limits to. Wait till women make the teams!

One part of the newspaper where women can go to the top fast is the morgue. Most newspaper librarians are female, and the term "librarian" is used loosely. No degree is needed in most places, and the pay is correspondingly low. Even here, where one would think no man would be caught dead, discrimination sometimes enters the picture. At one newspaper, a woman had been functioning as head of the morgue for over forty years at clerk's pay—about $140 a week. When a young male clerk in the newsroom expressed interest in working in the morgue, he was promoted to librarian at about $150 a week, and the woman was assigned to train him.

Some progress is being made for women in the newspaper industry. One positive force for change is the women's liberation movement itself. Women reporters, delegated as usual to "women's stuff," were sent out to cover the Liberation events in 1969, 1970, and 1971. They went, they saw, and they were instantly conquered. Much to the chagrin of male editors, there were demands for equal pay, merit pay, the right to wear pants to work, promotions, raises, and so forth.

This is not to say that our real-life comic-strip heroine has it good yet. Women reporters are still sent out for their editors' coffee, still denied promotions to rewrite and desk jobs, still assigned to cover schmaltzy stories on homeless collies.

Even in the one segment of the industry where women seem to be moving up—the hometown and suburban weeklies—the reason women have become editors, reporters, typesetters, and artists is economic; they're cheaper. Stagnating salaries on the small papers drove the men out. Newfangled typesetting equipment that "even a typist" could operate brought the women in to replace expensive craftsmen. The only people around willing to work on weeklies for next to nothing are women, primarily affluent women who would even work for free, just to have something interesting to do.

Where women have risen to policy-making positions on small papers, the results are sometimes revolutionary. Leatrice Spanierman, editor of the *Nassau Herald* in Lawrence, New York, launched a weekly radical-feminist section, four pages long, to raise the consciousness of her readers. The Queens *Tribune* gives space to a local women's liberation group to address the community, and numerous small papers across the country now have feminist columnists.

There's hope for the newspaper industry. The rising feminist consciousness of women journalists and the Guild's militancy for women's rights are having a very definite effect on the status of women on newspapers. Lois Lane has her flesh-and-blood foot in the door.

The Loners

FREELANCE WRITING FOR MAGAZINES

Envied and deplored by office-bound friends, stroked and bullied by editors, pronounced irresponsible by acquaintances, the freelance writer can do one thing that almost no other professional can do: take a walk at 3:30 in the afternoon. This experience is also rare for them, for no freelance has the time to walk, very often. Do you think it's relaxing to work at home? It isn't. Aside from the great advantage of working without shoes—the circulation of the blood from the feet to the brain is good for writers— most freelancing combines the frantic and the poignant, with the peril of the sordid always threatening.

First, deadlines tend to display a mutual attraction: three

major articles are due on Thursday the twelfth. Three different magazines have no reason to care whether you satisfy anybody else's schedules. Second, the essential source for the next piece— the biologist, or the Mafia expert—who must be interviewed for his or her unique information, has suddenly left the country, after abruptly canceling your appointment (sometimes they even die on you). Third, the flaking ceiling in your seedy railroad apartment has just released a stream of water that washes out the corrections inked in on your only typescript. Not only must the work be done again, but the presence of yelling plasterers and repairmen isn't helpful. Fourth, a revision of a piece—sold months ago and heartily forgotten—is now requested by an editor who had said he wouldn't alter a word; he must have it immediately, because he loves it. Fifth, a favorite cousin pleads to sleep on your sofa until she decides whether to get a divorce. "Sleep" is a euphemism, because she wants to talk to you all day long. Sixth, can you expand that little essay, only changing the point of view? Our readers are conservative, you know. Seventh, the rent is due.

As a writer addicted to freelancing, I would have strongly recommended both the work and the life a few years ago. It was possible then to make a modest living, if you gave up a few necessities. (As Dylan Thomas said, "I *want* a lot, but whether I *need* what I want is another question.") Now—not merely because of inflation and recession, but because the magazine world is dying fast—no one should consider beginning as a freelance unless she has some money of her own or helpful parents or—much as it's against my principles—an employed boyfriend or husband.

I loathe the notion that writing is momentarily limited to privileged people. Even the best hatcheries—such as *The Village Voice,* or the surviving bits of the underground—can't conceivably support you while you make a name for yourself.

Freelancing is such an individualized trade that there's no formula, no route to suggest to others. Aside from a very few magazines, such as *The Nation, The Progressive,* and *The Wash-*

ington Monthly—which are definitely friendly to new writers—most of our publications are changing character so quickly that it's impossible to predict what they'll be like a few months hence or if they'll even be around. As the palace revolutions accelerate and the editors she knows get fired, a freelance needs to be increasingly self-protective. There's a lot of sloppy commissioning and false encouragement around, and many editors do not have the authority to buy what they've blithely asked you to write. They'll let anyone write anything, and then discover that the style or the subject wasn't appropriate. (Probably the worst publication on this score is the *New York Times Magazine.*)

Always try to make certain that an editor really likes the subject you've suggested and that it's suitable for the nature of his particular magazine. For example, there's no use trying to plant anything on radical politics in most establishment magazines, any more than you can write about food for *Foreign Affairs* or the joys of polygamy for the *Ladies' Home Journal.* And don't write about anyone you respect for *Esquire;* they only want put-downs. Also, try to determine how much power the editor you're dealing with has—how much of a company commitment she or he can make to you. Recently, at *Harper's,* two top editors were so busy sabotaging each other's projects that a piece that pleased one was apt to be vetoed by the other.

At the beginning, don't take on pieces that require lots of research. Choose an accessible topic so that you won't have lost too much time if a piece isn't bought. (Never take on a theme that's really alien to you. You can't handle church reform if you're an atheist.) Beware of magazines in which all the pieces read very much alike: you're going to be either heavily rewritten—or rejected because you can't produce the house style. (You can expect a lot of rewriting from most of the women's magazines, especially *Cosmo.*) Keep in mind that the editors at a magazine whose style seems repulsive to you will rarely admire yours.

Above all, what any freelance needs is two or three editors on different publications who really like her work, and who can protect her from being messed over by their colleagues. I've been published in twenty periodicals (in some, only once). When that number astounds me, I remind myself that it was mainly due to editors' changing jobs. On the whole, I've had the best experience with editors who've done some writing themselves. Remember, many editors are frustrated writers who wanted to write and couldn't; as a result, they may be badly equipped to rewrite you.

Avoid editors who tell you that they love to be creative. They get possessive about your work and are apt to hash it up. Your last paragraph is likely to appear as the lead, and they enjoy adding what they call "transitions." If they demand a lot of "restructuring" from you, you may end up with a slice of Liederkranz that will be unsalable in any market. Despite the necessity of taking risks, no freelance can afford this experience very often.

To start with, you should specialize in a few subjects you know well. Later, you can branch out. But editors won't know what to do with you if you say you'd love to write "anything." Personally, I haven't had any problems with sexism; I've written a lot on politics and have never been offered fashion or furniture. And the pay has been equal; either my price is determined by my agent or I am paid a given magazine's set fee.

But some women tell me that they've been given the choice of "feminine" subjects or nothing. So be tough on this point. Don't let yourself get ticketed at the beginning, because it's hard to break away from a reputation for writing about cookouts or weddings or "Famous People and Their Dogs." Choose and solicit the magazines you most respect (if any) for the way they cover your field. And if you can't stand rejection, don't be a freelance writer. Anyone who stays in the profession continues to get rejections *and* acceptances; as Graham Greene has said, "Success is only a temporary condition for a writer."

One fact some are reluctant to face is that the freelance writer should be in New York. Of course a reporter can get good feature experience in California or Washington or Boston. But New York is the center of the storm and the seat of most magazine and book publishers' offices. Equally important, it's where you meet editors by chance: I've had quite a few commissions that resulted from casual conversations with strangers. New York also provides so many good subjects for articles, from the muck-ups of the city administration to the presence of alligators in the sewers. It's still the center of culture, heroin, and finance—of poverty and privilege, horror and delight. Anyone living in New York cannot help being assaulted by an infinite number of ideas for pieces. And for books.

Although most magazines are hurting these days, the field of original, shortish paperbacks on topical subjects is perfectly healthy. As many agents remark, contemporary paperbacks are becoming the new magazines—especially now that they can be published in three months. Hence it's useful to make the acquaintance of some editors at places like Avon, Bantam, Dell, NAL, Popular Library, Pocket Books, or others; some magazine piece you've written may give them an idea for a book.

One writer I know adds that all freelances should try to foresee "the 200th anniversary of *any*thing," and sell the idea to a publisher well in advance. Knowing book editors can also lead to freelance research work—usually for an author who needs background material. And doing research is always invaluable training for any freelance. You can quickly learn the techniques of gathering facts, how to interview someone, what libraries have certain specialties, and simply where to call for information. Also, the subjects are often appealing: my own first freelance research jobs were on the Loch Ness Monster, Murder, Inc., and the Battle of Shiloh; later, there was Whistler, Thomas Wolfe, and King Farouk.

You can discover whether you're a natural freelance by spending ten minutes alone with your own temperament. The most likely freelances are loners and renegades; they like to travel, they like their own company, and they like the fact that life can change rapidly within a week. They thrive on unpredictability and are apt to be fiends for privacy. (They're also fierce about interruptions, which many friends find hard to understand.) The freelance simply dislikes institutions and organizations; and the safety they offer feels like feet-in-cement to her. An unfettered life is merely a necessity—no less, no more.

Meanwhile, no staff job can offer such a range of subjects or experiences. (In the last year, my assignments have ranged from the Panthers to Iris Murdoch, from rebel GIs to the John Birchers, and from off-off-Broadway to Philadelphia politics.) Freelancing enables the same person to be a reporter and an essayist, a reviewer and a scriptwriter. The freelance may get a sudden offer to go to Iceland or New Jersey, be given such subjects as weather prediction, Proust, crime, dentistry, or sapphires, be asked to interview the authors she most admires or scorns, or be presented with a topic she despises.

Incidentally, it's nice if a freelance *likes* to write. (Certain writers—including some very good ones—simply hate it. They're usually better off in office jobs.) Freelancing is only for mavericks with a distaste for security and the kind of nervous system that cannot miss a deadline. It's definitely an impractical field, and the paradox is that it requires a host of practical considerations.

The freelance must have an agent. But she must have published some pieces before an agent can judge her work and take her on. She must also be able to write quickly—or freelancing won't work at all. Every article has a natural, in-built time span limiting the number of days or weeks that should be spent on it. Living with the subject longer than necessary will make you miserable and will deaden the way you write it. The freelance who's slow is in trouble sooner than anyone else. Not only is money lost, but the editor who has to assist in a high-forceps delivery for a late piece won't want to use the same writer again.

Actually, the experience of freelancing is very much like being a student; you have six papers due on given dates in the next four weeks, and you schedule them according to the difficulty or the ease of each subject, the appropriate length, and your sense of your own timing. You know that one piece will require far more research than another, and take that into account. A topic that's completely new to you—say, slumlords or nuns—will take longer than reviewing somebody's first novel.

To repeat: the freelance beginning in '74 will have a much rougher time than those who started in 1968 or 1969. Perhaps she will need a part-time job, or a job that pays enough to save for a year off. But the necessity to earn is also stimulating: it helps some to discover their priorities faster than those who need no cash at all. Some people who have spent years writing fiction or plays that never worked out might have been better at reporting, or writing essays.

Meanwhile, there are many dropouts from freelancing—those who have simply found it demoralizing. This unorthodox field demands a highly professional approach—and infinite contacts. But it's hugely rewarding to those who can stand it or afford it, and it certainly gives women far more authority and freedom than most staff-writing jobs do.

A Media (Pa.) Look at Newspaperwomen

by Lynn Martin Haskin

A brief look at the history of women in journalism shows that we've "come a long way, baby," from the days when women were relegated to women's departments on newspapers. Now, militant feminist reporters are demanding that child care centers be supplied by their bosses.

In many American cities women are organizing and contributing to journalism reviews in which they fault their editors for perpetuating sexist, stereotypical descriptions, for continuing to run want ads segregated by sex, and for granting what they consider unsatisfactory maternity-leave benefits. Generally the road for women in journalism has been rocky; in some cases it still is.

A recent study of 167 women who work on the news-editorial staffs of Pennsylvania's 111 daily newspapers shows: few women are complacent; some are satisfied; the majority are discontented or frustrated by the many different kinds of discrimination they experience daily.

Almost half of the women who anonymously participated in the study feel they receive less pay than men for equal work and that they are treated differently from their male counterparts. More than three-fourths of the women do not anticipate advancement on their newspapers.

The picture, however, is not entirely bleak. Some women are satisfied and said so. Like the woman who said, "I know men who are earning less than I." Or the one who reported, "I make sure the pay is equal. I set my own salary." The vast majority, however, do not find themselves in so fortunate a position. Among the women who know they receive less pay than men and know they are being discriminated against in other ways are several who seem resigned to accepting their lot. One woman who complained of pay inequality said, "It's a sorry fact of life and I accept it." Another dismissed the problem with, "Well, it's a man's world."

The overwhelming number of women who reported sex discrimination, pay inequality, assignment discrimination, or inferior treatment were angry or frustrated. Although newsroom salaries were generally poor, women on newspapers with larger circulations tended to feel that the pay there is equal for men and women. And almost all women who work on newspapers that belong to the Newspaper Guild are guaranteed equal salaries by union contracts.

Not all of the women were so lucky. A recurring sentiment was summed up by the woman who said, "This is poor pay for man, woman, or beast, but men and beasts get the edge."

No noticeable pattern emerged between the low salaries given to married as opposed to single women. Both seemed to be discriminated against systematically by male editors with interchangeable rationalizations. Married women were told, "You are paid less because you have a husband who can support you." Single women were told they received less pay because they "don't have a family to support."

The data on salaries support the women's complaints. One-fifth of the 167 women earn less than $100 a week and almost two-fifths (57 women) earn less than $125 a week. Of these 57 women, 52 work on newspapers with less than 50,000 circulation. As of March 1971, well over half (55.8 percent) were earning less than $150 a week. At the higher end of the scale, there were only 4 women (2.6 percent) who earned $250 a week or more; they worked on the state's largest papers. Individual salaries ranged from $57 to $336 for a 40-hour week.

Almost half the women (47.74 percent) said they do not receive salaries comparable to those of men with equal qualifications. When asked if the pay was equal, some replied, "Silly question" or "Are you kidding?" One representative comment came from a woman who explained, "Men with less seniority and experience would not go out and cover a fire at 3:00 A.M. as I do, yet they receive pay increases and promotions. The only pay increases I get are when the company grants a cost-of-living increase to all its employees."

But the instances of discrimination go beyond those of salary differences. While some complained of "subtle discrimination," others cited specific examples of assignments that are taboo for women. More than two-fifths (43.41 percent) said there were certain types of stories their editors would never allow them to cover. The biggest off-limits areas were police, riot, or accident stories. The second largest group of women said their editors would not let them cover party politics, city or township government, courts, schools, or education. One woman explained, "My

editor doesn't think women have the brains to cover politics."
Another, a reporter on a large daily newspaper, said, "I'm treated
like Blondie—people find it hard to believe I have a brain." Other
taboo assignments included sports, science, and women's liberation news.

Since it is possible that the reason an editor may not assign a
certain story to a woman is that she doesn't want to cover it, the
women were also asked what types of stories they refuse to accept.
Well over four-fifths (84.43 percent) said there are no stories that
they would refuse. In every story category, the women were willing
to accept more assignments than their editors were willing to give.
Only two women said they would refuse "bloody accidents" or
"dangerous assignments," while nineteen said their editors would
not give them stories like that. In short, women are willing to cover
more types of stories than their editors are willing to assign.

Other types of discrimination were reported by almost half
the women who listed one or more ways in which they felt they
were treated differently from their male counterparts. These comments exemplify the major gripes: "I've never heard the editor yell
'take an obit' to a man." "Discrimination is subtle—there are no
women doing general assignments." "My managing editor has no
respect for the ability of any woman."

Several women said they had to be "better than men" to
prove themselves to their male editors. One said, "More is expected of me as a woman." Others complained of "paternalism,"
"a lack of respect for my work," and "a refusal to take me
seriously."

The women were asked if they anticipated advancement on
their newspapers. More than three-fourths of them responded
negatively. A response typical of women on many smaller dailies
was this one from a woman's page editor: "I've gone about as high
as I can go unless the managing editor retires or dies." Others
expressed the futility of hoping for advancement with the remark,
"Not on this paper!"

Longer explanations included: "The editor will not have a woman in a decision-making news capacity." And "The editor has a Jehovah-complex: no one is allowed to leave his 'family'!" On a medium-sized newspaper, one reporter said she did not anticipate advancement "simply because I am a woman." And a younger, college-educated woman said, "There is a schism here and I am known as one of the 'rebels.' The editor is anything but pleased with us."

One explanation for the high percentage of negative responses to the question about possible advancement is that for reporters—male or female—there are now fewer editorships for anyone to move into. Many women who are currently editors saw advancement into management (to managing editor or executive editor) as almost impossible.

Several women saw advancement possible only to women who moved to a different newspaper or into a different field such as public relations. Others who responded positively defined advancement (for themselves) as increased salary, more responsibility, or a more desirable reporting assignment—labeled by a few as "lateral advancement."

The present crop of Pennsylvania newspaperwomen got their jobs via various routes—most of them were either secretaries or students when they got their first newspaper job. Other previous positions include public relations, homemaking, teaching, sales, and skilled or unskilled labor.

Most women now employed on large-circulation newspapers in Pennsylvania had previously worked on other newspapers, while many women on the smaller newspapers were getting their first editorial experience. The only female publisher and the only female managing editor who participated in the study both hold jobs on newspapers with circulations between 5,000 and 25,000.

From other information obtained from the five-page questionnaire, several conclusions can be drawn about the professional, personal, and educational backgrounds of the women:

—Younger women tend to work on newspapers with large circulations.

—Women on larger newspapers are more likely to be Democrats than women on smaller newspapers. However, there is no significant difference between the total number of registered Democrats and Republicans who participated.

—More than half the respondents were Protestant, more than one-fourth were Catholic, four were Jewish, and twenty-four reported "other" or "no preference."

—Women on larger newspapers are likely to have more formal education than those on smaller dailies.

Almost three-fifths (58.08 percent) attended or were graduated from college. Of those with bachelor's degrees, more than half received them in liberal arts subjects and more than two-fifths in journalism. Almost 15 percent of the college graduates had advanced degrees. Women with master's degrees were fairly evenly distributed among all groups while women with only bachelor's degrees were clustered on large-circulation dailies. The only woman with doctoral credits works for a newspaper in the third-smallest circulation group (10,001–25,000).

Several steps must be taken by management to alleviate sex discrimination on newspapers:

—Immediately equalize all salaries for persons performing similar jobs.

—Eliminate meaningless job classifications that create arbitrary categories and allow different salary levels for the same work.

—Develop general guidelines for salary levels and share them within and among news-editorial staffs.

—Rotate all staffers to various types of assignments for varying lengths of time to allow staffers to develop expertise without becoming stagnant.

—Remove stereotypical sexist descriptions and phrases from all news stories except where they are relevant.

—Encourage female staffers who desire equal treatment to

alter their image of themselves and to raise their levels of consciousness before they expect men to alter their images of them.

THE RESEARCH TRAP

by Patricia Beckert

The magazines of this country form an important segment of journalism. Unlike newspapers, magazines reach out to a nationwide readership with news, information, ideas, or entertainment. So that the facts given may be accurate and complete, most magazines maintain sizable research staffs. Whether called "researcher" or "editorial assistant" or "research associate" or "reporter/researcher," the job is more or less the same.

It is virtually always filled by women, well-educated (often with graduate degrees), talented, resouceful and, sometimes, ambitious. Basically, the researcher is required to provide the raw materials from which magazine stories are written: they cull material from libraries; they interview specialists on the subjects being researched; they write research reports and original analyses of pertinent sources. These women are performing one—or rather, several—of the basic chores of journalism. Sometimes, they perform *all* the duties of the newspaper reporter or magazine correspondent. Unquestionably, they earn the professional status of "journalist" as they spend years at such work.

And here is where the most damning evidence lies. Years *are* spent in research. Only the rare exception escapes upward out of that ghetto of research. Indeed, a woman with ambitions to practice a writing career or an editing career or a magazine-reporting career can usually see clearly where her ambitions will take her. A young woman may join the staff of a magazine soon after college graduation, if not as a secretary, then perhaps as a researcher from the outset.

In any case, once she becomes a "researcher," she has

entered a lifetime profession. As young men are hired and promoted around her, the woman remains at the same work. If she prefers to attempt writing or editing or reporting, she is told she does not have proper "experience." The stories from one magazine to another may vary a little in detail, but the deadening theme is the same: Research, my dear, is a woman's job. And very good at it you are!

The mastheads of the magazines are the most eloquent proof that there are well-defined cutoff levels for women employees. On *Time* Magazine's masthead, 15 names are listed in the editorial hierarchy before the first woman's name appears, and then she is one of two women among a total of 23 associate editors. Five women are among the 25 contributing editors. Fifty-seven reporter/researchers include one man. And in the Time-Life news service, out of 106 correspondents listed, there are 7 women.

At *Newsweek,* 29 names and two large categories are presented before the first woman's name is listed. And then she is the lone woman in the category of general editor among 20 men. Eight women are associate editors out of the total of 35. On the sixth level listed in order of rank, assistant editor, there are 11 women and 8 men. Thirty-eight women are listed as senior editorial assistants and editorial assistants, with 15 men in those categories. Fourteen women are in the *Newsweek* news bureau—and 61 men.

These two large magazines, major employers of women who are highly educated and highly qualified, are not exceptional in their placement of women. Smaller and different kinds of magazines generally share the same value system. And very often, those women given status on the masthead of a magazine do a "different" kind of work from men in the same category. Sometimes they are relegated to another "women's department"—copy-editing.

Women are rarely hired into the higher-ranked, higher-paying jobs at magazines, and it is probably as rare to find a woman promoted into a better position. The excuses are frequently feeble and meaningless, but they hold down women who ought to be meeting the challenges they set for themselves. A heavy weight indeed it is—one that strength of ability and capacity cannot even budge. Not once has the publisher of a major publication, a major magazine, provided the leadership to smash once and for all the walls of the ghetto. The women inside are doing it themselves, but the work is slow and painful.

Yet if this is the way that women with education, "advantages," and the other credentials to succeed in our society are being treated, think of the others without degrees and "good luck." What of them? Often they find themselves in circumstances that call to mind the sweatshops of the turn of the century.

IS TELEVISION A MAN'S WORLD? YES, MA'AM[1]

by Gloria Banta

"How can you write for children when you don't have any?" A simple question, asked of me last week by a simple man as I was doing what I do to pay the rent—working as associate producer of a late-night ABC program about television, "TV Times." I can't earn a living in New York doing what I'd rather do—write for television—and I'm not yet ready to give in and make the move West where all the work is—so, weekends I write and Monday through Friday it's "TV Time."

At "TV Time," one of the hundred-odd people involved in a show of this kind came up to me. He'd overheard I'd written the premiere episode of this year's "Afterschool Special" series for ABC, a children's show called "Rookie of the Year," and that's when he asked the question.

At first I thought he might be joking (true, I *don't* have any children, but I *do* have an imagination) until another man, his co-worker, came up with "Yeah, Gloria . . . how *did* you get to

[1] *The New York Times,* Sunday, September 30, 1973. Reprinted by permission.

be a writer, anyway?" There it is again, I thought. Why is it no one ever asks a man, "How *did* you get to be a doctor . . . cop . . . rapist . . . President?" As my friend Pat always says, "The only time they *don't* ask a woman, 'How'd you get to be . . .?' is when she's pregnant!"

Actually, I came to be a writer through luck and some hard work (and, of course, a brilliant, creative mind—which is, by the way, how I answered that curious duo). The luck came first, in the guise of the aforementioned friend, Pat Nardo. She was working in California on "The Mary Tyler Moore Show" as production assistant to Allan Burns and Jim Brooks, executive producers and creators of the show. Pat had even typed the original presentation, and was the first one ever to read and laugh out loud at their marvelous creation.

At that time I was in phase IV of my life in Europe. (Over a period of five years I would work six months, then take off six months and travel.) This time I was in Venice, in love, and had little to do with my days, so I wrote a lot of letters, most of them going to my three closest friends: Pat in Hollywood, Camille Marchetta, a Queens expatriate who'd moved to London and become a writers' agent, and Marie Squerciati, who was then hard at work on her Ph.D. at Columbia. They had been friends from early on, and when I met them upon moving to New York in 1963, I joined the circle. Our penchant for travel and variety often separated us for long periods of time, but we never lost touch, and our long, weekly letters kept the relationships alive and growing.

So the letters flew back and forth: Venice/London/New York/Hollywood. Pat's boss, Allan Burns, thought we were all bananas and even dared suggest the letters were those of frustrated writers. We were all very funny, he said, but why didn't we try writing for profit instead of self-amusement? Like why not try to write a script for "The Mary Tyler Moore Show?" "Sure," Pat said. "I mean it," he said.

The cable arrived next day: COME BACK STOP WE'VE GOT

CHANCE TO DO STORY FOR THE MTM SHOW STOP. . . . "Who, us?" I said, and left for California immediately. We wrote the script, with lots of help from Allan and Jim, and when we finally turned it in, they liked it and put it on the air.

Allan Burns and Jim Brooks had come through. In the 10 years we'd spent working in the business for various producers, writers, and executives, they'd all been full of adjectives about our hidden talents—"How smart!" . . . "How funny!" . . . "How clever!"—but not one ever suggested we come out of the closet.

No wonder we'd never thought seriously about writing as a career. When I moved to California from Denver in 1960, women writers were doing "soaps," and that was about it. I'd had a year of invaluable experience at the NBC affiliate in Denver and was eager to get to California where the real core of the business was. Of course, New York was my real goal. I was dying to be part of the endless stream of girls who poured out of the Seagram Building (as I'd seen them do in *The Best of Everything*). I'd have been content to join a typing pool, so long as it was in that magnificent structure! But I was too scared to try New York first, so Los Angeles it was.

I moved into the famous Studio Club for women in Hollywood where Kim Novak and countless others lived as starlets. You were allowed to take residence there as long as you had something to do with the business. I turned out to be the only non-actress in the place, which made me something of a freak, until I landed a job as assistant to the casting director of a daytime television show. Suddenly I was an accepted freak.

The following year, I heard that Steve Allen would be doing a network variety comedy show and I rushed to interview for a job on it. I was four months early—preproduction and staff wouldn't even happen till then—but in my eagerness I was promised a job, and four months later I was hired as secretary to the associate producer.

Steve Allen. Three men were my laugh idols: Sid Caesar on

"Your Show of Shows"; Robert Benchley ("Grandfather Twilly had been a mean man and had little spots of soup on the lapel of his coat. All his children were mean and had soup spots on their clothes, too"); and Steve Allen.

Although the show turned out to be a disaster in terms of ratings, it was a gold mine of new talent. There were the writers: Buck Henry, a brilliant, skinny comic/writer brought out from New York to be partnered with Stan Burns, one of the old "Tonight" show regulars; Bill Persky and Sam Denoff, also from New York; Arne Sultan and Marvin Worth, comedy veterans; Bill Dana (Jose Jiminez) as head writer, Leonard Stern as skit director. And besides all the writing talent, Steve introduced the Smothers Brothers, Tim Conway, Jim Nabors, and, of course, his famous regulars, Louis Nye, Don Knotts, Tom Poston. And, as if all that weren't enough, people like Mel Brooks and Carl Reiner were always dropping by.

So there I was, 20 years old and surrounded by some of the funniest men in the world. When writers' conferences were called, the whole staff would meet to test out new material. Was it or wasn't it funny enough? I wanted those meetings to go on forever. I was content to sit there and listen. Sometimes I had to take shorthand notes and would asterisk the jokes that got the biggest laughs, then transcribe them into script form. I used to be so careful the way I typed it up; a dash here, an exclamation point there, always trying to make it read as funny as it had sounded.

Once it occurred to me while transcribing those notes that if I tried, maybe I could write skits half as funny as theirs. (I'd done it in my head hundreds of times as a kid, watching "Your Show of Shows.") God, I wanted to be one of those guys! But whoever heard of a girl comedy-writer? Besides I'd never have the nerve to show anything to them. (A secretary, just out of her teens, pushing material!) I was just grateful for my job.

My boss, the associate producer, didn't help. He kept telling me to get out of the business. "This is no life for a nice girl—or a rotten one, either. They only end up having affairs with all these crazies, going from job to job . . . it's awful. So what do you want from it? Listen, I know this terrific winetaster. . . ." God bless him, he was always trying to fix me up with what he thought was "marriage material."

But what *did* I want from it? Everything. Maybe, if I worked hard enough, maybe some day I could even be an associate producer like him. I did know of one woman who made it, and she was only in her forties when she got her break! Then there were other alternatives: Acting? No, I was too realistic to go into that. Casting director? Well, there were a few women in that, but actors depressed me—somebody always lost. Agent? That was wrong, too. I wasn't interested in contracts or percentages. Nope, I wanted to be in the thick of it; I wanted to be involved in production.

After the show was canceled and my bubble burst, I did go from job to job, none coming close to the Steve Allen experience. Once I worked for Ernie Kovacs in his home for a whole week— and I never saw him! He even dictated letters over an intercom wired throughout the house, which had been Lon Chaney's. Mostly, Ernie was in the cellar playing gin, or poker, I can't remember what. He'd play day and night, with various actors and producers coming in and out—all action centering on that secret cellar.

When I decided I'd had enough of California and was ready to tackle New York, I was still uncertain of what I wanted to do, but I had enough production experience to insure a good job once there.

I remember the day I left my friends at the office gave me a party and one of the producers on the lot came over to me and confided he thought I was making a big mistake. "Why?" I asked, already knowing his answer. The echo came back to me: "Why don't you just get out of the business? New York's worse than L.A. Go find yourself a nice fella."

So. Here I am, 10 years later, still in New York. I've been a casting director, production coordinator, and script assistant. I've worked in the theater, films, and television, and finally I am that "associate producer" (and I didn't have to wait till 40!).

As for the original question about writing for children, well, that assignment was chance, too. And again through Pat. Back in New York as manager of children's programming for ABC (she hasn't got any kids, either), Pat was eager to dramatize a book she'd found called *Not Bad for a Girl*. It was based on the real-life story of Sharon Poole, a 10-year-old girl who wanted to play Little League baseball. When the coach let her join the team, the town went crazy—obscene phone calls, job threats to her father, and garbage thrown at her during games. It seemed unbelievable, but it was a perfect story for "Afterschool Special." After different writers turned in several unsuccessful outlines, Pat and the producer, Danny Wilson, came to me and said "Try." I hesitated; Pat was the children's expert, but she assured me she'd help as much as she could.

It was a lot of fun researching Little League games, interviewing boys about their feelings if a girl joined the team ("What would I do? I'd quit!") And finally turning in the last draft, ready to go into production.

As a result of "Rookie" and the Mary Tyler Moore show, I'm now represented by a major agency, have two pilot-development deals, a TV movie I want to do, and my agent tells me there's a lot of work waiting, if only I'd go West.

Oddly enough, my friends have all turned out to be writers as well. Pat spends weekends developing a screenplay; Camille just finished her second, which looks as though it'll be filmed; and Marie's articles have appeared in *The Village Voice* and other publications. We still write to each other—but only every other month or so.

Editor's Note: The following letter, published subsequently by the *New York Times,* speaks for itself:

To the Editor:

I was wholeheartedly (almost) delighted to see the story by Gloria Banta ("Is Television a Man's World? Yes, Ma'am," Sept. 30) telling how she, who wrote the TV play for ABC's "Rookie of the Year," made it in TV. Then Ms. Banta writes, "The manager of children's programming for ABC was eager to dramatize a book she'd found called *Not Bad for a Girl*."

It just happens I wrote that book. I am also a woman. But book writers get short shrift in this, the world of TV. Couldn't Ms. Banta have mentioned my name?

I guess not.

Isabella Taves

New York City

6

APPENDIX

EMPLOYMENT RIGHTS OF WOMEN

NEW YORK WOMEN are filing complaints against sex discrimination on the job in unprecedented numbers. Until 1970, only a handful of complaints a year were brought to the New York City Human Rights Commission. In 1970 the State Division of Human Rights (N.Y.) received 331 complaints; New York City received 141. In 1971 complaints in New York State numbered 500, although New York City's fell to 130.

Media coverage of neo-feminist demonstrations and the burgeoning number of books on the movement are having their effect; so, too, are widely publicized group complaints of women working for national magazines, as well as higher court decisions on sex discrimination, such as the Supreme Court's ruling in 1971 that eliminated the "sex plus" theory (women could be barred from a job because of their sex and one other factor, such as marital status) unless it also applied to men. Women are simply more aware of their legal rights, and are acting accordingly. And they are on firm ground. Many of the complaints have been settled by conciliation *in favor of the employee.*

What your rights are:

New York State employers are forbidden to discriminate against women in hiring, firing, salaries, fringe benefits, training programs, and in classified ads. Employment agencies in the state cannot discriminate in referring you for a job or a training program or in classified ads.

On the federal level, Title VII of the 1964 Civil Rights Act prohibits discrimination on the basis of sex in "hiring, upgrading, and all other conditions of employment." The Equal Employment

Opportunity Commission (EEOC) is the law's enforcer. It will handle complaints of a minimum of twenty-five people in upholding the law unless sex "is a bona fide occupational qualification." BFOQs must be proved by the employer and probably do not exist in publishing. This is what they do *not* mean:

Assumptions about the applicant's sex

Preferences of co-workers, employers, clients, or customers

Members of the opposite sex traditionally held the job

Heavy physical labor, manual dexterity, late night hours, overtime, isolated or unpleasant surroundings are involved

Travel or travel with members of the opposite sex is involved

Physical facilities not available

Personal characteristics not exclusive to either sex, such as charm or aggressiveness[1]

How to file a complaint:

A New York City resident should first file a complaint with the New York City Commission on Human Rights, 80 Lafayette Street, New York, New York 10013 (telephone: 212–566-5050). The agency whose lawyers act for defendants has the power to subpoena to testify. Following testimony, the agency can order an employer to hire, rehire, reinstate, or upgrade employees and rebate salary and compensatory damages.

Other agencies: (1) New York State Division of Human Rights, 79 Worth Street, New York, New York 10007 (telephone: 212–488-5832); (2) Equal Employment Opportunity Commission, Room 4000, 26 Federal Plaza (Foley Square), New York, New York 10007 (telephone: 212–264-3642).

In preparing a suit against a company, it is obviously wise for the group to present a strong, determined front to management. Since participation in the suit may be the first occasion on which many of the women have protested against, or even stood up to, their bosses, they may well be scared—beset by periodic seizures

[1] U.S., Equal Employment Opportunity Commission, *Toward Job Equality for Women,* 1969.

of panic, terrified that they will lose their jobs for "offending" the boss by "asking for too much" or being "too militant." One thing that can help is to keep in mind that you are not asking for unearned favors, but for your rights; that the company is breaking the law by maintaining job categories based on sex and discriminatory promotion practices. Also beware of management (and your own cowardice) when it suggests getting together informally (like one big basically happy family) and talking over what's making you "unhappy." Believe it that management will not make everything right the minute you raise your voices (in a ladylike way only, of course) to object to what is happening. The company (any company) will not change its ways unless it is really forced to, and formal action—probably legal—is the only force it will recognize.

Thus, stand firm and formal, and to help you do so, the advice of a good, actively involved lawyer cannot be overemphasized. It is vital to have some outside professional person as spokeswoman for the groups in *any* contact with management, particularly in negotiations. First, the company has a lawyer advising it, even if he is not in immediate evidence. Second, your outside lawyer has nothing personally to lose by offending management and so will not be inhibited, as women employees cannot help being, by the danger (imagined or real) of reprisals. Equally important, the lawyer is professionally skilled in the maneuvering of negotiations and can thus more effectively argue the case. She must, though, have had the time to fully sound out the feelings of the group, to go through and understand the specifics of the work situation, and to thrash out with the group the priorities of its demands so that she can accurately represent the women in getting what they want.

BEWARE: *Newsweek,* which considers itself an enlightened employer (and appears to suffer from "liberal guilt"), tried to play the women's demands off against a "prior commitment" to improve the racial balance of the magazine's staff. The tactic of playing one "minority" group off against another should be clearly seen through and denounced as the despicable maneuver that it is. The company has a duty to both groups. (It is interesting to note that while they countered with the plea that they felt more pressed to hire blacks, *Newsweek*'s management has not done so—on the editorial staff there is only one black researcher and only five or six black reporters. Period.) Also, don't be put off by alibis like "Well, the men don't have it any better." If that is true, and you agree that the whole company practice is bad, fight to raise the standards and improve the opportunities for all employees to the level of what you want for women.

If there is a union at your company, see if you can have your demands incorporated into the contract when union negotiations next come up. With an attack on a second front through the union, you will have the backing of a broader base of employees and can increase pressure on management accordingly.

CONCILIATION AGREEMENT BETWEEN TIME INC. AND WOMEN COMPLAINANTS

1. The respondent Publisher shall refrain from the commission of unlawful discriminatory practices in the future. The Publisher does not concede or admit that it, or any of its employees, had committed unlawful discriminatory acts in the past, and has agreed to all terms in order to avoid lengthy legal proceedings and to manifest its good faith and its intention to adhere in the future to policies which are not discriminatory.

2. All recruitment, hiring, interviewing, referral, promotion, setting of job classifications, training programs and compensation of personnel, by the Publisher, shall be without regard to sex. It is expressly understood that all job categories shall be equally open to qualified candidates, without regard to sex or marital status.

3. The Publisher will actively attempt to achieve integration of all job categories by sex, provided that this agreement shall not be

construed to mean that the Publisher will be required to maintain any particular level of personnel or to maintain quotas based on sex.

4. Applicants for employment by the Publisher will not be assigned to interviews on the basis of the sex of either the applicant or the interviewer.

5. Each person hired by the Publisher will be given a clear, full and accurate explanation of the duties, responsibilities, and career possibilities of the position for which she or he is hired.

6. The personnel department and department heads responsible for hiring shall be instructed by the Publisher to advise new employees that they are at all times free to have their résumés made available to any supervisor. The qualifications of each employee seeking another position will be appraised by the appropriate supervisors, and the employee will be notified of the disposition of his or her application. Training or tryouts may be given at the sole discretion of the Publisher, and the results of any such tryout will be discussed with the applicant involved upon its completion.

7. Terms 11 through 46 of the herein agreement cover certain other issues, pertaining particularly to the editorial departments of the Publisher's respective publications individually, which were resolved in the course of the discussions leading to this agreement.

8. (a) Any complaint of sex discrimination arising in connection with matters covered herein with respect to editorial department employees of the Publisher shall first be discussed by a committee composed equally of representatives of the complainant women staffers and of the editorial management of the publication within which such complaint arose. Any such complaints which have not been resolved by such individual publication committees may be referred for consideration to a company-wide committee, composed equally of representatives of the complainant women staffers and

the editorial management. In the event that any such complaint alleges discrimination in an individual's salary based on sex, the Publisher will make available to the company-wide committee, on a confidential basis and without names, data relevant to such allegation. If such complaints are not resolved by the company-wide committee, the individual involved has the right to file a verified complaint with the State Division of Human Rights.

(b) Any complaint of sex discrimination arising in connection with matters covered herein with respect to employees of the Publisher in other than editorial departments shall be discussed by a committee composed equally of noneditorial female employees of the Publisher and of the noneditorial management of the Publisher. Complaints which are not resolved may, with the consent of the individual involved, be referred to the State Division of Human Rights.

(c) Resolution of complaints by any such committee shall require the consent of a majority thereof.

(d) Information concerning any such complaints shall not be disclosed to any such committee without the written consent of the complaining employee involved; and relevant information with respect to individuals other than the complainant shall be made available on a confidential basis without names.

(e) Such committees shall periodically report the results of their meetings to the State Division of Human Rights.

(f) It is understood that all matters of traditional management prerogatives which are outside the scope of the Human Rights Law are not subject to review by any of such committees or by the State Division of Human Rights.

9. The Publisher shall prepare a quarterly statistical analysis showing; by sex and without names (a) the sex of the personnel department interviewer by whom individuals applying for employment to the personnel department have been interviewed (b) the

job categories for which such applicants applied (c) the job categories, if any, to which such applicants were referred, and (d) where applicable, the job categories in which such applicants were hired. Such analysis, insofar as it relates to applicants for editorial categories, together with a quarterly summary of transfers and promotions of employees covered by the contract between the Publisher and the Newspaper Guild of New York, shall be presented to the company-wide committee referred to in paragraph 8 (a) hereof. Such analysis, insofar as it relates to applicants for jobs in noneditorial categories, shall be presented to the committee referred to in paragraph 8 (b) hereof. In the event that the representatives of the complainants on such committee so request, the staff of the State Division of Human Rights shall have access to the data from which such analysis was compiled for the purpose of checking the accuracy of such analysis.

10. The State Division of Human Rights will conduct periodic compliance reviews in accordance with its normal procedures, initially on a quarterly basis, which reviews will include analysis of the relative salaries of men and women in the same job category.

A Voice from the Depths

READER'S DIGEST SUBSCRIPTION DEPARTMENT

The publishing business, like any other business, is not made up only of presidents and editors and chairmen of the board, but also of a lot of people who do menial and tedious tasks, tasks which are ultimately important to the well-being and success of the business. The people who perform these chores are often women, and their efforts are largely ignored.

Opening mail or shuffling and classifying subscriptions is certainly unstimulating work, but it need not be unbearable. At the *Reader's Digest,* it is made unbearable. Working conditions are deplorable. For one thing, we were crammed into outrageously small areas, fifty women in one corner and a few hundred in a not very large, but very drab, dreary, poorly ventilated room—not to mention the uncomfortable chairs and the tables that somebody upstairs in editorial had no use for anymore.

I found, as time went on, that these were only a few of the insults to my integrity as a woman and a person that I would have to put up with. Here are some of the abuses I recall:

(1) We were to raise our hands (and these are adult women, remember) to ask permission to go to the rest room.

(2) We were not to talk or make any noise.

(3) We were not given sufficient time for lunch or other breaks. Often the time of our lunch breaks was changed from day to day without any notice.

(4) We had to queue up to get our coats at the end of the day, then return to our seats and line up again to be dismissed.

(5) Our lounge areas, for what they were worth, were dreary (lots of reject furniture) and not all that clean.

(6) During the rush season, we had mandatory overtime two hours twice a week and all day Saturday, and the employee who balked soon found herself without a job.

(7) Our pay was pitiful, and I can think of an incident in particular that indicates it was discriminatory. There isn't much to opening mail, but it seems that men are considered more adept at

it than women. During the Christmas season, some college boys were hired to help open the mail. It was brought to my attention one day that the young man sitting next to me was being paid at least fifty cents more an hour than I was. I fail to see why his job was considered worth fifty cents more than mine, since we were doing the exact same thing.

(8) We were not permitted to wear slacks (not even pantsuits in the coldest of weather) although the boys could wear jeans and T-shirts.

(9) We were required to sign in and sign out in two or three different places.

(10) We were told not to ask questions about what we were doing but just do as we were told.

(11) We were required to bring in sick notes from a doctor if we were out.

Probably the saddest thing about this predicament was the constant harassment, ridicule, and scolding that these women were subjected to. Almost all of them needed the work and lived in constant fear of losing their jobs if they complained or asked for improvements. Some of them had worked there for twenty to thirty years. And what did this silent loyalty to the company get them? Laid off, sometimes with less than a day's notice and not so much as a thank you for your efforts and years of good work.

I have never heard of men being treated in such a way. What does the dismissed woman do? She goes out meekly and tries to find another job, hoping the pay is at least as good and the job no more menial.

As a woman and a human being, I don't think it's just, and I protest. I am no longer working in the publishing field, but I would like to see conditions there improve for women—and not only for the VIP. The "little guy" is just as important to the success of the business as good old Mr. What's-His-Name, the never-present chairman of the board.

Note: This report was a part of the testimony given at a hearing held by a New York State Joint Legislative Committee investigating fair employment practices in January 1972.

MEMORANDUM OF UNDERSTANDING[1]

(*Between* Newsweek *and Women in the Magazine's Editorial Research Department*)

This Memorandum of Understanding, dated June 1, 1973, has been adopted by the management of *Newsweek* Magazine and representatives of women employed in *Newsweek*'s Editorial Department (such representatives will be referred to as the "Women's Committee").

The purpose of this Memorandum is to further *Newsweek*'s policy of equal employment opportunity for women as researchers, reporters, writers, and editors for *Newsweek* Magazine.

This Memorandum supersedes a memorandum of understanding between *Newsweek* and *Newsweek* women entered into on August 26, 1970.

I. INTRODUCTION

This Memorandum is predicated on the current size, structure, and functions of the various departments of *Newsweek's* Editorial Department, which are described, as of June 1, 1973, in the Appendix to this Memorandum. It shall not in any way limit

---

[1] Upon the signing of this memorandum, the *Newsweek* Women's Committee withdrew charges of sex discrimination, filed May 16, 1972, with the Equal Employment Opportunity Commission.

the exclusive right of *Newsweek* to alter or change such size, structure, or functions, provided that where any such alteration or change will have an adverse effect on any rights of the women employed in the Editorial Department under this Memorandum, *Newsweek* shall negotiate with the Women's Committee concerning changes in this Memorandum so as to implement the purpose of this Memorandum in the changed circumstances. All provisions of this Memorandum unaffected by such alteration or change shall remain in effect.

II. DEFINITION AND EXPLANATION OF TERMS

(1) The term "Editorial Department" refers to the letters correspondents, researchers, domestic reporters and bureau chiefs, foreign correspondents, writers, copy editors, the senior editors in charge of major editorial departments, and the four highest ranking editors of the domestic and international editions of *Newsweek* Magazine.

(2) The term "major editorial department" refers to each group of writers and researchers who are subject to the supervision of a Senior Editor in Charge. As of the date of this Memorandum, there are seven major editorial departments: National Affairs, Foreign News, Business News, three Back-of-the-Book departments (including the following sections: (a) Theater, Music, Art, Movies, and Books; (b) Science, Medicine, Cities, and Sports; (c) Religion, Education, Life and Leisure, and Media), and International Editions.

(3) The term "Senior Editor in Charge" refers to a Senior Editor who supervises a group of writers and researchers.

(4) The term "writers" refers to permanent full-time writers who may be classified as assistant, associate, general, or senior editors, for either the domestic or international editions of *Newsweek* Magazine, but does not include columnists or Senior Editors in Charge.

(5) The term "foreign correspondents" refers to permanent

full-time reporters and bureau chiefs in *Newsweek's* bureaus outside the United States.

(6) The term "domestic reporters" refers to permanent full-time reporters in *Newsweek's* offices in New York and in its bureaus in the United States, but does not include columnists or bureau chiefs.

(7) The term "in-house tryout" refers to a tryout for a position as writer by a candidate who was a permanent full-time *Newsweek* employee immediately prior to the commencement of the tryout.

(8) The term "out-of-house tryout" refers to a tryout for a position as writer by a candidate who was not a permanent full-time *Newsweek* employee immediately prior to the commencement of the tryout.

III. RESEARCHERS

(1) The percentage of all researchers who are men shall be approximately equal to the percentage of all writers who are women. *Newsweek's* obligation under this paragraph shall be considered fulfilled if these percentages are either equal or as nearly equal as is mathematically possible (in view of the actual number of researchers, the actual number of writers, and the actual number of either women writers or men researchers). *Newsweek's* obligation under this paragraph shall also be considered fulfilled if the percentage of men researchers and the percentage of women writers would be equal or as nearly equal as is mathematically possible with an allowance for a total disparity of three persons. For example, suppose that *Newsweek* has 45 writers and 30 researchers. If 15 of the writers are women, then the obligation is fulfilled if the number of men researchers is from 7 to 13 inclusive. If 10 of the researchers are men, the obligation is fulfilled if the number of women writers is from 12 to 18 inclusive.

(2) In carrying out its obligation under paragraph (1) above, *Newsweek* shall avoid any unjustified concentration of men

researchers in any one major editorial department. The burden of justification shall be borne by *Newsweek*.

(3) No woman researcher shall be transferred involuntarily from one major editorial department or section of a department to another if the sole purpose of the transfer is to create an opening for a newly hired male researcher.

(4) *Newsweek* will continue to provide occasional writing opportunities for researchers.

IV. REPORTERS AND CORRESPONDENTS

(1) *Domestic Reporters.* Approximately one-third or more of all domestic reporters shall be women. Where the total number of domestic reporters is divisible by three (3), then one-third or more of the total number shall be women. Where the total number is one more or one less than a number divisible by three (3), then one-third of the total number, and approximately one-third or more of that divisible number shall be women. For example, if the total number of domestic reporters is 60, 20 or more shall be women. If the total number is 62 (one less than 63) or 64 (one more than 63), then in either case 21 shall be deemed to be one-third of the total number. *Newsweek*'s obligation under this paragraph shall be considered fulfilled if the actual number of women domestic reporters is within two of the number that constitutes one-third of all domestic reporters as herein defined. For example, if one-third of all domestic reporters is 20 (the total number of domestic reporters being 59, 60, or 61), the obligation is fulfilled if there are 18 women domestic reporters.

(2) *Foreign Correspondents.* From January 1, 1974, through December 31, 1975, one out of every three persons hired or transferred onto the staff of foreign correspondents shall be a woman. If a woman is or was hired or transferred to the foreign correspondents staff before January 1, 1974, she shall be counted toward *Newsweek*'s fulfilling of its obligation under this paragraph. A person shall be considered hired or transferred to the

staff of foreign correspondents as of the date when he or she actually assumes the duties of the position.

(3) *Training Program.* *Newsweek* shall conduct a summer training program for prospective reporters, in which at least two full positions out of the first six shall be made available to women letters correspondents, women researchers, or women editorial secretaries.

(a) Not fewer than one-third of all persons other than *Newsweek* employees who are included in the program in positions other than the first six shall be women. Where the total number of such persons is divisible by three (3), then one-third or more shall be women. Where the total number is one more or one less than a number divisible by three (3), then one-third of that divisible number shall be deemed to be one-third of the total number and one-third or more of that divisible number shall be women.

(b) The program shall normally last for at least thirteen consecutive weeks for each position.

(c) Any position may be split between two persons by the mutual consent of *Newsweek* and the persons involved.

(d) Notice of this summer training program shall be given at least three months in advance of the start of the program.

V. WRITERS

(1) *Newsweek*'s staff of writers shall include at least 11 women by December 31, 1973. *Newsweek* shall maintain at least that number of women writers in 1974, except that if the number of women writers falls below 11 at any time from December 31, 1973, through December 31, 1974, *Newsweek* shall have 90 days within which to attain that number of women writers again. Approximately one-third or more of the writers shall be women by December 31, 1974. Thereafter, during the term of this Memorandum, approximately one-third or more of the writers shall be women. Where the total number of writers is divisible by three (3), then approximately one-third or more of that total number shall be women. Where the total number is one more or one less

than a number divisible by three (3), then one-third of that divisible number shall be deemed to be one-third of the total number, and approximately one-third or more of that divisible number shall be women. For example, if the total number of writers is 60, 20 or more shall be women. If the total number is 62 (one less than 63), or 64 (one more than 63), then in either case 21 shall be deemed to be one-third of the total number. *Newsweek*'s obligation under this paragraph as of December 31, 1974, and thereafter during the term of this Memorandum shall be considered fulfilled if the actual number of women writers is within two of the number that represents one-third of all writers as herein defined. For example, if one-third of all writers is 20 (the total number of writers being 59, 60, or 61), this obligation is fulfilled if there are 18 women writers.

(2) No major editorial department shall be without at least one woman writer for more than six consecutive months unless (a) during that six months at least one woman candidate for a position as writer has been given a tryout, and (b) at the end of that six months at least one woman candidate for a position as writer is taking or is scheduled to take a tryout. If those conditions are satisfied, the period of six months shall be extended while *Newsweek* continues to conduct tryouts for women candidates for a position as writer in that department until a woman is employed as a writer in that department.

VI. TRYOUTS FOR CANDIDATES FOR POSITIONS AS WRITER

(1) *In General. Newsweek* shall continue to assure that *Newsweek*'s employees shall be offered tryouts in preference to other persons whom *Newsweek* determines to be equally or less qualified. *Newsweek* may in its discretion limit the number of tryouts conducted at any one time.

(2) *In-house Tryouts.*

(a) Requests for Tryouts. Any permanent full-time *Newsweek* employee desiring to try out for a position as a writer may submit a written request for such a tryout to the Chief of

Correspondents or to the Senior Editor in Charge of the major editorial department in which the tryout is sought. Such written requests shall specify: (i) the particular major editorial department, if any, in which the tryout is sought; (ii) whether the tryout is sought only when an opening for a writer exists, or without regard to whether an opening exists.

When the Chief of Correspondents receives a written request for a tryout in any major editorial department, the Chief of Correspondents shall promptly refer a dated copy of the request to the appropriate Senior Editor in Charge unless the Chief of Correspondents denies the tryout request. Additionally, whenever an opening for a writer occurs in any major editorial department, all permanent full-time *Newsweek* employees having pending requests for a tryout in that department shall be notified promptly of such opening.

(b) Processing of Requests for Tryouts. Any request for a tryout may be denied either by the Chief of Correspondents or by the Senior Editor in Charge of the major editorial department in which the tryout is sought. Where a written request for any tryout is denied, a written statement of reasons for denial shall be furnished by *Newsweek* to the applicant within one month from the date such request is made; and the statement shall include the identity of the person who made the decision to deny the tryout.

Where a request for any tryout is not so denied, then, within one month after the date such request is made, a written statement shall be furnished by *Newsweek* to the applicant setting forth the status of such request (for example: tryout will occur within three months; tryout may be granted after the current tryout of another applicant is completed; additional experience necessary before tryout given; or tryout is unlikely in the foreseeable future). No denial of a tryout by the Chief of Correspondents shall bar a permanent full-time *Newsweek* employee from resubmitting a request for a tryout to the Senior Editor in Charge of the major editorial department in which the tryout is sought.

(c) Conduct of Tryouts. If a request for an in-house tryout is granted, the tryout shall be conducted in accordance with the following rules (of which the candidate shall be informed), unless the candidate and the Senior Editor in Charge conducting the tryout mutually agree to different rules: (i) It shall last not less than eight weeks, unless an offer of a job as writer is made to the candidate before the eight weeks have elapsed; (ii) The candidate shall receive not less than one writing assignment each week during the tryout; (iii) During the tryout there shall be consultations at least once each week between the candidate and the Senior Editor in Charge conducting the tryout; (iv) At the end of the tryout, the candidate's work shall be reviewed by one of the three highest ranking *Newsweek* editors; and (v) In the case of a tryout for an open position, if within three weeks after the end of the tryout the candidate is not offered the position, an editor authorized to act on behalf of *Newsweek* shall furnish the candidate a written statement of the reasons why he or she was not offered the position and the identity of the person who made the decision. In the case of a tryout conducted without regard to the existence of an opening, if on the basis of the tryout it is determined by *Newsweek* that the candidate will not be offered a position as writer, an editor authorized to act on behalf of *Newsweek* shall, within three weeks after the end of the tryout, furnish the candidate a written statement of the reasons why he or she will not be offered a position and the identity of the person who made the decision.

(d) Effect of Denial or Failure. Denial of a request for an in-house tryout or failure in an in-house tryout shall not bar a permanent full-time *Newsweek* employee from consideration for another tryout.

(3) *Out-of-house Tryouts*. If an out-of-house tryout is granted, it shall be conducted in accordance with the following rules, unless the candidate and the Senior Editor in Charge conducting the tryout mutually agree to different rules: (i) *Newsweek* may terminate any out-of-house tryout at any time during the first

three weeks of the tryout; (ii) If *Newsweek* allows an out-of-house tryout to continue beyond three weeks, the tryout shall last not less than six weeks; (iii) The candidate shall receive not less than one writing assignment each week during the tryout; (iv) During the tryout, there shall be consultations at least once each week between the candidate and the Senior Editor in Charge conducting the tryout; (v) If *Newsweek* allows the tryout to continue beyond three weeks, at the end of the tryout the candidate's work shall be reviewed by at least one of the three highest ranking *Newsweek* editors.

(4) *Training Program for Prospective Writers.*

(a) *Newsweek* shall continue to make facilities and a reasonable amount of working time available to *Newsweek* employees for a training program for prospective writers, and shall continue to encourage appropriate persons to act as instructors in the program. Training of a total of thirty candidates for approximately eight weeks each shall be made available under the program by June 30, 1975.

(b) The program shall be conducted under the general supervision of the program instructors and the Women's Committee.

(c) Women and men researchers, letters correspondents, and reporters in New York shall be eligible for participation in the program in order of seniority as *Newsweek* employees.

VII. CHIEFS OF DOMESTIC BUREAUS

(1) By December 31, 1973, at least two women reporters shall have been acting bureau chiefs of domestic bureaus for not less than three weeks each. The three weeks need not be consecutive, but no period of less than one week shall count toward the three weeks.

(2) Of the first six persons appointed chief of a domestic bureau after January 1, 1973, two shall be women. Any woman who accepted a position as chief of a domestic bureau prior to

January 1, 1973, but who took up her duties as chief after January 1, 1973, shall be counted as one of those two women.

VIII. SENIOR EDITORS IN CHARGE

·(1) By December 31, 1974, at least one woman shall have acted as a Senior Editor in Charge for not less than four weeks. By December 31, 1975, at least one other woman shall have acted as a Senior Editor in Charge for not less than four weeks. The four weeks need not be consecutive, but no period less than one week shall count toward the four weeks.

(2) By December 31, 1975, at least one woman shall have been appointed a Senior Editor in Charge.

IX. WOMEN'S COMMITTEE

Newsweek shall continue to consult with the Women's Committee on matters of equal employment opportunity for women in the Editorial Department. The committee shall be chosen by the women in the Editorial Department.

X. REPORTING AND CONSULTATION

(1) On April 30, August 31, and December 31 of each year, *Newsweek* shall furnish a report in writing to the Women's Committee concerning performance under this Memorandum. (The initial report shall cover the period from the date of this Memorandum to the closing date for the report.)

(2) The reports referred to in paragraph (1) of this section shall include the following information:

(a) A completed copy of Form A, attached to this Memorandum, giving aggregate data about applicants during the reporting period who were sent letters containing a form rejection;

(b) A completed copy of Form B, attached to this Memorandum, for every candidate for a position as researcher who applied to or was approached by *Newsweek* during the reporting period (except those candidates who were sent a letter containing a form rejection);

(c) A completed copy of Form C, attached to this Memorandum, for every candidate for a position as reporter or bureau chief who applied to or was approached by *Newsweek* during the reporting period (except those candidates who were sent a letter containing a form rejection);

(d) A completed copy of Form D, attached to this Memorandum, for every candidate for a position as writer who applied to or was approached by *Newsweek* during the reporting period (except those candidates who were sent a letter containing a form rejection).

3) The information required to be included in reports pursuant to paragraph (2) of this section shall be limited by the following guidelines on confidentiality:

(a) For candidates who are already *Newsweek* employees, required information on experience about their current employment shall be limited to (i) the candidate's job classification at the time the candidate is considered for the position about which the report is being made and (ii) if the candidate is at that time working on the front-of-the-book or the back-of-the-book, in a domestic bureau or in a foreign bureau.

(b) For candidates who at the time of consideration for an editorial position are not *Newsweek* employees but who are working for another publication, required information about their current employment shall be limited to (i) name of the publication at which the candidate is employed; (ii) the candidate's skill or expertise—e.g., reporter, writer, editor, columnist; (iii) the candidate's substantive specialty—e.g., politics, sports, science; *provided that* if the supplying of information under (b) (i), (ii), and (iii) would identify a particular candidate, then the specificity of the information supplied in those three categories may be reduced, *provided further that* the reduction in specificity should be carried out first as to (b) (iii), then as to (b) (ii), and only as a last resort as to (b) (i). For example, instead of reporting that a candidate is the music critic for *Time,* the form might show that the candidate is an arts critic for *Time*. The name of the publication may be deleted only where such deletion is the only possible way to preserve the anonymity of the candidate. A candidate is deemed to be identified, and the candidate's anonymity destroyed, if the information supplied identifies the candidate as part of a class or group numbering five or less.

(4) The Women's Committee and representatives of *Newsweek* (including at least the Chief of Correspondents or one editor of the rank of Senior Editor in Charge or above) shall meet within one month after each periodic report has been presented to discuss the report and any other matters relating to equal employment opportunity for women employed in the Editorial Department.

XI. SETTLEMENT OF DIFFERENCE

If any issue arises out of an allegation of a violation of a specific obligation undertaken by *Newsweek* herein, this procedure shall be followed for resolving it:

(1) Any question by the Women's Committee shall first be given to the Chief of Correspondents for an explanation. If the question is why a particular *Newsweek* employee was not offered a position, the Chief of Correspondents shall give an explanation only if that employee has authorized him in writing to do so.

(2) Any difference or issue between the parties not resolved under paragraph (1) of this section shall be referred to a Joint Review Committee consisting of three persons designated by the Women's Committee and three persons designated by *Newsweek*.

(3) If the Joint Review Committee is unable to resolve the matter, it shall be submitted to arbitration by a single arbitrator, upon notice, under the Voluntary Labor Arbitration Rules then obtaining of the American Arbitration Association, and the parties shall abide by the award rendered.

(a) Any issue for arbitration shall be confined to matters arising out of or relating to this Memorandum.

(b) No such arbitration may be undertaken by a

woman employed in the Editorial Department of *Newsweek* except with the express approval of the Women's Committee.

(c) Every arbitrator shall be limited by the provisions of this Memorandum, and Title VII of the Civil Rights Act of 1964, 42 U.S.C. SS 2000e to 2000e–15, and the judicial case law applicable to Title VII.

(d) Any cost or expense of such arbitration shall be shared equally by *Newsweek* and the Women's Committee, except that neither shall be obligated to pay any part of the cost of a stenographic transcript except by its express consent.

(e) There shall be no stoppage of work by any woman employed in the Editorial Department over an issue that is in arbitration or that may be submitted to arbitration pursuant to this Memorandum.

(4) Any difference arising under this Memorandum shall be presented to the other party without delay, but in no event more than four weeks after the complaining party became aware or by reasonable diligence could have become aware of such difference. Either party may reject consideration of any issue that is not presented by the other party on or before July 15, 1975.

(5) No issue or other matter submitted to arbitration pursuant to any agreement between *Newsweek* and the Newspaper Guild of New York shall be submitted to arbitration pursuant to this Memorandum; and no issue submitted to arbitration pursuant to this Memorandum shall be submitted to arbitration pursuant to any agreement between *Newsweek* and the Newspaper Guild of New York.

XII. GUILD AGREEMENTS

Nothing in this Memorandum shall be interpreted or construed in any manner to supersede, contravene, or be inconsistent with any provision of any agreement between *Newsweek* and the Newspaper Guild of New York.

XIII. DURATION OF MEMORANDUM

Except where expressly provided otherwise, the obligations imposed under this Memorandum shall terminate on June 30, 1975.

XIV. CLAIMS AND COMPLAINTS

In consideration of the foregoing provisions of this Memorandum, each and all of the individual women who are signatories to this Memorandum and the Women's Committee, acting on behalf of all women previously or currently employed in the Editorial Department of *Newsweek* (except women who as of the date of this Memorandum have separate legal representation)

(a) do hereby release, acquit, exonerate, and forever discharge Newsweek, Inc., and The Washington Post Company, their officers, directors, employees, agents, servants, attorneys, and any others who may have acted in concert with them from any and all debts, actions, suits, complaints, proceedings, and any and all claims, demands, and liabilities arising from or relating to sex discrimination of any sort or character against any or all the women who are signatories to this Memorandum or women represented by the Women's Committee, or arising from or relating to any denial or abridgment of rights, privileges, opportunities, or benefits of employment affecting any or all of the women who are signatories to this Memorandum or women represented by the Women's Committee, occurring prior to the date of this Memorandum; and

(b) agree to withdraw forthwith any and all complaints, declarations, and similar documents commencing proceedings that they, or any of them, have filed with any agency of the United States or of the State of New York or of the City of New York arising under any statute, regulation, ordinance, or other law providing for equal employment opportunity, and to execute and file such further documents as may be necessary to terminate any and all proceedings which have been commenced on behalf of any or all of them in any such agency.

XV. This Memorandum contains the entire agreement between the parties concerning equal employment opportunity for women employed in *Newsweek*'s Editorial Department and shall not be modified except in writing.

INITIAL PRESENTATION BY THE CBS WOMEN'S GROUP TO CBS PRESIDENT ARTHUR R. TAYLOR

July 19, 1973

CBS WOMEN IN ATTENDANCE: Rene Burrough, Sylvia Chase, Judy Hole, Jane Tillman Irving, Anita Kopff, Ellen Levine, Barbara Lomholt Lingel, Marie Mahecha, Chin Mahieu, Nancy Perov, Lily Poskus, Susan Quigg, Janet Roach, Inge Schmidt, Lynn Sherr, Joan Stewart, Cheryl Taylor, Mary Gay Taylor, Priscilla Toumey, Louise Waller.

AGENDA

(1) Mutual Introduction of Women's Group and Management
(2) Introduction of Presentation
(3) Labor-Grade Problems
(4) Secretarial Problems
(5) Promotions, Opportunities, Training Programs, and Salary Differentials
(6) Benefits
(7) Women Counselors
(8) Image of Women at CBS
(9) Affirmative Action Plan and Conclusion
(10) Question and Answer Period

INTRODUCTION OF PRESENTATION

We represent CBS women in New York. We were chosen in fully publicized general meetings where every CBS division in New York was represented.

We appreciate this opportunity to meet with you. We know you are aware that women face discrimination at CBS. Since we are closest to the problem, we would like to work with you. We expect that this and subsequent meetings will lead us to solutions that will benefit CBS as a whole. Your policy notes indicate to us that you're willing to confront the situation and intend to change it.

We will talk about some of the most pressing problems women encounter as CBS employees and will make some initial recommendations.

LABOR-GRADE PROBLEMS

Fifty-one percent of the CBS work force is female.

The women of CBS are concentrated in labor-grade positions where the pay is low and the possibilities for change or advancement extremely limited.

Think of a switchboard operator. Does a man's voice come to mind? Think of a secretary. Can you picture a young man with a good education hitching his wagon to that star? And picture yourself living on their pay.

The vast majority of CBS women are employed in nonexempt jobs as secretaries, telephone operators, billers, clerks, computer operators.

And unless they themselves make extraordinary efforts that is where they stay—in the same departments, and the same jobs.

Despite the existence of the Career Inventory System and the posting of available jobs, women are not getting better jobs and greater opportunities. The statistics speak for themselves.

The major problem is a lack of communication between Personnel and most women. In addition, Company policy segregates labor-grade personnel facilities from MMC facilities. This bars traffic between the two categories and it becomes as difficult for a labor-grade woman to move into an exempt position as it is for an enlisted military man to become an officer.

The pay scale is biased to keep women in dead-end labor-grade jobs. The few E, F, and G level women who are offered entry-level executive positions are faced with substantial pay cuts if they choose to make a change.

A survey of CBS made in 1971 by the McKinsey Company set three years as "about right" for a high potential person to stay in one job.

We maintain that women are particularly stagnated in jobs because of lack of management interest in their promotion.

Because women have been conditioned to accept this situation, there must be active recruiting within CBS.

The minority training is the only in-house training program we have; job mobility for women has not been a Company priority. Limited as it is, the minority training program must not be compromised, but programs for both groups must be expanded, and additional funds allocated for that purpose.

CBS does have an Educational Assistance Program, but women who seek outside training for another job are often unaware of the program's existence. It would be interesting to know how many applications are received and how many grants given each year to men and to women.

According to CBS Personnel, there are only three women employed in broadcast union technical jobs. If CBS were to apply pressure on all its unions to hire women, new job categories would be opened up, and there would be women among the CBS staff carpenters, painters, plumbers, electricians, video-tape operators, and stagehands.

The job reclassification program is not well known, and should be better publicized. The annual personnel appraisal is a source of great distress; it can be used unfairly, and has been used as a threat. Many women are unaware that a post-evaluation conference is mandated. Employers should be required to verify in writing that the interview has taken place, and management might consider asking employees to evaluate their supervisors, on a similar form.

Older women at CBS have a particular problem. Some who have been with the Company for 10 and 15 years hold the same or same level job that they started with. For example, one accounting assistant, who started as a biller 14 years ago, now makes $198 a week. Obviously, she did not leave to get married or have babies, but that was the reason given for not promoting her, when she was passed over, in favor of a 20-year-old. Particular attention should be given to compensating these older women.

The few established programs leading to advancement for labor-grade personnel are described in the employees' handbook, but this written notice is insufficient. Active INTERNAL recruiting is required, combined with on-the-job training and encouragement from management to seek outside training under the Educational Assistance Program.

SECRETARIAL PROBLEMS
Fifty-one percent of the CBS work force is female.

The greatest single block of labor-grade women at CBS is concentrated in the secretarial category.

These are low-status jobs, as evidenced by the kinds of housekeeping chores that are added to a secretary's professional responsibilities, and by our salaries and the difficulties we have in moving into other job categories.

A poll of CBS secretaries turned up the following most common complaints, and I quote:

From a Magna Cum Laude College Graduate:
"When my boss occasionally loses a phone number or when he forgets an appointment that he has set up without my prior knowledge, he will often expect me to take the blame for his confusion. What is of great concern to me is that I want to get ahead in my department, and it is mortifying to me that I often must appear to be extremely stupid and inefficient in the eyes of executives whom

I want to impress with my abilities. My boss feels I should accept the blame graciously because protecting him is part of my job. He has told me, if the mistake is mine, no one will pay much attention to it because everyone expects a secretary to make little mistakes now and then, whereas executives cannot get away with that kind of error."

From a Secretary Whose Principal Duty Is Taking Care of Her Boss's Personal Business:
"While I would not mind doing this kind of thing part of the time, I find that he will stop me doing some work involving CBS in order to take on some personal task for him. When I tried to discuss with him the fact that I wanted to work for CBS in order to be involved with its business, not his, he showed me the portion of the secretarial manual that says a secretary should keep in touch with her boss's personal needs."

From Another College Graduate:
"It is galling to me to have to fetch and pour coffee four times a day, in his own special cup, or he won't drink it. I must also keep his water jug filled and cleanse it thoroughly every day because he is a very fussy Stillman dieter. My boss also complains that the cleaning people do not do a very good job on his desk at night; therefore, my first job every morning is dusting his desk. Please help me!"

How can the Company help?

(1) All secretarial jobs should be classified according to a secretary's responsibilities, not those of his/her boss.

(2) Women who apply for entry-level jobs should be offered the same variety of nonsecretarial positions as men.

(3) Offer monetary rewards for tenure in one position.

(4) Expand the Career Inventory System to include salary grade employees below G level, since there are so few secretarial positions at or above that level.

(5) Issue a manual directed to executives which states that

certain parts of a secretary's job should remain optional, such as doing his/her boss's personal business.

(6) Revise the secretarial manual to make it acceptable to intelligent, professional secretaries.

Historically, secretaries were men and the job was considered a training ground for management. Secretaries learned the inner workings of their departments and ultimately became managers themselves. As the job acquired a female label, it lost its training connotations and status.

We would like them to be restored.

PROMOTIONS, OPPORTUNITIES, TRAINING PROGRAMS, AND SALARY DIFFERENTIALS

Fifty-one percent of the CBS work force is female.

But the high managerial ranks are woefully lacking in female membership. "It's a men's club." The great majority of us hold low-ranking positions. This is illustrated by the CBS Telephone Directory.

—Of the 2,130 names listed, only 351 (16.5 percent) are women.

—Of the 400 managers at both the Headquarters building and the Broadcast Center, only 61 (15.2 percent) are women.

—Of the 379 directors, associate directors, and assistant directors, only 21 (5.5 percent) are women.

—Of the Company's 85 vice-presidents, only one is a woman.

There are only three women above (Executive) Level 10, where the Executive Incentive Program begins. There are none above 15.

Any way you cut the deck, women come out holding the low cards.

In our experience, when the logical candidate to fill a particular job opening in a department is female, the Company often goes outside or to other departments to find suitable male candidates. This rarely happens when the heir apparent is male. The Company shows definite prejudice against giving women high-level job titles and salaries, even when the candidate is experienced, educated, and efficient.

There are women achievers at CBS, holding responsible jobs and earning high pay. But we are few. And our earnings are paltry compared to men's. CBS women with management potential tend to be channeled into a few, familiar areas: Personnel, Promotion, Community and Audience Relations, Research, and Archives. Other lucrative areas seem to be closed to us in practice, if not in theory. A female executive in Sales, for example, is truly a rare bird.

Existing training programs, since they are directed toward management personnel, tend to be for-men-only because management women are so scarce.

We want to believe that CBS is committed to changing this picture. We suggest that the Company undertake several specific programs, comparable to those recommended by McKinsey in its Management Survey of 1971, so that next year at this time, the number of female managers, directors, and vice-presidents will be at least four to five times what it is today. From then on, there should be a balanced increase every year, parallel to men's advancement.

We hope that the Company considers the problems women face at least as serious and worthy of solution as the management turnover problem which necessitated the McKinsey study.

Following are several McKinsey suggestions for managers that we have adapted and recommend be applied to women:

(1) Create managerial career paths that would develop varied experience and skills for potential female senior managers.

(2) Ensure "fast track" for the top 20 percent of female managers.

(3) Increase intergroup transfers of female managers, where appropriate, to avoid pockets of long tenure.

(4) Provide challenging managerial positions to lower-level

female managers, and open all departments to qualified female candidates.

(5) Allocate sufficient funds to develop improved formal training programs for women, so that the existing inequity may be at least partially leveled-off in the short run.

BENEFITS

Fifty-one percent of the CBS work force is female.

Statistics show that women live longer than men. They are now employed longer, and in the near future companies will have significantly more female employees to retire. The present CBS pension plan is applied equally to men and women, but since most women are in the lower-paid jobs we naturally will receive less pension money. The Company, in introducing its investment fund planning, pointed out that an employee now needs 43 percent of his or her salary to live on after retirement. The difference between 43 percent of $40,000 and 43 percent of $10,000 is considerable. The employee investment fund with its maximum contributory factor of 5 percent does not add much to the picture when, again, you take 5 percent of $40,000 vs. 5 percent of $10,000. Not to mention the additional perquisite of the executive incentive plan for managers at executive level 10 and above.

Equal Employment Opportunity Commission guidelines indicate that payment of benefits shall not be based on any factors, actuarial or otherwise, which discriminate because of sex. If the CBS pension plan and group life insurance policies are based on male-female tables, they should be brought up to date to meet new guidelines.

In some respects, the CBS medical plan is quite adequate with regard to maternity benefits. If all CBS maternity benefits do not follow the new EEOC guidelines, however, they should be revised to do so. The guidelines state:

Disabilities caused or contributed to by pregnancy, miscarriage, abortion, childbirth, and recovery therefrom are, for all job-related purposes, temporary disabilities and should be treated as such under any health or temporary disability insurance or sick leave plan available in connection with employment. . . .

It should be noted that the cost of the current CBS maternity coverage discriminates against female executives. Female salary-grade employees are automatically enrolled, free of charge, for such coverage. Female executive personnel must enroll for dependent coverage at a cost of $2.60 per week. This inequity should be rectified.

We would also like to address ourselves to the question of nonmedical maternal or parental leaves for the purpose of child-rearing. At this time, there is no stated CBS policy on the subject. It should be considered, as there is increasing concern on the part of men and women regarding equal sharing of the responsibilities for the care of young children.

We would like you to consider at this point an additional benefit. At present, in Hollywood and in Terre Haute, CBS employees have credit unions. It is believed that an employee can get, for example, a $1,000 loan at an interest rate of four percent. What a savings that is to low-paid female employees who often find themselves refused bank credit unless they have collateral for the very fact that employment is not guaranteed if one is of child-bearing age. Most important, however, is that investing in shares of a credit union could prove a big boost in the final retirement income of the low-paid female. Almost like owning a piece of the "Black Rock."

WOMEN COUNSELORS
Fifty-one percent of the CBS work force is female.

Early this year, five women were appointed as counselors, on a part-time basis.

As stated in your Policy Notes, these counselors are "to deal with the gripes, the hopes, and the aspirations" of CBS women—a sizable group—the majority of CBS employees.

Traditionally, laborers' complaints are called grievances. The use of the term "gripes" offended many of us because it suggests the corporation does not consider the status of women at CBS a serious labor problem.

It seems to many of us that five women, assigned part-time, are insufficient to tackle the problems of 51 percent of the CBS work force.

We would like to see some advanced management techniques applied to the problem.

The five women currently are spending a great deal of personal time, as well as company time, in their capacity as counselors. It is our feeling that serious consideration should now be given to the idea of making these full-time positions.

Many CBS women, prospective recipients of this counseling, would like to add their ideas on how to improve the status of women at CBS.

IMAGE OF WOMEN AT CBS

As broadcast by CBS, the image of women is the most controversial and, we have found in our study of the subject, the most elusive of all the issues which have been raised. It is also basic to any change in the status of women here at CBS. Our product reflects what CBS feels about women. As internal policy changes, so should our air product.

There are at least three reasons to alter our perceptions of women: First: Self-respect. Women are organizing because they want to get a fair shake. To some of us that means we aspire to hold positions of responsibility within this Company. (Who knows? As we sit here, someone may be wondering how her paintings would look in this office.) Any executive will be proud to say that her company was in the vanguard, was first to determine that something should be done to portray the new woman as she really is.

Who is she?

She is a worker. Forty-one percent of the women in the United States are full-time workers.

More than six million children under the age of six have mothers who work full time. Of the families in question, 40 percent of the women work because their incomes are NECESSARY (that is, their husbands earn less than $7,000 annually).

Forty-two percent of working women are single, widowed, divorced, or otherwise without husbands.

If these statistics fail to convince us that the average American woman is not always middle class and/or married and/or a mother, then consider these:

The rate of divorce increased 80 percent from 1960 to 1972. The Bureau of Census estimates that by 1980, 25 to 30 percent of the marriages of people now in their thirties will have ended in divorce. As a Census Bureau official said, "There's been a social revolution going on and nobody has been paying attention to it." There is a new American woman out there watching us, with intellectual and practical needs which are not being served by much of current television programming.

This brings us to the second reason why we ought to adjust our perceptions of women: Women are consumers. In broadcast marketing, women, ages 18 to 49, are the advertisers' targets. Yet, Nielsen figures show that in May [1973] only 4,830,000 women (11.1 percent of the total population) even *watched* prime-time television. We know that television audiences are declining. Bold and innovative programming seems very much in order.

If at least part of that new programming spoke to the needs of the new women, yet a third purpose would be served. This is the time of license challenges. Everybody knows that affiliate relations are vital to our company. If the network takes the lead in serving needs which are articulated in these license challenges, it will be doing affiliates a good service.

Now that we have discussed some of the reasons why we feel the image of women must be a part of CBS's new policy, let us explain what that image now is.

We have not conducted a survey of CBS network television. We hope it will never be necessary to do so because that kind of thing usually is part of a legal action. But the work done by license challengers to WRC and WABC is worth reviewing.

Their monitors of daytime television produced a generally unflattering and unrealistic portrait of the American woman. She emerged a caricature: either a neurotic misfit or a fatuous homebody. We submit that workers and wives are neither.

Remember the old days of radio? Ma Perkins was a loving, supportive grandmother, chockful of wisdom which, if sometimes platitudinous, provided women with a model for loving and nurturing their offspring. Helen Trent tried to find out if a "woman 35 or over" could "find happiness."

She didn't find much of that, but along the way, she solved mysteries, got her friends out of jams and was, in general, the sort of career woman you'd turn to in a pinch. Our Gal Sunday was a model of American virtue. Married to an English lord, she upheld traditional American values and emerged triumphant in a field of usually rather decadent players.

Recently, CBS News Correspondent Marya McLaughlin spent a day watching CBS "soaps." She found that these dramas were, in fact, dealing with some very current issues: abortion, divorce, women's liberation, the working woman. However, she observed that the women characters who became involved with these issues always seemed to end up in jail or a hospital bed. In fact, it seems to us that soap operas seem to prey on the fears of women. Even their titles suggest a sort of twilight world . . . a place where you'd expect to find only disaster: "The Young and the Restless," "Edge of Night," "Secret Storm," "Search for Tomorrow." (On the plus side, we must say we are wholeheartedly in favor of, at least the title, "Love of Life.")

If you're a quiz show fan, you're denied the pleasure of seeing a woman as Mistress of Ceremonies.

If you're a Sunday afternoon watcher, you'll seldom see women as guests or panelists on "Face the Nation."

If you look at the promos for WCBS Television News, you'll think there's not a single woman employed in that news room. The copy doesn't help a bit when it refers to "newsmen."

To develop this fleeting and too general commentary on the image of women at CBS, many womanhours were spent with CBS marketing and sales people and figures. In the process, we learned much, but not enough. We would like to learn more. We are confident that, if you will give us access to your professional expertise, you will be rewarded. We would like to help CBS find new vehicles which will sell to the market we need and which will do credit to the Company. In the process, we hope you will discover the talents of your women work force and put them to work in the programming department.

Certainly, the addition of some women, ages 18 to 49 or over, will give you a vital marketing resource.

As we say in the promos, CBS has been the leading television network for 17 years. We'd like to keep it that way. Let us help.

AFFIRMATIVE ACTION PLAN AND CONCLUSION

We are sure you're not surprised by the issues we've raised this afternoon about the status of women employees at CBS. They are the same concerns being raised by working women all over the country—from those in tiny companies with a couple of dozen employees to those in corporate giants like AT&T. They are issues that federal agencies such as the Equal Employment Opportunity Commission have made top priority.

With the hindsight gained from the older civil rights struggle, both women and the government have learned which methods seriously combat discriminatory policies and practices and which do not. What has proved totally ineffective over the years is the simple issuance by companies of statements proclaiming nondiscriminatory policies. What has proved much more effective is the institution of a strong affirmative action program backed by top management and including employment goals and a timetable for reaching them. These kinds of affirmative action plans are so well thought of that they are required of government contractors. We believe such a program is the only way CBS can show its sincere commitment to its female employees even if CBS were not a federal contractor.

We propose that CBS draw up a single corporate affirmative action plan for women. It should include, but not be limited to, the recommendations noted throughout this presentation, as well as those that follow. Ideally this affirmative action program will compensate in part for past wrongs and guard against future discrimination.

(1) A Women's Advisory Council should be established immediately, made up of elected representatives from each division or group.

(2) The entire labor-grade personnel structure should be overhauled so that many of the jobs that are now dead-end would instead be steps on a longer-term career ladder. Since a large majority of women at CBS are secretaries, this job category should be the first to be restructured.

(3) The next two openings on the board of directors should be filled by women.

(4) Serious consideration should be given to the creation of permanent part-time positions. The availability of such jobs would benefit both men and women who need time for child-rearing, study, or other nonsalaried projects.

(5) Borrowing from the precedent-setting AT&T affirmative action program, CBS's promotion pay schedule should be totally revised. For instance, the new salary a secretary would receive on promotion should be determined mainly on her length of service with CBS, not on her salary at the time of promotion, or necessarily on the salary set for the new job category. This mechanism would go a long way toward compensating women who have been unfairly passed over for promotions.

(6) A complete review of the educational background, ex-

perience, and current qualifications should be undertaken immediately of all female employees with at least four years' tenure. In this way, CBS can ascertain who should be promoted or upgraded immediately.

(7) CBS should allocate sufficient funds to develop training programs tailored to the unique needs of each division. Apprenticeship programs with unions should be drawn up and funded jointly by CBS and the unions. Like a new promotion pay schedule, training and apprenticeships in some degree compensate women for past discrimination.

(8) Consciousness-raising programs for both male and female employees should be instituted so that men and women can come to understand all the ramifications of sexism and how to eliminate it from the day-to-day working environment.

(9) Internal recruiting and training must be the primary method for filling all open positions. If qualified women cannot be found in this manner, the corporation should actively recruit women from the outside.

(10) CBS should set up a monitoring system to ensure that its affirmative action program is carried out at all levels. An integral part of the monitoring system should be the hiring of an EEO officer specifically for women. The EEO officer would be in addition to any kind of counselor and/or Advisory Council.

(11) Last, but most crucial to the ultimate elimination of discrimination, is the establishment of employment goals and a timetable for reaching them. For instance, the *Newsweek* settlement announced last week has a goal that by January 1975 one-third of its reporters and writers will be women. Knowing the labor pool of qualified women is at least that large for many of CBS's job categories, we think similar goals and target dates are reasonable objectives. EEOC broke more new ground in the AT&T case by setting employment goals for men in previously all-female jobs. By the same token, we think 25 percent of CBS secretaries should ultimately be male.

So that no time is lost, we would like to establish the Advisory Council immediately and schedule a meeting one month from now with you and whoever else should be present to discuss which of our proposals can be implemented most quickly and to set up a realistic time schedule in which to do that. Also at that meeting, we can arrange a longer range timetable for those proposals requiring much further study and set up task forces to undertake the work.

You have already taken some initial steps on the long road toward eliminating discriminatory policies and practices at CBS. Your top management includes people like Franklin Thomas on the Board of Directors; Jack Schneider, whose Broadcast Group underwrote the Conference Board study on women; Richard Salant in the News Division; David Nelson at WCBS Radio; John Backe at Holt—all of whom have publicly expressed their eagerness to eliminate sexism in their divisions. Because of these things, we feel confident that with a strong commitment and hard work on your side and continued pressure and hard work on our side, CBS can become a leader among American corporations in the effort to raise the status of women in the labor force.

CBS RESPONSE TO WOMEN'S GROUP PRESENTATION

August 17, 1973

At the meeting held on Thursday, July 19, 1973, we had agreed to respond promptly and fully to the many points raised in the presentation submitted at that meeting. While there are some issues on which we are not completely in agreement with your views, there is no question that the area of agreement is more significant and extensive than the area of disagreement. We want to continue to discuss our disagreements; meanwhile, the fact that there is such broad agreement is a very important consideration for the future.

As has been pointed out in the President's Policy Note on Women, there is no dispute that over the years women have not progressed in the same manner and to the same extent as men and that, in consequence of this, serious inequities exist. This is, of course, a national problem, existing extensively throughout business and industry as well as government—a problem really only focused on in the last couple of years. We think that most fair-minded people would concede that CBS's record to date has been significantly better than that of others. Nonetheless, there is still much to do.

We believe that the drive for the equality of opportunity for women in business and industry has reached the point where there can be no turning back, where it has an inevitability and momentum of its own. All of business, CBS included, obviously has a lot of catching up to do. However, not a great deal of purpose will be served by either excusing or condemning the past; the key standard for all of us is our present and future commitment and whether programs are developed and carried out effectively to give meaning to that commitment.

One important disclaimer: No one should expect instant perfection. Many of the problems and inequities raised in your presentation, even with the best will in the world and with maximum effort, will take time to correct; that is inherent in effecting change in any large organization. It is true whether we are dealing with issues relating to women, men, or minorities, or even nonpersonnel issues that do not so intimately involve the human equation.

Suffice to say that CBS has always cherished its role as a leader in an environment of change; in the same way, we expect to provide constructive leadership in finding solutions to the flood of problems being identified by the women's movement. You should bear in mind, however, that those who lead the way on un-chartered paths are precisely those who are most likely to stumble from time to time. We hope, therefore, that if we occasionally seem to be groping for our way, you will not mistake our intentions. We also hope that you will not reject ideas simply because they come from management. The management of CBS—even if it is composed predominantly of men at the present time—has the practical business experience to bring to bear on the problems facing us.

In fact, most of the progress that CBS has made to date—and that progress since the beginning of the year has been significant—has come from the initiation of CBS management. We think it is pertinent to review briefly and in general terms what that progress has been.

(1) *President's Policy Note on Women.* This Note, which was issued on February 13, 1973, expresses the commitment of the Company to the advancement of women in the Company structure and contains the categorical promise that means will be provided to fulfill the commitment. Mr. Taylor has followed through on this in his travels around the Company by emphasizing this commitment in numerous meetings and discussions with thousands of CBS employees.

(2) *Appointment of Woman Counselors.* The concept of "Woman Counselor" was a CBS invention, and the creation of this position underscores our traditional willingness to provide innovative leadership. We believe that with the creation of this position, we have opened an important new channel of communication—for those women who wish to avail themselves of it—between the women of the Company and management. This enables the Company not only to be better cognizant of those women's thoughts and needs, but also provides the women of CBS with the means of learning, on a day-to-day basis, the actions that are being taken by management to improve the situation of women. It is also a means

of providing better access for women to management for redress of individual grievances. The contributions made by the Woman Counselors have been inadequately recognized. Perhaps most importantly, they have influenced management in its thinking; it is hard to visualize how we could have made such progress between February and August without them. We will be saying more about the evolving role of the Woman Counselor later in this response.

(3) *Centralized listing of all open positions.* Last year the Company began centralized listing of all open positions with the personnel office at each location. This ensures that all vacancies are known to all personnel functions and opportunity is not confined within single divisions or units. Moreover, exempt positions throughout the entire Company are listed with Manpower Management, Compensation (MMC) in New York.

(4) *Two-week waiting period to search for women and minorities.* The establishment of a two-week waiting period before a vacancy can be filled has been—and is—an extremely valuable and effective device in giving the Company time to search out qualified women and minority candidates prior to filling the vacancy either internally or externally.

(5) *Posting of lower level executive positions.* Recently the Company has provided job posting for all vacant exempt positions in executive levels 1 to 4 to facilitate the movement of women from salary grade to executive levels. We will expand the posting procedure to keep the posting open until the job has actually been filled and to include additional higher executive level positions, probably up to grade 10.

(6) *Career Inventory System.* This system, which represents the master inventory and skills bank of CBS employees, is being used successfully to identify qualified candidates, both men and women, for promotion. Recently the system was extended to include employees in salary grades G, H, and I. It is our intention, after the resolution of technical problems, to extend the system to all employees whose career objectives include executive level jobs.

(7) *Recruiting techniques.* All sources of recruitment and all

labor unions with which we have contracts have been advised country-wide of our special desire to see women candidates for executive, professional, and craft positions. All advertisements for executive, professional, and craft positions carry the statement, "Male/female applicants from all races desired."

(8) *Consultants.* Recognizing the scarcity of sound professionalism to deal effectively with many of the women's issues now being raised, the Company has intentionally sought out supplementary professional help wherever available. This has included the employment of the consulting firm of Boyle/Kirkman and making available the service of an industrial psychologist.

(9) *Awareness sessions.* In recognition of the fact that deeply ingrained male attitudes do represent an obstacle to the progress of women, the Company has been piloting awareness sessions with supervisory management. These sessions are being very well received, and we anticipate they will be extended.

(10) *Individual management meetings.* For over a year MMC has been conducting meetings with group and division presidents and other managers, not only to emphasize our commitment to equal opportunity for women but also to encourage the recognition of "fast track" women in the normal promotion process. In addition to the individual meetings, presentations to this effect have been made at the annual meetings of the Broadcast Group and the Finance and Development Departments. The MMC Report, which has had wide circulation, also includes a section on our policies in respect to women employees.

(11) *Orientation programs.* In recognition of the fact that another significant obstacle to expanding opportunities for women is their very unfamiliarity with the kinds of jobs that might be available, we will begin to pilot a series of orientation programs to familiarize employees with various positions in each of the divisions and groups.

(12) *High-potential women.* We have instituted a system for the identification of "high-potential" women.

(13) *Secretarial positions.* A study has been initiated, in

conjunction with the Employee-Management Committee, to identify dissatisfactions of women in relation to secretarial positions
and to propose solutions. The secretarial guide is in the process of
being rewritten to eliminate any objectionable portions and will be
reissued in the near future.

(14) *Pay patterns.* A study of the pay patterns and job
classifications for men and women in comparable positions, taking
into account performance, service, and other relative considerations, is in process. Any inequities that may be found will be
corrected as they are revealed. We believe unqualifiedly in the
principle of equal pay for equal work.

(15) *Training.* We are working hard to define the need for
internal and external training and will be developing programs to
meet these needs. This will have to be a continuing and long-term
effort. One new course we are planning will give training in supervisory techniques. We are looking for additional ideas as to what
kind of training courses would be of value. We believe that the
best overall program will be based primarily on on-the-job training
supplemented by specialized supportive training courses.

(16) *Job restructuring.* Another important but long-term
study looks to restructuring of positions, which has begun in
selected areas. In addition, we are reviewing job description so as
to identify and create more entry-level jobs that have upward
mobility and offer logical career potential in order to expand the
opportunities for women.

(17) *Management incentives to progress.* CBS recognized
that incentives are as much a spur to progress on this as on other
issues, and consequently we are including general goals and targets
for operational management as a key part of their executive incentive compensation programs.

All of the foregoing represents an action program for which
no apology is necessary.

(Mr. Wool noted that the statistics cited by the women's group
were derived from listings in the CBS New York Telephone

Directory, which is neither an authoritative source of grade information nor all-inclusive. It does not cover all New York City CBS offices.)

SALARY (LABOR) GRADE PROBLEMS

We would not want to quarrel here with the underlying premise expressed in your presentation that the women of CBS (who, incidentally consist of 43 percent, not 51 percent, of the CBS work force) are concentrated in salary grade positions at the lower end of the pay scale, and that insufficient opportunity has been presented to enable women to develop the experience necessary to be promoted to higher level and more remunerative positions. This is what the dialogue between us is all about.

We do, however, have some differences relating to the implications of some of your statements, on which we would like to comment.

—While it is true that in the past women have had to make extraordinary efforts to be promoted out of their existing jobs into executive levels, it is our view that that describes a past condition and that the beginning of change is already in effect.

—The Career Inventory System and the posting of available jobs has resulted in an increasing number of promotions to better jobs for women.

—While there may have been some lack of communication between Personnel and most women, our Personnel Department never wanted it that way. We recognize that having women personnel executives in charge of placement is not sufficient to ensure the necessary dialogue. We feel that the appointment of the Woman Counselors was an important initiative on our part and that it has opened up lines of communication. Moreover, we have now brought the Personnel Department and Manpower Management, Compensation under a single vice-president to ensure improved communication between these two staff departments.

—The pay scale is not intentionally designed to keep women in dead-end salary grade jobs. A woman moving from a salary grade job to an exempt position would not be taking a pay cut in making this move unless she is foregoing significant overtime earnings, which are, in any case, taken into account in setting the new salary. Within reason, we shall try to mitigate this, but this adjustment is not unique to women; it is a decision that men must make too as they progress in their careers.

—We plan to deal with the "stagnation" of women in their current jobs through a positive career development program. We agree on the need for training programs, and as indicated above we are working in this area. These programs will not be a substitute for minority programs, and within reasonable bounds, funding will not be a problem.

—We believe that the CBS Educational Assistance Program is in fact more widely known to women than you think. During the most recent past period, 30 percent of the participants in the program were women, and there is no restriction on the eligibility. Nevertheless, we will underscore open eligibility in future announcements.

—The issue of cooperation with unions in training programs is a difficult and complicated one. Our union contracts typically have antidiscrimination clauses. We will investigate the possibility of securing the unions' assistance in hiring and training and will be reporting back on a piecemeal basis during the remainder of the year. A major problem is the very low turnover in craft jobs; in New York, the overall union turnover figure for 1972 was 8 percent. Among technicians, the turnover was only 4 percent. Also, you should recognize that until recently few women have expressed an interest in many of the jobs that fall under union jurisdiction. In the meantime, we are pleased to note that CND has hired its first camerawoman in New York and a soundwoman in Washington. This is an area where orientation programs will help.

—We will attempt to better publicize the job reclassification procedures. We have already, prior to our previous meeting, adopted some of your recommendations with respect to performance appraisal, which has become a mandatory procedure this year. Postappraisal interviews are now required, and the supervisor must sign the form. The form now also reflects the employee's aspirations, short- and long-term, as stated by the employee. We will not ask employees to evaluate their supervisors on a similar form at the present time.

—The problem of women with long tenure is indeed particularly difficult. Every grade has a salary range, with new employees generally starting at the lower end, and the ranges are increased from time to time in light of competitive and economic conditions, so that some salary progression within grade is possible. We will examine what other companies are doing in this area, and we will see if the woman with long tenure can be given some preference in career advancement.

—We agree with your final comments that a key element of the ultimate solution is active internal recruiting, combined with on-the-job training and outside training under the Educational Assistance Program. We are working to provide better programs.

SECRETARIAL PROBLEMS

We think it might be useful to state some general propositions, which might help to put the issue of the appropriate role of the secretary in context.

The management of CBS believes strongly in the perhaps old-fashioned virtue that all employees, men and women, are entitled to be treated with dignity and respect. We believe that we have no jobs that are inherently demeaning; but it is unfortunate that in practice some may not share this view. We also believe that it is sound business practice for CBS employees to abide by a rule of maximum separation of their personal and business affairs. It is not unreasonable, however, that some managers, in organizing their daily affairs for reasonable efficiency, will wish to deal with some of their personal business affairs during business hours, in the same way that they very frequently take business papers home to deal with in the evenings and on weekends. As long as a rule of reason is practiced, we see nothing objectionable in this or in secretaries assisting their managers in these personal affairs—if that assistance is based on a spirit of willing cooperation. So that there will be no doubt, the Company does not require secretaries to assist their managers with their personal affairs, and no secretary who objects to this will have it held against her in her CBS career. Beyond this, it goes without saying that the CBS secretary is not a personal servant.

Turning now to your specific recommendations:

—We agree that secretarial jobs should be classified according to a secretary's responsibilities—in other words, job content—but we do feel that the position and responsibilities of the supervisor are among the several criteria impacting on this job content. This has always been the intent, although there are undoubtedly secretarial positions improperly classified. In the short term, we are examining these misclassifications as they come to our attention and taking appropriate action. Further on, we discuss the issue of identifying those secretarial positions which can be made into meaningful training jobs, and their job classifications will reflect this.

—It has always been our policy to try to expose women candidates for employment at CBS to the highest level available opening consistent with their education, training, and experience. Unfortunately, as noted on several occasions, much has to be done to define more entry-level positions so that greater opportunities are available to women and to ensure that those entry-level positions are truly significant rungs on the career ladder.

—We are not in favor of offering monetary rewards for tenure in one position beyond the salary increases that are available within the range for the job.

—As noted above, we are expanding the Career Inventory System to those interested.

—We do not think it necessary to issue a separate manual to

executives on the secretary's job, but we have commented above on our views as to the secretary's responsibilities in relation to the supervisor's personal business.

—We are revising the secretarial manual along the lines suggested and expect that the new manual will be issued in the near future.

Finally, it is our view that the secretarial position at CBS should be offering two distinct types of career opportunity. First, as you suggest, it should be one of the significant entry-level positions providing knowledge, training, and experience leading to other career opportunities. At the same time, it should provide an opportunity for advancement with respect to job content and consequently financial reward for those employees who view the secretarial position as a sufficient career unto itself, offering its own pattern of rewards and satisfactions.

PROMOTIONS, OPPORTUNITIES, TRAINING PROGRAMS, AND SALARY DIFFERENTIALS

We believe that the two-week waiting period, the Career Inventory System, and job posting—all already instituted—will go a long way toward eliminating the risk of passing over qualified women candidates for promotions. Beyond this, we must more broadly define job specifications so that capable women candidates are not precluded from opportunities based on an unnecessarily narrow definition of experience requirements.

We agree that we must break out from the tendency to limit women to a few familiar promotion channels.

We agree that we need an extensive effort to promote a sufficient number of women managers and executives until such time as we can be comfortable with a balanced increase every year comparable to men's advancement. We are not sure whether the right number of promotions is four to five times today's level, or more, or less.

Again, turning to your specific points:

—We agree on the need for managerial career paths, and this program is in development.

—We agree on the need for a "fast track" program. We do not think your 20 percent figure is meaningful—probably virtually all of our women managers today can be considered as being on a "fast track." As our pool of women managers grows, you will have to remember that a "fast track" program, by its very nature, must be confined to relatively small numbers to be effective.

—We agree that an increase in intergroup transfers for women managers is appropriate. It is appropriate for men as well. The Career Inventory System should help in this respect.

—We want to provide more challenging managerial positions for women and to open all departments to qualified candidates. It will take time to develop programs and make progress.

—We agree on the need for improved training; we have indicated that this is being developed and have said that, within reasonable bounds, funding will not be a problem.

BENEFITS

As you have indicated, the CBS Pension Plan applies equally to men and women, but to the extent that women are concentrated in lower paid jobs, their pensions tend to be smaller in absolute terms. The Company believes that the Pension Plan cannot be modified to take this problem into account. There is, however, at least one saving grace. Our Pension Plan relates the level of an employee's pension payments to his or her final pay; to the extent that we can, from here on in, move women up the career and salary ladder, these women will have pensions which do not penalize them for their years of service at the lower pay levels.

We do not believe that any provision of our Pension Plan is in violation of EEOC guidelines. Needless to say, we will at all times comply with those guidelines.

On the subject of the CBS Medical Plan, as it relates to maternity benefits, we frankly have a divergence of view. We do not believe that a normal childbirth should be considered as a disability. In our view, maternity leave is more analogous to military leave than to disability leave, and the guiding rule should be—and is—that the woman employee is given a reasonable leave of absence and assurance that the interruption of service will not prejudice her career opportunities.

You note that women executives must pay for the cost of their dependent coverage while salary grade employees receive such coverage free. This is not a discrimination issue, but simply a difference in benefit packages available. Nevertheless, we would like to do something for what we believe to be the relatively small number of women executives affected, but we have thus far been unable to work out any acceptable method with our insurers. We will continue to work on this issue.

We disagree with your comments in respect to non medical leave, maternal or paternal, for the purpose of child-rearing. The granting of such leaves to employees can interfere with the career opportunities of the employees who remain. It is Company policy, however, not to be arbitrary in evaluating requests for leaves of absence.

On the issue of a credit union, the Company has considered this from time to time and is in no way opposed. The particular difficulty has been getting people who are willing to spend time in the operation of the credit union. If a real demand exists for a credit union, we are willing to lend the conventional Company support to such an operation.

WOMAN COUNSELORS

You have made a particular point that the use of the term "gripes" in the President's Policy Note on Women tended to offend. Any offense was unintended. We will not use the word "gripes" in the future. We hope for your part that you will not unduly make an issue of the use of words. If every single word has to be chosen with absolute care, communication will become impossible. Let us concentrate on our substantive problems rather than worrying unduly about form or words.

We are in general agreement with your comments in respect to Woman Counselors. As indicated previously, the appointment of Woman Counselors was a major new initiative arising out of the President's Policy Note. The general intent was to provide a vehicle for open communication between the women of CBS and management and to provide a means by which individual women could discuss grievances and inequities and seek advice with respect to career opportunities and aspirations.

Being a Woman Counselor has turned out to be a pretty tough job, consisting mostly it sometimes seems, apart from long hours and hard work, of a broad misunderstanding by others of what they are trying to accomplish. It is, therefore, all the more satisfying to see how much the Woman Counselors have helped us achieve in such a relatively short time. The threads of this contribution are woven into many of the actions discussed in this response.

In defining the responsibilities of the Woman Counselors, we had no previous experience on which we could rely. It was always intended that the role of the Woman Counselor would evolve with experience and that the Company would make appropriate changes over time. Our present thinking is that in the short term we will in fact be moving in the direction of making the Woman Counselors full time, and that they will be given increased management responsibilities in helping the Company develop and implement specific action programs. They will, of course, continue to be an important channel of communication.

Beyond that, the future role is less certain, but it is possible in the longer term that the responsibilities of the Woman Counselors will give way to more professional in-house counseling and program planning. Moving in that direction will enable us to better ensure that career counseling is available to all employees. It would also be an important step in our longer term program of providing a better integration of the Personnel, Manpower Management, and group management development functions, so that we can have a more meaningful career development program for all employees.

AFFIRMATIVE ACTION PLAN AND CONCLUSION

CBS has an active plan for women. It derives its corporate authority and commitment from the President's Policy Note on Women and is in fact the summation of all the actions we have outlined. It does include, where appropriate and where we are able to do so, definite goals and objectives.

With regard to your specific points:

(1) We are willing to see, and in fact encourage, the creation of a CBS Women's Advisory Council. The strong emphasis must, of course, be on the word "Advisory," since as we have indicated there is no way that the Company can delegate its policy-making responsibility in this area. This includes the responsibility for balancing the priorities between this issue and other issues facing the Company. We think there should be further discussion as to the procedures for establishing the Advisory Council. It would be destructive to allow an electioneering and adversary atmosphere to intrude into the sensitive and delicate dialogue we are trying to establish between the management of the Company and its women employees. We would hope the Advisory Council could be constituted in such a way as to provide maximum recognition of the great diversity of views that exists among CBS's women employees. We would anticipate that the Advisory Council would meet on a periodic basis with the Vice-President, Development and his senior staff and with other members of management as necessary. We also contemplate that the Advisory Council would work closely with the Woman Counselors. Mr. Taylor could, of course, also meet with the Advisory Council when necessary and appropriate, but we think it advisable to schedule such meetings only on an as-needed basis.

(2) As we have stated previously, we agree that changes are needed in the salary grade structure to provide more entry-level positions into management and logical career progression opportunities. This is a long-term and continuing effort which is in process.

(3) While we note our point of view, we think it inappropriate to discuss in this forum the election of additional women to the Board of Directors, which in any case is the responsibility of stockholders of the Company.

(4) The suggestion that we create permanent part-time positions requires further study. We looked at this subject a year or more ago and decided it wasn't practical. It may be that some of the difficulties will evaporate in the current environment.

(5) We do not agree that, as you have requested, employees who are promoted should be given an increase based on their length of service with the Company rather than on salary levels for their new jobs. This would bring distortions and ultimately a multiplication of inequities to our salary structure. It is our belief that as a matter of policy promotional increases should continue to be determined on the basis of the level and salary range for the position. The real answer, as we have all recognized, is to effectively open up more higher level positions into which qualified women can be promoted.

(6) Your presentation suggests that a complete review of the educational background, experience, and current qualifications should be undertaken immediately of all women employees with at least four years' tenure. We have, for more than a year now, been giving attention to the backgrounds of both women and men in our attempt to identify high-potential candidates. This effort is being significantly expanded as part of our program to accelerate "fast tracking" of high-potential women employees. The Career Inventory System, particularly in its expanded form, will provide us with additional insights in this area. We are not sure whether your

words "complete review" anticipate actions beyond this. If so, we could consider what else might be practical.

(7) In the area of training programs and apprenticeship programs with our unions, we have previously in this presentation indicated our willingness to work with you. Every union we deal with has been contacted and told of our desire to see women candidates.

(8) In the area of consciousness-raising programs, as indicated, our efforts have already begun. These programs are taking the form of awareness sessions for managers and counseling and orientation programs for interested employees. These programs will be expanded as rapidly as practical as we gain experience.

(9) We agree that internal recruiting and training must be the primary method for filling all open positions. We also agree that if qualified women cannot be found in this manner, we should be actively recruiting women from the outside. All the recruiting sources with whom we deal have been so advised.

(10) We agree that, as you noted, it is of course essential that CBS have a monitoring system to ensure that its action program is carried out at all levels. The issue is no different from that of having effective controls and progress reporting for the implementation of any program. Statistical reports, broken down by city, group, and division, are prepared quarterly and copies are sent to top management to keep them informed of progress. The Vice-President, Manpower Management, Compensation and the Director of Personnel, reporting to the President through the Vice-President, Development, are specifically charged with the successful implementation of our action program. Whether we should proceed to the appointment of an EEO officer specifically for women as part of this monitoring and control system is under consideration. We would not want to leave you with the impression that it is other than an open question, but we have already indicated our thinking that ultimately in the longer term the role of

the Woman Counselor might evolve into a permanent function charged with the responsibility for program development and implementation as well as counseling. This is probably not dissimilar to the role of the EEO officer you visualize. We need time to determine the appropriate means for achieving these commonly agreed objectives.

(11) Your final point relating to the establishment of employees goals and timetables is a critical question; we must be extremely careful not to create seeming differences between ourselves as to the goals when no differences in fact exist. As we have said earlier, all of the positive things that we are doing constitute the CBS action program. We are committed to correcting inequities and to do this with all the energy and good will we can command, and we want to see just how far and how fast we can go on the basis of this energy and good will. Already, in just over four years, we have increased the number of women officials and managers from 8.8 percent to 16.1 percent, and the number of women professionals from 17.5 percent to 24.4 percent. With these facts in mind, we think it wrong to establish numerical goals at this time. We realize that AT&T and *Newsweek* have, in their settlements, established such numerical goals and timetables. But we do not feel that these agreements, literally extracted after painful periods of significant ill will, are appropriate precedents for CBS. One problem with the establishment of numerical goals is that such goals, by their nature, would impose a degree of caution and an urge to minimize targets that the CBS management does not currently feel. A second problem, equally serious, is that the existence of numerical goals or quotas (which is what they really are) would create strong pressure on management to fill those quotas by the simple expedient of outside recruiting. Building training programs and career opportunities for our existing women employees will take time and hard work but should be much preferred to the simpler course of putting the recruiters to work. Even without such numerical goals, it should be recognized that CBS already has

a record of more action, more progress, and greater participation by women in its affairs than most other companies. We have our problems, but we recognize them; it is our goal to work with all of you in a mutual effort.

CBS is going to move forward in its action program for women at the fastest possible rate that is practical, very simply because it is just and because it is in our interest to do so. We very much hope that you can find the way to agree with our approach and give us your good will, help, and cooperation.

COMPLAINT FILED BY THE WIRE SERVICE GUILD AGAINST THE ASSOCIATED PRESS

In late September 1973 the Wire Service Guild filed a complaint with the federal Equal Employment Opportunity Commission (EEOC), charging the Associated Press with discriminating against women and members of minority groups in past and continuing violation of the 1964 Civil Rights Act. The nine-page complaint charged that the discrimination occurs not only in the AP's recruitment and hiring practices but also in its training, transfer, and promotion opportunities.

Eight individual cases were cited to illustrate the AP's pattern of discrimination.

Statistically, the complaint says that of the approximately 1,300 domestic AP employees represented by the Guild, roughly 30 are black, 170 are women, and 30 are Spanish-surnamed. These figures "are grossly out of proportion to the population as a whole and especially to that of major cities where the AP has bureaus."

Among the sources of minority employees cited as ignored by the AP were lists of journalism graduates gathered by the Newspaper Guild and passed on to AP and UPI by the Wire Service Guild, names provided by AP employees and former employees such as Austin Scott and minority people who have acted as temporary correspondents for the AP during periods of racial tension in large cities.

Further, the Guild says that while management claims to have established a training program for minority group members, those hired as "trainees" do not receive adequate training. Participants often receive little or no special training and some have received less training than new regular employees.

In at least one case a trainee who had been given less training than that given ordinary employees was then fired with the explanation that she could not perform the job as well as a regular staffer.

This woman commented about her nine months with the AP, "I feel that rather than being trained, I was programmed to fail."

The Guild complaint notes that the alleged training program set up by management has produced few minority employees for the regular AP staff. Moreover, efforts by the WSG to create a meaningful training program have been rejected by management during contract negotiations.

The complaint also says management's establishment of a "training program" without consultation or negotiation with the Guild violates the rights especially of minority employees but also of all employees to have their wages, hours, and working conditions negotiated through the collective bargaining process.

As for advancement and promotion opportunities, the Guild complaint charges that the AP has no female general executives, bureau chiefs, or foreign correspondents. There are only two female domestic correspondents.

The complaint notes that because the AP has failed to recruit and hire any significant number of minority persons, it has not yet had much opportunity to discriminate by refusing to promote minority persons. However, the Guild says, the pattern of discrimination in promotion against women suggests that a similar pattern would prevail in the case of minorities.

In response to the Guild's charges, the AP's "A" wire story on the filing of the complaint quoted a management spokesman as saying the Guild's figures are not accurate and the charges are "groundless." He also "noted that the Guild is scheduled to begin contract negotiations with the AP next month and that the complaint probably was a prelude to the opening of bargaining."

AP management also is quoted as saying the company two years ago filed with the federal government an affirmative action plan concerning minority employment and that the plan was approved by the government and the goals were met or exceeded.

The Guild told the EEOC that neither the affirmative action plan submitted to the government two years ago nor the AP's repeated agreement to a "no discrimination" clause in its contracts with the WSG have resulted in any meaningful reduction of its discriminatory practices.

The Guild asks the federal agency to try to conciliate the AP's discrimination against women and minority group members by the establishment of effective recruiting and hiring programs, meaningful training programs, and fair transfer and promotion programs through negotiation with the union.

The Guild also asks specific relief including back pay for the individuals cited in the complaint, as well as for others that an EEOC investigation may find are entitled to it.

Failing such conciliation, the Guild asks the agency to bring suit in federal court and/or to authorize the Guild to bring suit.

Note: Condensed from WiReport (published by permission).

74 75 76 77 78 10 9 8 7 6 5 4 3 2 1